THE COMPLETE BOOK OF SHOOTING

THE COMPLETE BOOK OF SHOOTING

A

GUIDE TO GAME HUNTING WILDFOWLING AND COMPETITION SHOOTING

FID BACKHOUSE, PETER ELIOT,
ROB KNOWLES, CRAWFORD LITTLE
& COLIN LAURIE MCKELVIE

OCTOPUS BOOKS

First published in 1988 by
Octopus Books Limited
a division of Octopus Publishing Group
Michelin House
81 Fulham Road
London SW3 6RB

© Bookbourne Limited 1988
The Old Farmhouse
Newton, Sleaford
Lincs NG34 0DT

ISBN 0 7064 3187 1

Printed by Mandarin Offset in Hong Kong

FOREWORD

Sporting shooting of live game and other quarry, with shotguns, rifles and handguns, is a widespread and popular recreational activity, eagerly pursued by several million enthusiasts in Britain, Europe and North America. Like the separate but closely-related sport of target shooting, it is an important pursuit with an ancient and historically significant background.

Today's sporting shooter has unique opportunities to acquire the most ancient skills of fieldcraft, and also the most modern guns, rifles, ammunition and other equipment, and apply them jointly in the sporting pursuit of many species of birds and mammals. Speedy international travel and increased leisure have also widened our sporting horizons, bringing faraway places and unfamiliar quarry within easy reach. Modern sporting practices and game management techniques have also strengthened the sportsman's traditional relevance as a practical wildlife conservationist, a role often forgotten or conveniently overlooked by many anti-shooting commentators.

The modern sportsman may find himself confronted with a bewilderingly wide range of species to pursue, of guns and rifles to choose from, of dogs to provide and share in his sport, and of techniques and sporting skills to practise and to master. In the pages which follow, experienced international sportsmen have joined forces to provide an up-to-date guide to the guns, the dogs, the quarry species and the techniques which comprise the wonderfully varied and exciting world of modern live-game shooting.

COLIN LAURIE McKELVIE MA FLS MIBiol

CONTENTS

GUNS & EQUIPMENT

Modern sporting shooting has reached a high degree of technical and technological sophistication, thanks to innumerable developments in the design and construction of firearms, cartridges, shot and bullet loads and many associated items like scope sights, binoculars and telescopes, plus a host of other aids to sport, like four-wheel-drive and all-terrain vehicles. However, recent developments should not blind us to the fact that sporting shooting – the pursuit of wild quarry with missiles – actually has a very ancient history.

Although the detailed origins of man's hunting activities are matters for scholarly discussion by palaeo-anthropologists, we can say with some certainty that men's lives as hunter-gatherers go back many tens of thousands of years. A semi-nomadic life, gathering available wild foods and catching wild creatures for food, undoubtedly preceded men's more settled communal lives as farmers and herdsmen. Among early hunting methods the simplest and most obvious projectile must have been the stone or the stick, probably picked up at random and flung when the chance of securing a likely bird or animal presented itself. The aboriginal's throwing stick, still used among some peoples today, is direct evidence of a simple link with an ancient past.

The throwing stick and the flung stone were to be followed by the stone-firing sling and later by the bow and arrow, and the evidence suggests that bow hunting for food is at least 30,000-40,000 years old, and possibly very much older.

The blowpipe, using a hollow pipe or reed as a primitive barrel through which a short, bolt-like dart could be propelled by air pressure from the firer's lungs, is an obvious precursor of the metal-barrelled, shot- and bullet-firing weapons as they were later to evolve. But it was the invention of gunpowder which was to enable weapons to be developed for propelling single bullets or charges of small shot at sufficient speed and with sufficient accuracy to make them effective, for food gathering and in warfare.

In the early days of firearms they were regarded as an important new aid in the serious business of killing wild animals for food. This was, and under some circumstances still remains, an important affair, but it later developed into a recreational activity which its followers found satisfying in its own right. Skill with a birding-piece or a rifle, and the fieldcraft necessary to achieve success against live game, became exciting and worthwhile ends in themselves, and from this the worldwide activity of sporting shooting in all its many forms was to develop, from the late 18th century onwards.

The 19th century was above all an age of exploration and colonization, as man's natural instincts for exploration were fuelled by eager national aspirations to conquer new territories and acquire colonies. The early explorers and settlers in Africa, India, the Far East, South America and many parts of North America were confronted by landscapes teeming with game and wildlife of all shapes and sizes. Shooting for self-defence and for the pot was a necessity, but it was not long before the sporting potential of the newly-acquired colonies was recognized. Thus began the golden age of African safari, Indian shikar, of buffalo hunting and the shooting of other large game in North America, and countless forms of gamebird and wildfowl shooting worldwide.

Today the world scene has changed, and the almost untrammeled freedoms of the early explorers and the settlers who followed them into unknown countries have been replaced by wise and well-regulated national and international legislation and agreements about the conservation of wildlife and the statutory regulation of sporting shooting. The sportsman's world has shrunk with the advent of high-speed air travel and the development of speedy communications of all forms. Even the toughest modern safari or a long trek into wilderness country in pursuit of elusive game would seem tame and safe by the standards of a century ago.

The game may be less abundant, the regulations more inhibiting and the modern shooting expedition less of an adventure than it used to be, but there are compensating advantages. Today's sportsman has guns, ammunition and other equipment which is powerful and efficient to a degree our ancestors would have found incredible. The sportsman of today, seeking a few hours' relaxation away from a busy working life, can jump into his car and drive off for a day's shooting to distances which would have taken many days of travel by horse. A shooting holiday in another country, once a matter of long sea voyages and protracted cross-country treks, now involves little more than a few hours travel by air and road.

But today's sporting shooter is motivated by the same challenges which historians and anthropologists can trace back to those earliest hunters with their stones, sticks, blowpipes and bows and arrows. Technology may alter the outward face of sport, but there remains a very basic, atavistic impulse, and a sense of excitement and achievement in testing personal skills against wild creatures, and above all by doing this in a way which requires very special mastery of a difficult technique. Once you have pressed the trigger your bullet or charge of shot flies free. You have no control over it, and unless your first aim was good the target will be missed. The same is equally true of the aboriginal with his throwing stick or the Indonesian hunter with his blowpipe. There is something infinitely satisfying in launching a missile on an accurate path and watching it connect successfully with a distant target. That, in essence, is the common bond which links the modern sporting shooter with the hunters of prehistoric times. The hunter's skills, the challenges of the pursuit and the satisfactions of success remain as important as ever.

CHOOSING A SHOTGUN

Your choice of a suitable sporting shotgun will be decided by a combination of your personal preference, the style of shooting you intend to pursue and the quarry species involved, the legal restrictions and, sometimes, the conventional requirements in your country or locality, and (not least) how much you wish to pay.

If your sport involves a range of different species and a variety of clay pigeon shooting disciplines, you may find you need more than one shotgun. The real enthusiast soon acquires a small battery of shotguns.

The table below shows the main points to bear in mind when making your choice.

CHOOSING A SHOTGUN

- **Bore:** Choose a bore which will fire a cartridge load suitable for your quarry. .410 and 28-bores are ideal boys' guns, and fine for short-range shooting. The 12-bore is universally dominant, and the 20-bore is increasingly popular.
- **Break-action shotguns:** Single barrelled shotguns are useful working tools. Double-barrelled shotguns dominate the sporting scene. English-style side-by-side guns are traditional in the UK and best for driven game, covert shooting, etc. Over-and-unders predominate in Europe, and for clay pigeon shooting.
- **Pump-action and semiautomatic:** Popular in N. America and among wildfowlers and rough shooters, and also for clay shooting. Legal restrictions for live game use in some countries – check local regulations. Can be heavy and badly balanced.
- **Actions:** Primarily boxlock and sidelock actions for double-barrelled guns. Both proven actions, but buy a good boxlock in preference to a cheap sidelock.
- **Barrel lengths:** Usually from 25" to 30". Choose according to personal preferences, though longer barrels better for wildfowling.
- **Chokes:** Moderate choke for gamebird shooting and skeet clays. Tighter choke for long-range wildfowling and trap clays. Variable and adjustable chokes available.

drop at heel

heel

stock (English style)

comb

drop at comb

top lever

fence

triggers

length of pull

trigger guard

recoil pad

toe

French stock

semi-pistol stock

pistol grip stock

Monte Carlo stock

right shoulder

comb

left shoulder

rib line

cast off

cast on

CAST *The cast is the angle between the stock and the barrels, which brings them correctly to the line of sight when the gun is mounted.*

OVER-AND-UNDER BARRELS *The barrels of an over-and-under gun lie one above the other.*

BOXLOCK ACTION *The action is contained within a solid action body. When the trigger is pulled, the sear releases the tumbler, which is then driven by the mainspring to strike the cartridge.*

PUMP OR SLIDE ACTION AND SEMIAUTOMATIC SHOTGUNS

GAS-OPERATED ACTION

SEMIAUTOMATIC ACTION *Part of the propellant gas is siphoned off to compress the recoil spring, eject the fired shell and recock the firing mechanism. Then the recoil spring chambers a fresh round, and gun is ready to fire.*

SIDE-BY-SIDE DOUBLE-BARRELLED SHOTGUN

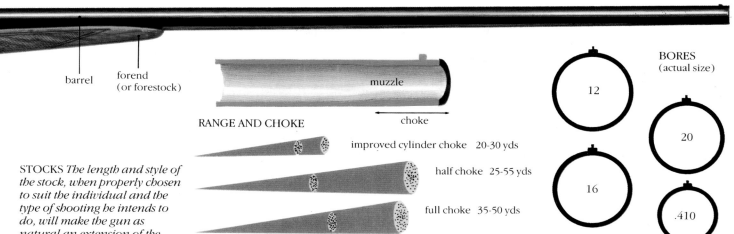

barrel

forend
(or forestock)

muzzle

choke

RANGE AND CHOKE

improved cylinder choke   20-30 yds

half choke   25-55 yds

full choke   35-50 yds

BORES
(actual size)

12

20

16

.410

STOCKS *The length and style of the stock, when properly chosen to suit the individual and the type of shooting he intends to do, will make the gun as natural an extension of the shooter's body as possible. The pistol grip is used on single-trigger guns where, unlike double-trigger guns, no repositioning of the hand is needed for the second shot.*

CHOKE *The amount of choke determines the effective range of the gun for different types of game: a gun choked improved cylinder is suitable for grouse, quail or pigeon at 20-30 yards; with half (modified) choke it is suitable for pheasant or rabbit at 25-55 yards; and with full choke, for duck or geese at 35-50 yards.*

BORE *The bore of a shotgun barrel (except the .410) is the number of lead balls, each fitting the barrel exactly, which add up to 1 pound weight.*

OVER-AND-UNDER SHOTGUN

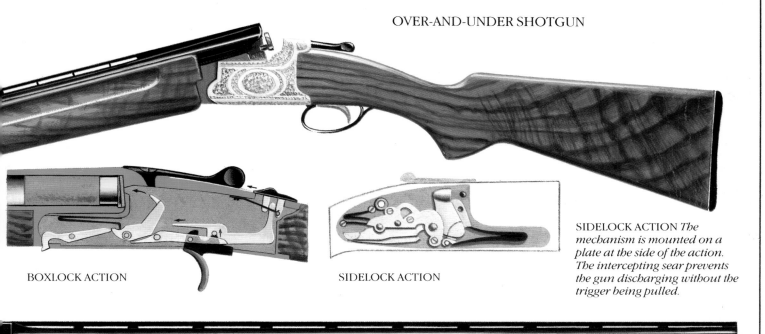

BOXLOCK ACTION

SIDELOCK ACTION

SIDELOCK ACTION *The mechanism is mounted on a plate at the side of the action. The intercepting sear prevents the gun discharging without the trigger being pulled.*

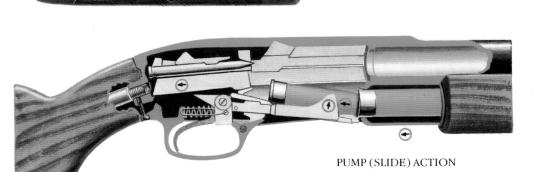

PUMP (SLIDE) ACTION

PUMP ACTION *The mechanism of a pump-action shotgun is operated by the shooter sliding the forestock to the rear and then forward again, to eject the spent cartridge, recock the firing mechanism and reload the chamber with a fresh round from the tubular magazine contained within the forestock.*

CHOOSING RIFLES & HANDGUNS

Sporting rifles and handguns suitable for live quarry shooting come in a bewilderingly large range of styles, actions and especially calibres, from the tiny but effective and universally popular .22 rimfire to the mighty .458 Win Magnum and the .44 Magnum handgun load.

Choose your rifles and handguns to suit your own style of shooting, the weight you are prepared to carry in the field, the amount of recoil you can accept, the game you pursue and the calibre and power you require.

Below and opposite are quick check-lists of the main points you should consider when making your choice.

CHOOSING A RIFLE

- **Air rifle:** For small quarry at close range only. Ideal for beginners and experts alike.
- **Rimfire (.22) rifle:** For small game and mammals up to fox size only. Ammunition cheap and universally available. Minimal maintenance.
- **Centrefire rifle:** Calibres from .222 to .458. Choose according to quarry species hunted.
- **Bolt-action rifles:** Wide range of models from many manufacturers. Strong and reliable actions. Left-handed shooters should choose a left-handed action, not available on all models.
- **Lever-action rifles:** Popular in N. America. Best suited to short-cased ammunition (eg .30-30, .444).
- **Pump-action rifles:** Used mainly in N. America. Strong and reliable, suitable for right-handers and left-handers. Tubular magazines can have feeding and safety problems unless carefully maintained.
- **Semiautomatic rifles:** Tend to be heavy. Risk of jamming. Check semiautos are legal for live game shooting before you buy.
- **Single-shot rifles** Some top-quality falling-block types available. Not a beginner's action.
- **Calibres:** Ensure calibre is adequate and legal for chosen quarry.
- **Barrels:** Long barrels produce higher bullet velocities and energies. Short barrels an advantage in close cover. Heavy barrels give maximum long-range accuracy.

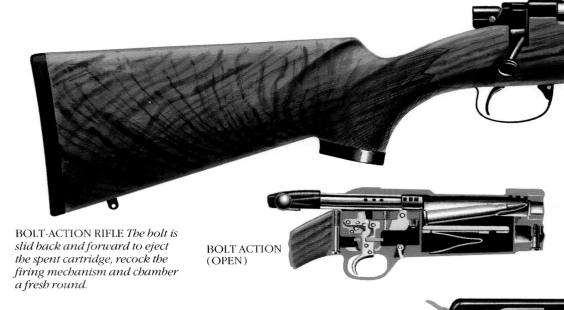

BOLT-ACTION RIFLE *The bolt is slid back and forward to eject the spent cartridge, recock the firing mechanism and chamber a fresh round.*

BOLT ACTION (OPEN)

LEVER-ACTION RIFLE

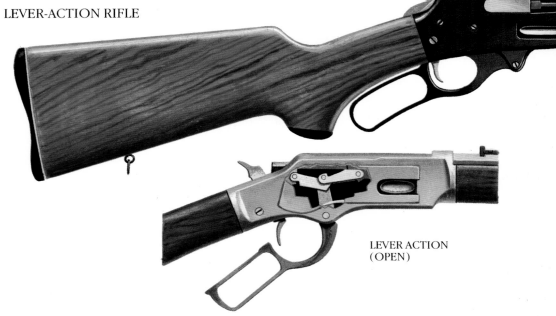

LEVER ACTION (OPEN)

REVOLVER

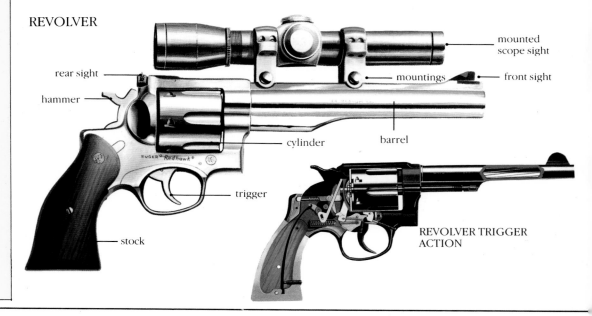

mounted scope sight

rear sight

mountings

front sight

hammer

cylinder

barrel

trigger

stock

REVOLVER TRIGGER ACTION

BOLT-ACTION RIFLE

BOLT ACTION
(CLOSED)

RIFLING *The spiral ridges and grooves cut into the bore of the barrel make the bullet spin, stabilizing its flight.*

SIGHTS *Telescopic sights contain various styles of reticle (sighting mark) which can be superimposed on the target. Open sights (bottom right) consist of front and rear sights which are aligned on the target.*

BOLT ACTION *When the bolt is fully open, a fresh round is pushed up from the magazine. When the bolt is pushed forward the cartridge is chambered, then the bolt is turned to lock it and seal the breech.*

LEVER ACTION
(CLOSED)

CHOOSING A HANDGUN
● **Single-action revolvers:** The hammer of a single-action revolver must be manually cocked before each shot. The hammer fall is longer and heavier than that of a double-action revolver.
● **Double-action revolvers:** With a double-action revolver, pulling the trigger both cocks and fires the gun. As a result, the trigger pull is relatively long and heavy, which can upset the aim, so hunters usually cock the hammer manually
● **Autoloading pistols:** Autoloading or semiautomatic pistols are generally not as

powerful as revolvers.
● **Single-shot pistols:** Reliable and accurate, single-shot pistols are becoming increasingly popular with hunters
● **Calibres:** The best calibres for small game are .22 and .32; for medium game, .38/.357; and for large game, .41 Magnum and up.
● **Scope sights:** A good scope sight can be a great aid to accurate shooting but it makes a pistol more bulky to carry, and not all pistols can be scoped.

LEVER ACTION *When the lever is pushed down and forward, the spent shell is ejected and the firing mechanism recocked. Pulling the lever back up chambers a fresh cartridge from the magazine and closes the breech ready for firing.*

REVOLVER *In a single action revolver, the hammer must be cocked by the shooter's thumb before the trigger is pulled. In a double action mechanism, pulling the trigger both cocks and releases the hammer.*

SEMIAUTOMATIC ACTION *When the gun is fired, gas pressure disengages the slide from the barrel and drives it back to eject the spent shell, recock the firing mechanism and allow a fresh round to be chambered.*

front sight
barrel
rear sight
hammer

COLT GOVERNMENT MODEL AUTOMATIC PISTOL CAL.45

locking ribs
spent case
slide
recoil spring
firing pin
trigger
stock

RECOIL ACTION

magazine spring
mainspring

SEMIAUTOMATIC PISTOL

magazine

13

SINGLE-BARRELLED SHOTGUNS

Single-barrelled, smooth-bored shotguns and, in earlier days, 'birding pieces' have always played an important part in sporting shooting, in the British Isles and around the world. Despite today's overwhelming predominance of double barrelled guns, both side-by-side and over-and-under varieties, the single-barrelled sporting gun designed to fire a cartridge containing anything from the smallest birdshot to heavy buckshot and single ball and Brenneke-type rifled slugs, remains popular and widely used. Indeed, despite the apparent sophistication of many double-barrelled shotguns, they are in essence nothing more than an amalgamation of two single-barrelled guns, to provide the sportsman with an immediate opportunity for a second shot. Similarly, pump-action and self-loading (semiautomatic) shotguns have developed from the basic single-barrelled gun, with the addition of mechanical aids to fast reloading.

The single-barrelled gun consists, like all shotguns, of the traditional triple combination of lock, stock and barrel. The barrel may be as short as 25 or 26 inches in the case of a light game gun, especially in the smaller bores like the 20-bore or the little .410, and such guns may weigh as little as 3½ to 4 pounds, making them light and easily manageable for youngsters learning to shoot. Many of the most celebrated shotgun shooters started their careers with guns of this type.

The 12-bore single-barrelled gun is more likely to have a 28-inch or 30-inch barrel, while the heavier magnum-type single barrelled guns may have barrel lengths of 36 inches or more, especially for 8-bore and 4-bore types, the latter being generally regarded as the largest bore of shotgun which a strong man can be expected to fire accurately from the shoulder.

Short-barrelled, small-bore, single-barrelled shotguns and 12-bore game guns will generally have the barrel bored with only a moderate amount of choke, to give the wider, even spread of shot which the rough shooter and game shooter normally find most suitable. The magnum and big-bore single-barrelled guns, still popular among specialist goose shooters and coastal wildfowlers, may be

Two 12-bore guns – a Russian-made Baikal (top) and a Fias Monocanna (bottom) – and an English-made 20-bore gun (centre), sold by dealers under their own brand names.

heavily choked to concentrate the charge of shot and maintain tight pattern densities and high pellet energy at long range.

The action of a single-barrelled gun may be of the boxlock type or, in the higher quality grades from the workshops of eminent makers, sidelock actions may be fitted. Older examples of the single-barrelled shotgun often have a sidelock or back-action type lock with an external hammer, which can be placed at the fully-cocked or half-cocked positions. Single-barrelled guns with external hammers are still produced, but the modern trend has been to

use a simple hammer action not unlike that of a single-action, single-shot pistol.

One of the most successful and universally respected single-barrel shotgun actions is the Greener GP martini-type mechanism. Whereas hammer guns, boxlocks and sidelocks are all of the familiar break-action, drop-down type in which the breech is opened and the barrels lowered for loading and unloading of cartridges, the martini or falling-block action has a barrel and action receiver firmly jointed together, with a falling block mounted within the action body.

A metal grip or loop, to the rear of the trigger guard and incorporating the grip or wrist of the stock, is pulled downwards to open the breech, causing the falling block to move downwards and to the rear through a short arc. Extractors or ejectors pull the spent cartridge clear of the breech, and a fresh cartridge is inserted by being slid manually down the grooved ramp on the top of the falling block. This is seated firmly in the chamber before the lever is returned to the upper position, which completes the recocking of the firing mechanism and seals the new cartridge

firmly in the chamber, ready for firing.

This type of action, although not common among sporting shooters in Britain, has enjoyed generations of popularity among gamekeepers, rough shooters and wildfowlers and, further afield, among game rangers and hunters in Asia and Africa. If chambered for the longer, magnum-type cartridges it can be used for the heaviest loads of buckshot, ball and rifled slug, and when fitted with interchangeable choke tubes it provides a combination of great versatility and reliability.

The clear disadvantage of the single-barrelled shotgun is the fact that only one shot is readily available to the shooter without an appreciable delay while he reloads. This makes the single-barrelled shotgun quite unsuitable for shooting driven game or covert shooting, in which the sportsman must expect to maintain a high rate of fire during the course of each drive. Anyone with a single-barrelled shotgun would be at a very serious disadvantage in this type of shooting.

However, the rough shooter, the vermin hunter and the wildfowler may not normally need to fire a rapid succession of shots, and the relative lightness of the single-barrelled gun may have a lot to recommend it, especially on shooting days when there may be many miles of walking and only comparatively few shots fired. An important school of thought also maintains that the single-barrelled gun encourages concentration and care, since the firer knows he has only one chance when a bird is flushed.

The single-barrelled shotgun has become a less common sporting gun than formerly, mainly owing to changes in the way shooting is carried on, and also to the advent of excellent quality, mass-produced double-barrelled shotguns at a price which is well within the reach of most modern sportsmen. Nevertheless, the single-barrelled style of sporting gun still has its place, especially where a simple, robust and light sporting gun is required. In addition, a great many sportsmen get great pleasure from owning and occasionally using some of the finely-made and beautifully-crafted single-barrelled shotguns which were produced in earlier generations by such eminent gunmakers as Purdey and Holland & Holland of London or Parker of the USA.

DOUBLE-BARRELLED (SIDE BY SIDE)

For most sporting shotgunners worldwide, the standard style of shotgun which overwhelmingly dominates the scene is the double-barrelled, break-action breech loader. This takes one of two possible forms: the side-by-side gun in which, as the name suggests, the two barrels are jointed together side-by-side; and the over-and-under style of shotgun, in which the two barrels are jointed one on top of the other.

It is generally agreed that human eye/hand co-ordination means that an individual's hands can be readily positioned so as to point quickly and accurately towards the spot on which his eyes are fixed. A gun which lies comfortably and easily within those hands and which comes readily and smoothly to the shoulder and at the correct angle therefore becomes part of that natural pointing of hand and eye. The double-barrelled shotgun, and especially the side-by-side type, achieves this better than any other design.

With side-by-side shotguns in particular, both barrels tend to lie low down within the cupped forward hand of the firer, and thus the axis of the barrels closely follows the natural direction of the firer's leading hand. (Slenderly made over-and-under shotguns, without heavy forestocks, achieve much the same 'hand-to-barrel' relationship.)

Side-by-side shotguns are readily available in a wide range of calibres, from the little .410 through the larger bores like the 28-bore, 20-bore, 16-bore and 12-bore (most popular of all), with the heavy, magnum-type 10-bore and 8-bore calibres also available in certain models from specialist manufacturers. Just as the double-barrelled gun, and especially the side-by-side style, has come to dominate the sporting shotgun scene in Britain and British-influenced countries, so the 12-bore has become the overwhelmingly predominant calibre for shotguns worldwide. By general agreement a double-barrelled 12-bore is capable of firing cartridges which are ballistically adequate for most sporting situations, without undue recoil, and the loaded gun, as carried by the sportsman, is of an acceptable weight. Generally speaking, a loaded, side-by-side 12-bore shotgun weighs be-

tween 6¼ and 6¾ pounds.

The mechanical actions used in side-by-side shotguns fall into two basic types – the boxlock and the sidelock – although individual manufacturers and gunmakers have created many variations on these two basic themes.

The boxlock style of action is a proven combination of mechanical efficiency and simplicity combined with toughness and reliability in action. The most popular type is known as the Anson & Deeley lock, recalling the names of two important early designers. It comprises five principal parts: the sear (activated by pulling the trigger); the tumbler (basically an internal hammer or firing pin); the V-shaped mainspring; the sear spring; and the cocking rod. The action of breaking and opening the gun forces down the leading edge of the cocking rod, which pivots the tumbler and compresses the mainspring of the action. A notch in the rear of the tumbler engages with the sear, which is held in position by the sear spring, and in this way the gun's firing mechanism is cocked and held ready to fire when the trigger is pulled. When the trigger is pulled, the sear disengages from its notch in the rear of the tumbler, which then pivots forward, driven by the mainspring, forcing the firing pin through the standing breech face of the action, to strike the detonating cap in the cartridge head, thus firing the gun.

All these moving parts are contained within a roughly box-shaped action which lies below and slightly behind the rear of the barrels, and there are no exposed moving parts as with the old style of hammer gun. The only outwardly visible moving parts are the top lever, the customary way of locking and unlocking the breech, and the safety slide or safety catch, normally placed behind the top lever on the top tang or strap of the action, and recessed into the upper part of the wrist of the stock.

The sidelock shotgun is rather more sophisticated and complex. Outwardly, the sidelock action normally appears as two elongated, semielleptical plates lying to the rear of the breech and set into the sides of the stock, above the trigger guard and forward of the wrist.

Those sideplates conceal an intricate mechanism, and in its most fully developed form this is known as a bar-action sidelock. The sidelock shares certain fundamental principles with the boxlock, including the presence of an internal hammer or tumbler; an engaging sear which holds it in position until it is released by the pressing of the trigger; and a mainspring to provide the driving force of the firing mechanism.

The sidelock mechanism also employs additional mechanical devices which allow for very careful regulation of the crispness of the trigger pulls and, perhaps more importantly, there is a secondary safety mechanism in the form of an intercepting safety sear. This blocks the fall of the tumbler if the main sear is accidentally disengaged by the gun being knocked or dropped. The sophistication of the sidelock

SHOTGUNS

mechanism allows for a high degree of fine-tuning of the action, and the best sidelocks provide a very fast 'lock time' (the time which elapses between the pulling of the trigger and the firing pin striking the cartridge cap) and particularly crisp, finely-regulated trigger pulls. These attributes, combined with the additional safety features, mean that the sidelock action is invariably chosen for the finest quality shotguns, of the type made by classic London gunmakers like Purdey, Holland & Holland and Boss, as well as many top-quality manufacturers elsewhere in Europe.

The simpler and cheaper boxlock action has nevertheless always been popular, and some exceptionally fine examples have been produced from the workshops of top quality British, European and North American gunmakers. It is particularly highly regarded for its simplicity and reliability, an important factor when a gun is intended for use in remote parts of the world, far from the nearest competent gunsmith's workshop. The basic boxlock lacks the graceful flowing lines and the large, exposed sideplates of the sidelock, but this is occasionally overcome by the fitting of so-called dummy sideplates, which enhance the appearance of the gun and give full scope for fine hand engraving of the action.

Among the many other types of patent shotgun action developed by individual gunmakers, it is worth mentioning the 'triggerplate action', sometimes known as the 'round action'. This compact action, externally rather similar in appearance to the boxlock action, has all parts of the lock mechanism connected to the triggerplate which is set into the bottom of the action frame.

The guns shown here are, from the top, a Winchester 23 Magnum 12-bore, a Parker-Hale 20-bore, and an AYA Yeoman, a Browning B-SS and a hand-built, sidelock action Holland & Holland Royal (all 12-bore).

It is a compact and very strong action, and the locks can be readily removed to be cleaned, checked and, if necessary, over-hauled. The origins of this action are credited to the Scottish gunmaker James MacNaughten of Edinburgh, whose patent was developed and made widely popular by another Edinburgh gunmaker, John Dickson.

Most side-by-side shotguns have twin triggers, one for each barrel. Conventionally, the front trigger fires the right barrel and the rear trigger fires the left. Likewise, it has become customary to bore the right barrel so as to provide only a slight degree of constriction or choke while the left hand barrel is more heavily choked. In a typical British-style game gun the right barrel might be choked improved cylinder with the left barrel bored half choke. In practical terms this means that the right (improved cylinder) barrel will deliver a moderately widely-spread pattern of pellets, 50 percent of the pellets falling within a 30-inch circle at a distance of 40 yards. The half-choked left barrel, with its greater degree of constriction towards the muzzle, will fire a tighter pattern, and should place approximately 60 percent of the pellets in a 30-inch circle at 40 yards.

Double-barrelled guns can be bored to suit the user's requirements, and these may vary from true cylinder (with no constriction of the nominal bore diameter) to full choke, which concentrates the shot pattern very tightly, placing 70 percent of the pellets within a 30-inch circle at 40 yards. Individual sportsmen often develop a decided preference for a certain combination of choke borings in their right and left barrels, depending largely upon their own marksmanship and the sort of sport and quarry they pursue. For example, wildfowlers and goose shooters often favour heavily-choked borings, while most low-ground game shooters prefer an open-bored right barrel and a moderately-choked left barrel.

Among specialist driven grouse and partridge shooters will be found some who prefer to have their right barrel moderately choked and a more open left barrel, reversing the normal layout. They may choose this because, for oncoming driven birds, their first shot, discharged by the front trigger firing the right barrel, is often fired at a

The upper two are a Parker-Hale (top) and a Fias Sirio, both 12-bores. The lower two are a matching pair of Famar 12-bores.

more distant target than the second (left) barrel. In this, as in so many aspects of sporting shotgun shooting, each individual needs to make his personal decision, in the light of his experience and perhaps with the guidance of a watchful shooting school coach or game shooting instructor.

While the presence of two barrels and often of two different choke borings (and, perhaps, two different cartridge loadings) has meant that the classic side-by-side game shotgun traditionally has double triggers, many British, European and North American gunmakers have devised and developed single-trigger mechanisms. A single-trigger mechanism on a double-barrelled shotgun means, in essence, that one pressing of the trigger discharges one barrel, the trigger then being released and pressed again to fire the second barrel. This is achieved by various mechanical modifications, which may involve the location of first one sear to release one tumbler, after which the trigger mechanism shifts to engage and activate the second sear, firing the second barrel. Alternatively, the mechanism may make use of the energy created by the gun's recoil when the first barrel is fired, part of the kick being used to switch the so-called inertia mechanism from one barrel across to the other.

Although the twin-trigger mechanism is generally acknowledged to be more simple and dependable, the single-trigger mechanisms, of whatever type, do confer some advantages. The shooter's trigger hand need not be moved for the second shot, whereas some hand movement is necessary with twin triggers to bring the trigger finger to bear on the second or back trigger, placed some three quarters of an inch to the rear of the front trigger. There may also be benefits in cold climates, where low temperatures numb the fingers, reducing manual mobility and often making gloves a necessity.

A further refinement of most single trigger mechanisms is the incorporation of a switching system, so that the first pressing of the trigger can be made to discharge either the right or the left barrel first. Under normal field conditions, however, this 'single selective trigger' mechanism must be set in advance, for there is seldom time to make the selection when a fast moving animal or bird offers an opportunity for a shot.

The classic side-by-side shotgun, as developed in England since the 1880s, will make use of a good boxlock or sidelock action or, in the case of a few makers such as Perazzi, a triggerplate action, usually with twin triggers, and a further important aspect of the gun's mechanism is the ejectors.

Once fired, each cartridge must be removed from the chamber of the gun before another shot can be fired from it. A simple extractor mechanism, usually comprising a recessed plate at the breech which lifts the cartridge heads slightly to the rear and exposes their rims as the gun is opened, is normal. The firer can then grasp the spent cartridge by the rim and pull it clear of the chamber, to be pocketed or discarded and replaced with a fresh one. However, many practical game shooting situations call for rapid reloading, and the automatic, selective ejector plays an important part in this.

Boxlock, sidelock and trigger-plate action shotguns can all be modified to incorporate single selective ejectors, which are activated individually when either or both barrels of a double-barrelled shotgun are fired. As the tumbler falls and the barrel is fired, a separate ejector spring is released and when the shotgun is subsequently broken and the action opened, the ejector for the fired barrel springs to the rear, extracting the spent cartridge and flinging it well clear as the gun is opened, allowing the shooter or his attendant loader to reload a fresh cartridge immediately into the empty chamber. Modern ejector mechanisms are extremely reliable, and it is rare to find a modern sporting shotgun which is not equipped with them, except in the cheapest grades and among certain specialized, large-calibre shotguns used principally by coastal wildfowlers.

A further aid to swift reloading, especially for driven game shooting, was the evolution of the 'self-opening' and 'assisted opening' shotgun actions. With a normal shotgun action the firing of one or both barrels releases one or both mainsprings, which are recompressed and cocked by the act of opening the action and pulling the barrels downward into the 'broken' position. This requires a little effort, and the firer must use both hands to do it. An alternative mechanism, usually found only in top-quality London made shotguns or European copies of them, is the self-opening action, in which the top lever need only be pushed to the side for the action to break open, assisted by springs, releasing the selective ejectors and preparing the gun for reloading. Using such a mechanism, the firer can break his gun and prepare to reload using one hand only (his right, in the case of a right handed shot), while his left hand reaches for one or two fresh cartridges.

However, the main action springs must still be recompressed, and the self-loading action is therefore much heavier and stiffer to close than the normal, unassisted action. But familiarity soon overcomes this, and a self-opening shotgun in experienced hands is capable of a remarkably high rate of sustained fire-power which makes it ideal for driven gamebird shooting when sport is fast and furious.

The assisted opening action is something of a compromise device, in which the stiffness in opening the normal action is slightly relieved by the assistance of springs, while closing the gun is less of an effort than with the true self-opener. These features, like many other shotgun action refinements, do not suit all individual sportsmen, who should experiment to find what type and style of action is best suited to their sporting requirements. Their decision will, of course, also be influenced by how much they can afford to spend on a sporting shotgun.

DOUBLE-BARRELLED (OVER-AND-UNDER) SHOTGUNS

The modern double-barrelled shotgun, loaded and unloaded by breaking the action at the breech, and firing modern cartridges (usually with plastic cases and today's reliable nitro-cellulose powders), is by far the most important shotgun for the majority of sporting users in every country.

Double-barrelled shotguns come in two styles, the side-by-side gun in which the barrels are placed one beside the other in a horizontal plane, and the over-and-under or 'superimposed' style, in which the two barrels lie one above the other in the vertical plane, jointed together either with a continuous rib or a series of smaller joints, and often with a further top rib lying above the upper barrel.

The majority of modern over-and-under shotguns have a single-trigger mechanism, whereby both barrels are fired in turn by pressing twice on the trigger. A selector switch makes it possible for the firer to choose which barrel is fired by the first pressing of the trigger, and the selector switch is usually built into the safety slide on the top tang or strap, lying along the wrist of the grip and to the rear of the top lever opening mechanism. Double-trigger over-and-under shotguns are also available, however, but these tend to be most common in either the cheapest, production line grades or in top quality, hand-built examples. The double-trigger mechanism probably suits the firer best when it is accompanied by a straight-hand stock, which enables the firer to carry out the slight repositioning of the hand between shots which is necessary when operating two triggers which are lying one behind the other. The single-trigger mechanism, however, requires no repositioning of the firer's hand, and therefore most over-and-under shotguns have a pistol or semi-pistol grip instead of the straight style of stock.

Another distinguishing feature on many over-and-under guns is the raised, ventilated rib on top of the upper barrel. Unlike the conventional smooth, concave upper rib recessed between the barrels of a typical English-style side-by-side shotgun, the over-and-under gun's top rib has always tended to be of a raised, file-cut or matt-finished type, ending with the small bead foresight found on virtually all types of shotgun. However, the widespread use of the over-and-under type of shotgun for clay pigeon shooting from the 1940s onward, with large numbers of cartridges being fired from one gun in quick succession, meant that gun barrels often became very heated, to the point where a shimmering, mirage-type effect was achieved by hot air rising above the barrels and disrupting the firer's sight picture. This problem became even more acute in warm summer weather. To reduce problems caused by overheating, manufacturers started incorporating ventilation slots in the raised top rib, to enable air to pass freely around a larger area of the metal surfaces, thereby encouraging the heat to dissipate more easily. This feature has now become almost universal in over-and-under shotguns, especially those designed specifically for clay pigeon shooting.

The superimposed positioning of the barrels on this type of gun inevitably means that the design and operation of the action are rather different from those of side-by-side shotguns. The action, cocking and ejection mechanisms remain fundamentally the same, but the actions of loading and unloading inevitably mean that the barrels must travel through a much greater arc than with the side-by-side design. This means that over-and-under guns have a wider action gap and are, in general, more difficult to manipulate and slower to reload than their side-by-side equivalents, and very much slower than assisted-opening or self-opening side-by-side actions. In most over-and-under shotguns the front trigger, or the first pressure of the single trigger, fires the lower barrel. The over-and-under action is placed under rather less strain when the lower barrel is fired, and if a succession of single shots is to be fired it is best that the lower barrel should be used for this.

Consequently, the lower barrel will normally have to be reloaded first, which means breaking the action and depressing the barrels through an arc of approximately 45° in order to bring the chambers clear of the standing breech, eject or extract the spent cartridges and insert a fresh cartridge without fouling the mechanism. To achieve the wide action gap necessary for this, the underside of the action block and forestock must be shaped and cut away accordingly. A result of this is that an inexperienced firer, or a newcomer to over-and-under shotguns, may nip his hand or catch his clothing in the bottom of the action as the gun is opened, although familiarity soon overcomes this problem.

Over-and-under shotguns, like side-by-side types, are available with either boxlock or sidelock mechanisms, although these are inevitably somewhat modified to allow for two tumblers and firing pins to be placed one above the other rather than side by side. The selective ejection system and the action locking are also different with the over-and-under barrel configuration. Despite these necessary changes the gunmaker and the sportsman have a fairly clear choice between the robust simplicity and reliability of the boxlock system and the greater sophistication and relative complexity of the sidelock, with its intercepting safety sears and other distinctive features.

In practice, this means that boxlock actions are normally found on the less expensive grades of gun, with sidelock actions reserved for more expensive models and the individually made, hand-crafted guns. As with side-by-side guns, boxlock actions are often accompanied by ornamental or 'dummy' sideplates, and the gun appears at a quick glance like a sidelock. The use of sideplates is not intended as a deception, however, and is perfectly legitimate, for it often improves the gun's lines and appearance, and gives much greater scope to the engraver, who has a greatly increased area of flat metal upon which to work.

Over-and-under shotguns are manufactured in a wide range of barrel lengths, depending upon the users' preferences and requirements. 26-inch barrels are popular among those who like a lighter, fast-handling gun for light game shooting, and for clay pigeon shooting disciplines like skeet. 28-inch barrels are widely popular for all normal use, while 30-inch barrels are often favoured by wildfowlers and others who shoot at high-flying game, including high driven pheasants.

32-inch barrels, while they are unusual, are also available from some manufacturers, to cater for the special requirements of those in pursuit of coastal duck and geese, where long-range shooting of heavy loads is often normal.

Like the side-by-side action, the over-and-under shotgun is available in a wide range of bores, from the tiny .410 up to the massive 10-bore magnum. This selection of bores caters to a wide range of shooting requirements, from a first gun for a young boy or girl up to the heavy shoulder guns favoured by some wildfowlers. 16-bore over-and-under guns are quite popular in continental Europe but are seldom seen elsewehre. In North America the 20-bore, often chambered to accommodate the 3-inch magnum cartridge firing one ounce of shot, is very popular and highly successful for everything from quail and upland game shooting to

These four guns are, from the top, a Baikal, a Miroku 6000 Sport GR1 and a Perazzi MX12 SCO, all of which are 12-bore, and a Famar Jorema 20-bore.

The upper two guns are a Winchester 5000WF (top) and a Browning Citori GR3. The lower two are an AYA Yeoman and below it a Beretta S686L. All these guns are 12-bore.

flighting duck and pass-shooting migratory wildfowl.

In Britain and Ireland, and throughout the world, the 12-bore still maintains its pre-eminence, although there is a significant and growing trend towards the 20-bore, which offers no significant disadvantage for normal game shooting while affording a considerable saving in weight.

Over-and-under shotguns tend, in general, to be heavier than their side-by-side equivalents. A typical English-style by-side 12-bore shotgun with 28-inch barrels and firing a nor-

mal game load of 1¹⁄₁₆ ounces will weigh about 6½ pounds, while an equivalent over-and-under gun will weigh a little over 7½ pounds, although special lightweight models are available from certain manufacturers. However, the 20-bore over-and-under, even with 30-inch barrels and chambered for the 3-inch cartridge, should not weigh much more than 6½ pounds. This apparently small saving in weight can be quite significant, especially if the shooting day involves several hours of walking.

Although side-by-side shot-

guns can easily be supplied with two sets of barrels, perhaps of different lengths and with different chamber lengths and choke borings, it is more common to find optional sets of barrels with over-and-under shotguns. A number of manufacturers sell production models with two sets of barrels as standard equipment, and this is probably a reflection of the tendency for many over-and-under shotgun owners to use their guns for live game shooting and also for one or more of the various clay target shooting disciplines.

The result is, in effect, two

very different guns, and typically this will comprise one pair of shorter barrels, probably 26 inches long, with 2½-inch or 2¾-inch chambers and a small degree of choke. The other set of barrels may be 28 inches or 30 inches long, with 2¾-inch or 3-inch chambers and tighter choking, and these options give the owner a choice between a light, fast-handling gun for skeet shooting or light game shooting, and he can readily change to a semi-magnum gun suitable for firing a much heavier load from more tightly choked barrels, which is a better combination

open choke borings and then change his choke tubes as dusk approaches, if an evening's duck or goose flighting is planned, with longer shots and heavier loads called for. The interchangeable choke system has been applied successfully to some side-by-side shotguns, principally in the USA, but it is most often seen on over-and-under guns.

The user of an over-and-under shotgun will find that the length and shape of his stock are just as important in ensuring comfortable, accurate use as with a side-by-side shotgun. However, the actions of over-and-under guns incorporate a stock bolt, a long metal rod running rearwards from the gun action and deep into the stock. This means that the stock of an over-and-under gun cannot so readily be steamed and bent to create the sort of cast and drop which can be achieved fairly straightforwardly with side-by-side shotguns. However, most manufacturers and competent gunsmiths can arrange for the purchaser of an over-and-under shotgun to be measured and fitted so that his gun and its stock are suitably regulated for him, and some modifications can also be made to secondhand or off-the-peg guns.

Additional cast, whether to the right for a right-handed firer (known as 'cast off'), or to the left for a left-handed firer ('cast on'), can be achieved by shaving away some wood from the inside and the upper surface or comb of the stock, enabling the firer's eye to be brought more directly behind the axis of the barrels. This, like all structural or mechanical work on any type of shotgun or other firearm, is best carried out by a professional gunmaker or gunsmith, and it is usually unwise to attempt do-it-yourself changes, alterations or repairs.

In choosing a double-barrelled shotgun and deciding whether to buy a side-by-side or an over-and-under gun, certain considerations should be taken into account in making your choice. The serious competitive clay pigeon shooter will invariably choose an over-and-under gun, and this style is now universally used for almost all clay pigeon target shooting disciplines up to international level. The field shotgunner, who may also wish to do a little occasional clay pigeon shooting, may find the choice more difficult.

For those whose sport will consist principally of driven gamebirds, the traditional English-style side-by-side shotgun may be the best choice. It allows for rapid reloading, especially if an assisted-opening or self-opening mechanism is incorporated, and the light, fast handling qualities of a well made side-by-side shotgun are rarely equalled even by the finest over-and-under gun. In addition, the traditional conventions of driven game shooting mean that the presence of over-and-under guns among pheasant coverts or on grouse moors is still somewhat unusual. It must be acknowledged that some shoot organizers and shooting hosts still look askance at over-and-under guns, however reactionary and unreasonable such an attitude may be, and those who wish to conform may therefore feel more comfortable with the conventional side-by-side shotgun. However, experience soon teaches each sportsman which style of shotgun best suits him as an individual, and it is increasingly common, even in the most traditional driven shooting circles, for over-and-under guns to be used.

For the rough-shooter, the wildfowler and the sportsman who shoots over pointers and setters the choice is rarely influenced by traditional tastes and conventions. If you shoot better with an over-and-under gun, and if your sport means that exceptionally rapid reloading is not normally necessary, you would be wise to choose an over-and-under gun and stick to it for all your normal shooting. Similarly, if the side-by-side suits you better, opt for that. Also, remember that every ounce of your gun's weight must be carried, often over rough and steep ground.

A lightweight over-and-under gun may weigh about the same as a traditional side-by-side English-style game gun, but you may find problems with greater perceptible recoil, especially if a large number of shots have to be fired. However, if your day's shooting involves several miles of walking and firing no more than a handful of cartridges, the lightweight over-and-under has much to commend it. Similarly, the wildfowler firing heavy cartridge loads at high-flying duck and geese will appreciate the inertia and recoil-absorbing qualities of a heavy over-and-under gun, where the perceptible 'kick' of each shot will be much less punishing to the firer.

for wildfowling and also for trap or down-the-line clay pigeon shooting.

Recent developments in the design of over-and-under shotguns have also included the introduction of interchangeable choke tubes. Whereas the more conventional forms of choke boring involve machining the bores of the barrels to create some degree of constriction in the last few inches of each barrel towards the muzzle, interchangeable chokes allow the firer to unscrew and remove a tubular muzzle liner and replace it with another choke tube which provides a different degree of constriction and thus a different nominal choke boring. The best and most modern types of interchangeable chokes are unobtrusive in appearance and lie flush with the barrels at the muzzles. They can readily be positioned and removed by using a special spannerlike tool.

Enthusiasts for the various types of clay pigeon shooting often have very specific choke requirements and make extensive use of interchangeable chokes, while the field shooter may wish, for example, to shoot during the day with relatively

PUMP-ACTION SHOTGUNS

The 'pump-gun' is a reliable, popular and proven design of shotgun, extensively used worldwide and traditionally very popular among North American sportsmen. This style of gun could more appropriately be called the 'slide-action' shotgun, since the distinctive working of this action involves the sliding backwards and forwards of the gun's forestock to eject a spent cartridge, recock the firing mechanism and reload the chamber with a fresh cartridge, ready for another shot.

The slide-action mechanism is one of a number of different mechanical developments which allow the sportsman to fire a number of shots in fairly quick succession, by successively ejecting expended cartridges and reloading with fresh cartridges held in reserve in a magazine. It is therefore a multi-shot development of the basic single-barrelled shotgun, the other types available being the self-loading or 'semiautomatic' types and, very occasionally, bolt-actioned shotguns. (The Winchester-type lever action, so successful with certain types of rifle cartridge, has not proved suitable or popular for shotgun users.)

The pump-action shotgun has a number of important advantages which have contributed to its popularity. The action is generally simple, very strong and reliable. In practised hands a second shot can be fired very quickly, sometimes just as fast as with a double-barrelled gun. In flighting or pass shooting, a pump-action shotgun with several cartridges in the magazine (where permitted) can perform at its best, allowing the firer to get off three or four shots in very quick succession, at a speed only achievable with double-barrelled guns by having a pair ready loaded and by working as a two-man team with a loader. While this is not uncommon in driven grouse or pheasant shooting, it is not practicable under more rugged and informal conditions.

The pump-actioned gun looks superficially similar in many ways to the semiautomatic type, and in skilled hands its rate of fire can be as fast, while its mechanism is simpler and there is less risk of malfunction due to rough handling, dirt or grit. Another advantage of the pump-

Four popular 12-bore pump-action shotguns. The gun at the top is a Winchester, the Ranger 120. Below that is a Remington 870 Magnum, which is especially suitable for wildfowling and turkey hunting, and the third gun is a Mossberg 500A. The gun at the bottom is a Browning BPS with Invector screw-in choke system.

action system is that when the forestock or slide lever is in the rearward position, the breech is held open, which gives instant safety and enables a quick and reliable visual check to be made to ensure that the chamber is empty and the gun unloaded.

Despite these important plus points, the pump-action shotgun also has some significant drawbacks. The sliding pump mechanism and the long, tubular magazine which lies below the single barrel mean that the gun's point of balance is much further forward than with a double-barrelled shotgun, and this makes the pump-gun less well balanced, slower and less pleasant to handle by comparison, a drawback it shares with the semiautomatic type shotgun. The slide action can be noisy in operation, which some shooters find disagreeable and which may disturb quarry, especially if the mechanism or forestock are inclined to rattle slightly, as many are, when the gun is being carried. Rattles can be impossible to overcome, for the pump action is designed to have a fairly loose mechanism.

In addition, the action receiver is narrow and the magazine loading port on the underside, forward of the trigger guard, creates two narrow metal surfaces or rails. When the gun is carried in the crook of the arm these can dig uncomfortably into the user's forearm, even through quite thick clothing. Few sportsmen will want to carry a pump-action gun for long distances in this position, especially if there is a full maga-

Some manufacturers, however, including the American firm Mossberg, have modified the safety systems on their pump-action shotguns to provide a top tang type safety, which is widely regarded as an important improvement.

The pump-actioned 12-bore shotgun is normally chambered for 2¾-inch or 3-inch cartridges, which reflects the pump-action style's popularity with goose shooters, wildfowlers and others who use heavily-loaded and magnum-type cartridges. The strength and reliability of this shotgun system is particularly important for this type of shooting, and it can withstand the harsh weather and rough conditions of use which the wildfowler's gun often inevitably receives.

Finally, the pump-action shotgun has another important application in sporting shooting: it can be used to fire heavy buckshot, a single spherical ball or a rifled slug of the Brenneke type for hunting deer and wild boar. While all of these cartridge loadings can be fired safely and fairly successfully from double-barrelled guns, the accurate ranges are short and rarely exceed 50 yards.

The pump-action system, however, means that the firer has only a single barrel to deal with, rather than two separate barrels which are almost certain to have been jointed together in such a way as to fire to two quite different points of impact, in slightly converging or diverging directions. When a slide-action shotgun is fitted with a simple sighting system, such as a blade or bead forsight and a V-type rear sight, it can be zeroed under range conditions, and properly-loaded Brenneke-type cartridges firing a single rifled slug can give groups of 9 to 10 inches at 100 yards, which is adequate for deer and wild boar in close cover; and when a good slug gun is fitted with a telescopic sight, it can fire groups of 3 inches at 100 yards – sometimes better.

The use of shotguns for deer, with heavy buckshot or rifled slugs, is largely prohibited in the British Isles (with certain rare exceptions) and the purchase, possession or use of rifled slugs requires possession of an appropriate Firearms Certificate, in addition to the normal Shotgun Certificate.

zine of cartridges to add additional weight to the gun.

Like all shotgun and rifle actions incorporating a tubular magazine, there is always some risk that cartridges will not feed evenly if the magazine spring becomes weakened or if blockages occur, perhaps caused by grit or mud. Extra care must be taken to ensure that a cartridge is not accidentally or negligently left in the magazine.

Recent hunting legislation in Britain and many parts of North America and Europe now means that pump-action shotguns and other multi-shot guns may not be loaded with more than a certain number of cartridges, normally not more than three. This restricts the capabilities of this action, which can cope with four or five cartridges in most normal magazines, and up to seven or eight cartridges where a magazine extension tube is fitted. This is now illegal for live game shooting in many countries, so if you are thinking of buying or using a pump-actioned gun for your live quarry hunting, check first that its use is legal in your hunting areas.

The traditional type of safety catch on pump-action shotguns is in the form of a button seated within the trigger guard, usually to the rear of the trigger. Shooters accustomed to the top tang slide safety usually found on most double-barrelled shotguns may find it difficult to adapt to this unfamiliar position, and extra care therefore needs to be exercised when changing from one style of gun to another.

SEMIAUTOMATIC SHOTGUNS

Taking the basic single-barrelled, single-shot smooth-bored gun as the starting point for all shotgun design, various methods have been devised to give the sportsman the ability to fire several shots in quick succession. Multiple barrels, individually loaded and combined within the one weapon, is one solution to the problem, and has resolved itself into the popular double-barrelled styles of shotgun, in side-by-side and over-and-under configurations.

The alternative path taken by other gun designers was to retain a single barrel and develop methods by which reloading could be carried out swiftly. A few adopted the turn-bolt action, more familiar and successful in rifles. Much more successful and widely adopted has been the slide or 'pump' action, in which a sliding movement of the forestock moves the standing breech and firing mechanism to the rear, ejecting a spent cartridge and reloading a fresh one as the firing mechanism is recocked.

The semiautomatic action, which should more accurately be described as the 'self-loading' action, was developed from similar principles, but replaced the manual actions of the shooter with inbuilt mechanical actions within the firearm itself, using the explosion of the cartridge to generate the energy necessary to eject the spent cartridge, reload with a fresh one and recock the firing mechanism ready for a second shot.

The earliest successful self-loading shotguns, designed by the celebrated John Browning in the USA, employed the long-recoil system, in which the 'kick' of the cartridge and the forces of reaction generated within the gun were used to force the action to the rear, extracting the spent cartridge and throwing it clear, before the breech block began its forward travel, picking up a fresh cartridge from a tubular magazine and feeding it into the breech, with the firing mechanism cocked and ready. A further pull on the trigger discharged the shot, and thus the firearm effectively reloaded itself.

(The term 'semiautomatic' is useful only to help distinguish this type of action from the fully-automatic or machine-gun type action in which shots continue to be discharged for as long as pressure is maintained on the trigger. The self-loading gun requires a separate pressing of the trigger with each shot.)

The Browning long-recoil system is still made and is widely popular, especially in the FN Browning gun. But most self-loading shotguns made nowadays work on a shorter-travel gas-operated system, in which the action makes use of a proportion of the propellant gases which expand rapidly and violently when the cartridge is fired. Siphoned off through a port in the barrel wall, gas pressure is made to bear upon a piston whose connecting rod forces the gun's action rearwards, compressing the recoil spring and ejecting the fired shell, while also recocking the firing spring and returning the firing pin to the ready-to-fire position. Once fully recoiled and compressed, the spring forces the action forwards. This lifts a fresh cartridge into the chamber and the gun is once again ready to fire.

The 12-bore remains by far the most popular calibre for the self-loading shotgun, as for all other sporting shotguns, but this system has been successfully used on everything from the tiny ·410 to the hefty 8-bore. Even within a single bore size such as the 12-bore, the same gas-operated recoil system can cope successfully with light training loads weighing as little as ¾ ounce up to 3-inch magnum loads weighing 1⅞ ounces. The gas system, if properly designed and well maintained, is self regulating and retains whatever gas pressure may be necessary to operate the action, venting excess gas through escape ports.

The self-loading shotgun can give reliable, trouble-free service in the field, but its relatively complicated and delicate mechanism requires careful cleaning and maintenance. If the moving parts of the action, the slides or the gas ports become

From left to right, the three semi-automatic shotguns shown here are the lightweight Browning B-80, which with its standard 26-inch barrel weighs only 6½ pounds, the Winchester Ranger Semiautomatic and the Beretta A303. All are 12-bore models, and have gas-operated actions.

clogged with grit, sand or dust, excess cleaning oil or unburnt powder residues from fired cartridges, the system can malfunction and cartridges will not feed smoothly. This can be prevented by stripping down the gun at the end of every shooting day, and giving it a thorough cleaning using a powder solvent to remove residues, and by taking care to clear the action of fragments of plastic debris which plastic-cased cartridges tend to leave behind.

Like the pump action shotgun, the self-loading gun has a tubular magazine which lies below the single barrel and within the chunky forestock of the gun.

This can mean certain disadvantages, with the gun's point of balance well forward of the action, which makes it less lively to handle than most double-barrelled shotguns. All tubular magazines are prone to stoppages and faulty feeding of cartridges unless kept scrupulously clean, and there remains the perennial problem of ensuring that the magazine does not hold a live cartridge which has become jammed out of sight.

When pulled to the rearward position and locked open, the semiautomatic action should be quite safe, but careful handling is still important and it is never so easy to be certain that both

magazine and barrel are clear of all obstructions as is the case with the break-open type of shotgun action.

Like the slide action shotgun, the self-loading mechanism can be allied to an extended tubular magazine providing up to as many as eight cartridges in reserve. This gives a rate of fire which is extremely rapid but which is rarely likely to be of use to the sportsman under normal circumstances. A full length, fully-loaded magazine extension makes the gun extremely muzzle-heavy, and the use of magazine extensions is prohibited by law in most European countries.

Bore for bore, the self-loading shotgun will always be heavier than its double-barrelled, break-action counterpart, but this may be offset by the much reduced recoil occasioned by the gun's greater inertia and the way in which the action absorbs recoil. The self-loading shotgun may be an ideal choice for the clay pigeon shooter who fires a large number of cartridges during the course of a day's practice or competition, without having to carry his gun very far. However, the field shooter who expects to walk several miles and fire only a few shots may find the additional weight a disadvantage.

TRAPSHOOTING GUNS

When clay shooting first became popular, the most widely used gun was the side-by-side twelve-bore game gun. As traps became more powerful and the clays faster, so shooters learned to appreciate how the slim profile of the over-and-under adds considerably to accuracy.

A clay gun doesn't have to be carried for long periods and is therefore somewhat heavier than a game gun. The extra weight assists swinging and also absorbs recoil. The majority of over-and-under trapshooting guns weigh around 7 or 8 pounds. So many cartridges are fired by clay shooters that recoil problems can reach medical proportions. One of these is flinching at the moment of pulling the trigger, another is the jolting meted out to neck bones during a season's shooting.

A single, selective trigger is preferred for clay shooting. This is another aid to fast gun handling, obviating the need to move the hand back down the pistol grip to the second trigger.

A major contribution to precise shooting is the raised, ventilated rib on the barrels. It is file-cut to produce a matt, glint-free surface, which causes the foresight and midsight to stand out most clearly. When these two are correctly aligned with the eye, the rest is down to the shooter. The ventilated rib also helps dissipate the heat generated by shooting, but it does this to only a small degree, which is why the fore-end of a clay gun is so much fatter than that of a game gun: it prevents fingers from getting burnt.

The beavertail fore-end is so named after its similarity in shape to the beaver's broad, flat tail. In America a full beavertail shape is preferred, while in Europe a less bulbous modified beavertail is more popular. Stocks tend to be of the Monte Carlo style, with a pistol grip, although some shooters prefer a straight comb for trench shooting. It all depends on which discipline the gun is intended for. In down-the-line (DTL) shooting, all of the targets rise in a consistent trajectory, and a higher comb raises the sighting line so that the clay is more readily visible above the gun's muzzle. In Olympic trap shooting, the birds fly at all angles, and a lower plane of sight keeps the shooter more firmly on their track. One very successful international claybuster has an unusually high comb, keeping his line of sight a good 1½ inches above the barrels. It doesn't look right, but he rarely misses.

The fit of a gunstock is essential to accuracy. It is not unusual to see top shooters with bits of foam rubber taped to the stock. There are no points for elegance on the clay circuit, only for birds killed, and a quarter inch on the comb may be all that a shooter requires to adapt his skill to local conditions.

Where the same gun is to be used for a variety of disciplines, variable chokes enable the shooter to select precisely the grades that the layout requires. Several makers supply guns that accept interchangeable choke tubes – the Winchester Winchoke is one such system. Guns for skeet have the barrels choked skeet and skeet or, less often, improved cylinder and quarter choke. In common with most trap guns, they are chambered for 2½-inch cartridges loaded with 1⅛ ounces of shot.

While most British shooters rarely so much as try using a

Guns for clay target shooting are usually heavier than game guns, and most have Monte Carlo-type stocks. The guns shown here are, from top to bottom, the Winchester 6500, the Italian-made Beretta 5682, the Browning GTI and the Japanese Miroku 3800 Grade 5.

twenty-bore at skeet, in America this discipline is shot with twelve, twenty, twenty-eight and .410 gauges. Experienced shooters have little trouble killing 100 straight even with these light loads. The standard skeet gun is lighter than those used for trap shooting. At 7 to 7½ pounds it weighs the same as a gun used for sporting clays, and barrel length is around 28 inches, keeping the gun quick in the hand. The rubber recoil pad differs between guns used for ISU skeet and those used for American skeet. ISU shooters start in the gun down position, so consequently the heel is often rounded off and the pad finished in wood or plastic to ensure fumble-free mounting.

American skeet shooters may start with the gun either up or down.

DTL guns have long barrels of 30 inches or over, weigh 7 to 8 pounds or more and are choked half and threequarters. Some shooters prefer more choke than this; however, the clay leaves the trap just 15 yards in front, suggesting that shooters who use fully choked guns should endeavour to take the bird sooner. The same gun may be used for Olympic trap. However, as the clays are less predictable in their flight path, a degree more choke gives the shooter a fraction more time to judge their trajectory and to take his shot, so most OT guns are bored threequarters and full.

CLAYS AND TRAPS

Each year, countless millions of clay pigeons are sent winging across the world's skies. Few of them get very far before being pulverized by a charge of shot, and the ones that are missed carry on flying until they run out of energy and hit the ground.

Clays are made out of pitch and powdered limestone, a mixture which shatters easily, is cheap to make and mould, and is unaffected by rain and wet. The smashed shards settle on the ground, and start to decay within a few weeks. They have to break easily, even when hit by just one pellet from the gun's shot pattern, and top shots are adept at spotting a little chip being flaked from a clay target – it marks the difference between a kill or a loss.

The basic design of a clay pigeon is similar to that of a Frisbee. It is shaped like an inverted saucer, and as it spins through the air, the motion of spinning provides a high degree of stability in flight so that the flight pattern of these targets will be consistent from release to release. This is important because some branches of clay shooting, like skeet and down-the-line, require the clays to follow a set flight path. If they don't, the shooter has reason to complain to the referee.

The standard clay pigeon weighs 4½ ounces and is not quite 4½ inches wide. This design is shot all over the world, but it is not the only design. The midi clay, for instance, is 3½ inches in diameter, and there is also the 2¼-inch mini clay often used on Sporting layouts. The mini is fast, tiny, and quite capable of spoiling anybody's clear round.

Equally difficult to hit is the battue design of clay, which is shaped like a biscuit rather than being domed like a standard target. It is about the same weight and size as a standard clay, but as it spins through the air, this design sideslips and lifts on the wind. It is whimsical in its flight path and is frequently found on the Sporting field, and like the mini, it sorts the good shooters from the indifferent ones on the international circuit. Similar to the battue, but with a wider rim, is the bolting rabbit design. This is made to roll and bound over the ground on its edge, so it's not an easy mark to hit.

The standard colour of clays

is black, which shows up well against a wide open sky, but they are often coloured differently to make them show up against difficult backgrounds. Coloured clays are most widely used on Sporting layouts where thick cover makes spotting tricky. Under these conditions,

fluorescent orange is popular, as is white, although white isn't easy to see in mist. White clays are used for floodlit shooting at night, the birds showing up clearly against the darkness and disappearing in a puff of white powder when hit.

Although it is not strictly a

clay, the ZZ target is the closest approximation to a live pigeon in flight. The centre is white plastic and shaped like a clay, but it has red wings which have to separate from the body for a kill to be scored. This discipline is shot with five machines which spin the birds before releasing

one at random. The flight is erratic, demanding precise shooting, but this sport has yet to win great popularity.

All clay pigeons are thrown from traps, a term which hails from the time when live birds were released from a wooden box. Nowadays, a trap is a spring-loaded arm which throws either one clay or a pair when it is released.

The most basic type of trap is the hand launcher, with muscle power providing the momentum, and it is claimed that this design is useful for novices. Hand-thrown clays, though, are slow and fly erratically in direction, and the man with the trap is not particularly safe unless he is concealed by a tree or a wall.

However, any group of clay enthusiasts can readily afford to buy a couple of good spring-loaded traps for setting up in a field. A wide range of designs is available, some being more heavy-duty than others. Some have seats on which the trapper anchors himself to facilitate re-cocking the throwing arm, but others recock automatically.

Many traps are designed to throw clays at specific angles: the springing teal trap sends a pair of birds rocketing upwards between the trees, the bolting rabbit trap has its arm set vertically so that the bird is thrown in an underarm movement, causing it to bounce over the ground, and the driven pheasant trap, set high on a tower, re-leases its clays horizontally so that they glide out over the shooter. Other designs of trap can be adjusted to alter the angle and speed of the birds they throw.

Shooting grounds often use automatic traps fitted with magazines that are loaded with over 1000 clays. Some of these are computer-controlled so that the angle and direction of the clay differs from release to release, as in the Automatic Trap discipline. These traps make it hard for the shooter to predict the flight of his birds. Older designs were less random and shooters could recognize a pat-tern in the release system.

The release itself happens in three ways. In Sporting, for ex-ample, most clays are released by the trapper. He either hears the shooter call 'pull' or the referee relays that instruction by pressing a buzzer that sounds in the traphouse. In some discip-lines, like Olympic Trench, a microphone in front of the shooter releases the clays elec-tronically the moment he calls for them. Under tense competi-tive conditions, this obviates delays caused by the trapper not being ready, or the referee being slow on the button.

The trapper's safety should always be of paramount import-ance: many have been injured because their only protection was a sheet of corrugated iron. A proper trench with a roof is ideal for DTL and other forms of trapshooting, and in disciplines like Sporting, safe trap houses can be made from thick wood, and covered with steel plating at least an eighth of an inch thick where extra protection is neces-sary. After all, it is unrealistic to expect a trapper to be on the ball if he feels his life is being seriously threatened every time somebody shouts 'pull!'

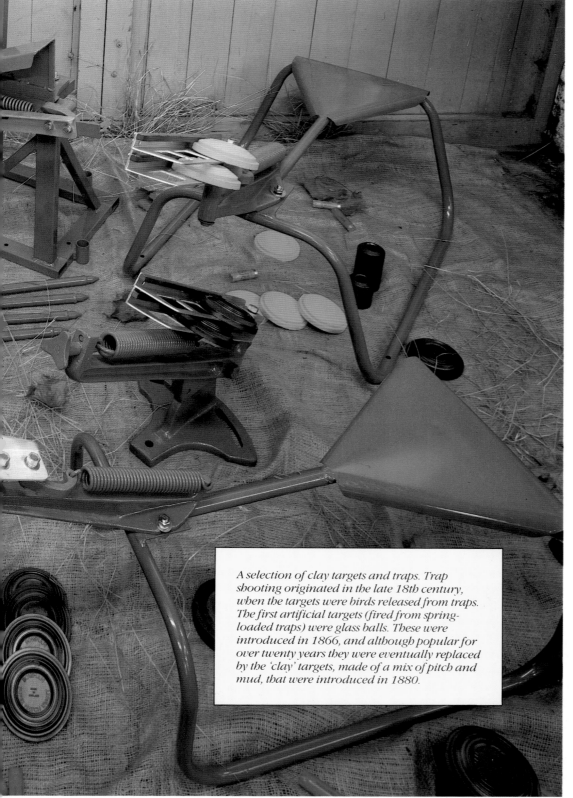

A selection of clay targets and traps. Trap shooting originated in the late 18th century, when the targets were birds released from traps. The first artificial targets (fired from spring-loaded traps) were glass balls. These were introduced in 1866, and although popular for over twenty years they were eventually replaced by the 'clay' targets, made of a mix of pitch and mud, that were introduced in 1880.

SHOTGUN AMMUNITION

The modern shotgun cartridge combines the detonator, propellant and shot in one convenient little unit. This takes the form of a firing cap, centred in the metallic head of the cartridge, just below a charge of nitrocellulose, granular powder above which there is an over-powder wad or the base of a plastic shot cup. Above or within this lies the charge of small shot, buckshot or single ball or slug.

The contents of the cartridge case are usually held in place and the case closed by a crimped squeezing together of the cartridge casing material, to form a square end, although a top wad and a rolled turn-over is often used as an alternative form of closure for magnum loads and large-shot cartridges. The vast majority of modern shotgun cartridges have a plastic casing, although the so-called paper cased cartridge (actually a thick cardboard, lacquered to give some water resistance) also remains popular.

The size of a shotgun cartridge, whatever the size or type of the shot pellets or slugs contained in it, is measured in three closely-related ways – by the calibre or bore of the gun for which the cartridge is intended; by the length of the cartridge case; and by the weight of the shot charge it contains. Apart from the little .410 and other miniature smooth-bore calibres, such as the 9 mm 'garden gun' and the tiny .22 rimfire smooth-bore shotshell, shotgun calibres are designated by a bore size, reckoned by the number of balls of pure lead the same diameter as the internal bore of the barrel tube which together weigh 1 pound Imperial weight. Thus the 12-bore shotgun, the most popular and widely used of all, has a barrel tube which accommodates a spherical lead ball weighing $\frac{1}{12}$ pound. (Its bore normally measures .729 inch, but it is never referred to as a '.729 shotgun'.)

A shotgun cartridge designed to fire a normal charge of small shot from a 12-bore sporting shotgun will measure 2½ or 2¾ inches in length. While 2½ inches remains the British standard, all American cartridges have until recently been of the 2¾-inch variety, in common with most cartridges from continental Europe. For heavy, magnum-types loads in shot-

guns of all bores from 20-bore to 12-bore the 3-inch cartridge case is used, and in the heavier shoulder-gun bores like the 10-bore, the 8-bore and the 4-bore, the cartridge case becomes progressively longer, extending from 3¼ inches to over 4 inches.

The greater length of the magnum cartridge requires a suitable chamber length within the barrel of the shotgun from which it is to be fired, even though it is physically possible

to insert a 3-inch cased cartridge into the chamber of a 2½-inch chambered gun. Great care must be taken only to use cartridge lengths which do not exceed the lengths of the chambers in the gun you are using, otherwise serious damage to the gun (and possibly its firer) may result.

It is also essential to ensure that cartridges of different bores do not become mixed. For example, if 12-bore and 20-bore cartridges become mixed, it is

possible for a 20-bore cartridge to be slipped into the breech of a 12-bore gun, where it will fall forward and lodge in the cone of the chamber, allowing a normal 12-bore cartridge to be chambered behind it. If that cartridge is fired with such a solid obstruction in the barrel a burst is inevitable, with potentially fatal results either to the firer or to someone else standing close by. The same can happen if .410 and 20-bore cartridges become mixed or 28-

bore cartridges are mixed with 16-bore.

In addition to these variations in the bores and lengths of shotgun cartridge cases, there is also considerable variation in the weight of the shot charge they can carry. For instance, the traditional standard shot load for a 2½-inch 12-bore cartridge loaded with size 6 or 7 shot, as normally used for shooting most forms of game birds, will weigh 1¹⁄₁₆ ounces. However, the same length of cartridge

case for a 12-bore can also be obtained with a shot charge as light as ¹³⁄₁₆ ounce, as a light training cartridge, and up to 1⅛ ounces, which some sportsmen prefer.

Apart from the increased use of plastics to form the cartridge case, there have been a number of other recent developments in the design of sporting shotgun ammunition in recent years, although the fundamental principles remain unchanged. For example, the old felt over-

powder or driving wad, above the powder and below the shot charge, is now often replaced by a plastic shot cup, not unlike a miniature eggcup. This comprises a flat or slightly concave circular base which functions as the over-powder wad, while the shot charge is contained within a thin-sided plastic cup. The shot cup and its contents are driven forward as the cartridge is fired, and they leave the barrel of the shotgun together, after which the cup falls away leaving

the shot charge to fly forward.

The shot cup prevents the shot pellets from coming into contact with the barrel walls, and this eliminates pellet deformation caused by abrasion. Undeformed spherical pellets fly truer, which should improve the evenness of the shot pattern, but the shot cup also holds the shot charge together and creates the same effect as a slight additional measure of choke boring in the gun barrel, which the shooter may wish to avoid. Many brands of game cartridge are still made with the traditional felt driving wad, which many shooters prefer. Quite apart from questions of shot deformation and the effects on shot pattern, many sportsmen wish to avoid littering the countryside with non-biodegradable plastic shotcups.

For over 200 years, ammunition manufacturers and sportsmen have experimented with ways of hardening lead shot, by 'chilling' it, by the addition of antimony, and by plating the shot with various gilding metals such as nickel. Most lead shot loaded in cartridges nowadays is hardened or coated in some way, which reduces pellet deformation, increases the penetrative power of pellets and greatly reduces 'leading', the fouling of the barrel caused by the abrasion of soft lead pellets which leaves a lead residue on the barrel wall.

Shotgun pellet development has gone a stage further with the recent advent of steel shot, which is now mandatory for duck shooting and wildfowling in many parts of North America. Lead is a poison, and significant mortality can occur among dabbling waterfowl which ingest lead pellets in heavily-shot areas. Steel shot avoids this, but the smaller mass of the steel pellet has lower energy and is less likely to result in a clean kill, when compared size-for-size with lead pellets.

Research and development will expand the range and suitability of steel-shot cartridges in the future, but those currently available are quite unsuitable for use in many shotguns, especially older guns and the traditional English and European types. If you are going to switch to steel shot, first check with your gun's manufacturer, or your dealer or gunsmith, to ensure that it will be safe.

With the wide range of bores, cartridge types, loads and charges to choose from, the selection of a suitable cartridge may seem difficult. The experienced shooter will invariably have his or her tried and tested favourites, while the novice should take expert advice from a shooting school coach or a friendly senior shooter. Once you find a cartridge which suits you and the gun you use it is wise to stick to it. Experimentation and constant changing are likely to lead to inconsistent shooting, and dissatisfaction.

AIR RIFLES & PISTOLS

The technology of air weapons has covered huge strides within the last few years. Although their power is still slight when compared with the massive muzzle energies that are developed by cartridge rifles, modern good-quality air weapons are effective, elegant, accurate and beautifully engineered.

Only a few years ago, airgun enthusiasts had the choice of just two power systems – spring or pump-up pneumatic. Nowadays there are other ways of propelling a pellet at high speed, and these include the precharged air cylinder, pneumatic cartridges, and the sealed gas ram piston.

The major advances in air weapon technology have taken place in Britain and Germany where severe restrictions on the use of cartridge rifles have made necessity the mother of invention. In England, the legal limit is twelve foot-pounds of muzzle energy. In Germany, it is even less, while in Northern Ireland special permission is required from the police – in the form of a firearms certificate – to use any air weapon. Such a certificate is required in England for high-powered rifles whose muzzle energy is over the twelve foot-pound limit.

These restrictions have generated an enormous amount of research into the design and engineering efficiency of airguns. At the same time, sighting systems, triggers, and woodwork have been considerably refined – they are very different from the airguns that grandad used. Not all types of air weapon are suited to hunting, however. Pistols deliver so little power that they are effective against only the smallest and least consequential quarry. Indeed, it is illegal to use air pistols for hunting in Britain, where they are used only for target shooting.

This is a minor matter, though, because there are so many fine rifles around. Some power systems are more suitable than others for field shooting. Most pump-up pneumatics, for example, need several strokes of the lever before they reach full power, and this is both time-consuming and noisy – not ideal when hoping for a quick shot at an easily-spooked quarry.

The spring-powered, break-barrel air rifle has reigned supreme for years. Many models are available, right up to a full 30 ft-lbs muzzle energy. The Weihrauch HW80 is one of the best-known rifles in this category. In its standard form, its power has obviously been restrained in deference to British and European legislation; custom rifle builders, however, have been creating some very interesting weapons out of this basic chassis.

The spring rifle is available in many different styles. Several models have to be cocked with a lever that is fitted either to one side or underneath the barrel. Although side levers can never be called elegant, they do permit a neat auto-loading system to be fitted. One of the best methods, and one which permits quick, accurate shooting, is made by Air Arms in England.

The system is simple enough. A tubular magazine is fitted above the air chamber, holding about 20 pellets. The cocking stroke allows one pellet to slip into the breech. Close the side lever, and the rifle is ready to fire. The makers of this system have toyed with the idea of creating a semiautomatic pneumatic rifle, with the power coming from a precharged air cylinder. Such a rifle will be interesting to check out – when it happens.

Pneumatic rifles look set to take over the industry during the coming years. They offer a major advantage over spring-and-piston rifles because they have no recoil, and several manufacturers are already exploring this theme. Air Arms, Sportsmatch, and Daystate make pneumatics that require a special reservoir – built into the rifle – to be precharged with air. The Daystate system allows the shooter to carry spare air cylinders, but the others require a visit to either an air bottle or to special charging equipment once the power falls off, and this can be a nuisance when far from base. Another manufacturer has designed a sensible compromise, though: Air Logic's Genesis air rifle is a pneumatic that can readily be recocked with one stroke of a side lever.

Less suitable for the hunting field are rifles that require pneumatic cartridges to be charged at home. These are fairly bulky and, naturally enough, need a large pocket to

These four air rifles and one pistol are, from top to bottom, the Air Logic Genesis, the Crosman 2200 Magnum, the BSA Supersport, the Weihrauch HW45 pistol, and the customized Weihrauch HW80 rifle from Venom Arms. All of these guns are .22 calibre. The separate scope sights and mounts are from Venom, and the knock-down targets from Airmasters.

take the discharged shells so they can be reloaded for next time. This type of power system is less convenient than others and detracts from the basic simplicity which is, for many people, the main attraction of air weapons.

Modern air rifles come with ramps to accept most shapes and sizes of telescopic sight. Because of the hefty recoil from a powerful spring rifle, many shooters fit solid one-piece scope mounts and an arrestor block to prevent the mount from sliding backwards in its rails. Recoilless pneumatics don't require such rugged sights as spring rifles do.

With the exception of a few models, trigger mechanisms on air rifles are subtle and adjustable, generally with a first and second pressure to ensure smooth release of the firing mechanism. Not many years ago, good triggers, like the Weihrauch's Rekord type, were a rarity on air weapons.

Ammunition for air weapons now comes in an abundance of shapes and designs, with the main calibres of .177, .20, .22 and .25 being generously catered for. Nearly all pellets are stamped out of lead wire, although some are steel and mounted inside a plastic sheath. Because of the curved trajectory of most pellets, it pays to find a brand which works well with a particular weapon, then stick with it and learn how it performs under different conditions of wind and weather. Pellets differ in weight from make to make: a heavy .177 can weigh as much as a light .20, while a .25 solid spitzer bullet requires a great deal of power to propel it in something resembling a straight line of flight. The .177 is the favourite of field target shooters because of its fast, flat trajectory. However, this type of pellet tends to drill rather than to drop quarry. Consequently, hunters generally prefer a heavy .20 or .22.

BOLT-ACTION RIFLES

The bolt-action rifle unquestionably dominates the world of sporting rifle shooting in every country, and has done so throughout the 20th century. The manually operated turn-bolt mechanism, allied to a single barrel and a magazine holding additional rounds of ammunition in reserve, has won enormous popularity for its strength, its reliability, its ready ease of operation and the way it provides the rifleman with a dependable system for firing accurate single shots, which can be followed by speedy ejection and the fast reloading of a fresh cartridge ready for a second shot, if required.

There are two main types of bolt actions, the turn-bolt and the straight-pull styles, but the latter is a now-obsolete military system with little relevance to sporting rifle design.

The turn-bolt, as its name suggests, involves a solid rod or plug at the breech which is rotated to lock and unlock it from the receiver at the rear of the barrel, while its movement back and forward is designed to extract and eject spent cases, and recock the mechanism as a fresh cartridge is pushed forward into the chamber. Raising the handle of the bolt turns the bolt body and disengages the large locking lugs which pro-

trude from the bolt cylinder, freeing the bolt from the forward, locked position in which the bolt face seals the rear of the breech behind the head of the cartridge. Once raised fully, the bolt handle can be drawn to the rear, extracting and ejecting the fired case while forward movement picks up a fresh round from the magazine and pushes it forward into the chamber. The final action of turning the bolt handle downwards re-engages the locking lugs, locking the action and sealing the breech.

Any consideration of the turn-bolt rifle action must begin with some reference to the designs and developments of the Ger-

man rifle manufacturer Peter Paul Mauser (1833-1914), one of a family of seven brothers who were all gunmakers. From his workshop at Oberndorf, in Germany, Peter Paul Mauser developed their original Model 71 action, which comprised a receiver forged or cast from a single piece of steel and bored lengthwise to accept a free-moving turn-bolt. The end of the rifle barrel was screwed into the forward end of the receiver, and an open slit or loading port long enough to admit a loaded cartridge was cut through the upper right side of the receiver. A cylindrical steel bolt with large ribs running along its

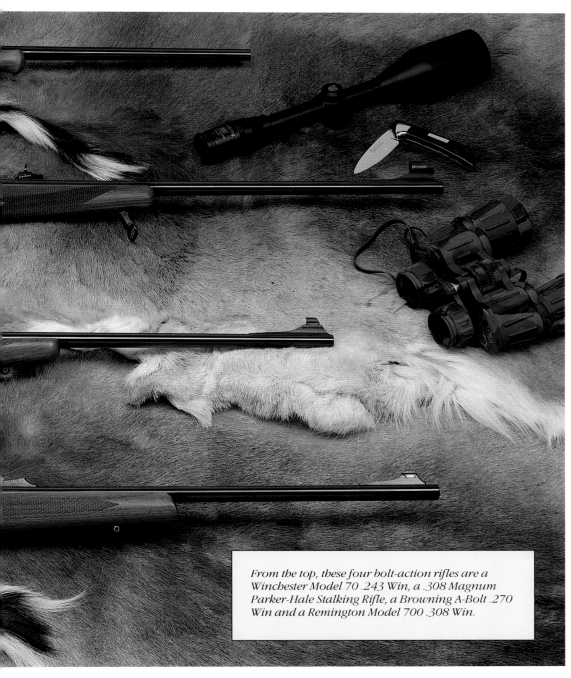

From the top, these four bolt-action rifles are a Winchester Model 70 .243 Win, a .308 Magnum Parker-Hale Stalking Rifle, a Browning A-Bolt .270 Win and a Remington Model 700 .308 Win.

length moved to and fro within the receiver, guided and turned by a bolt lever or handle with a rounded knob on the end.

The action of sliding the bolt forward and turning down the bolt handle served to chamber a cartridge and lock the breech in the ready-to-fire position. After firing, the bolt handle was raised and pulled back to extract the cartridge, held by small claw-type extractor hooks. The rearward pulling of the spent cartridge case brought it sharply against a flange in the receiver, causing the spent case to flick sideways and outward clear of the action, leaving it free for the bolt to return, cocking the

firing-pin mechanism and feeding a fresh cartridge into the chamber before the breech was sealed by the rotational movement of the bolt as the handle was returned to the downward position.

Mauser's eventual production of the Model 98 bolt action established a design which has been the foundation for most turn-bolt rifle actions throughout the world this century. The M98 has two forward and one rear locking lug which gives it massive strength, ideal for modern high-pressure ammunition even of the most powerful magnum type, and the upward rotation of the bolt handle begins

the recocking of the firing pin, which is completed as the bolt is moved forward, picking up the top cartridge from the magazine and pushing it into the chamber. The final forward movement of the bolt causes the cartridge head to slide under the extractor hook before the bolt handle rotates and engages the three locking lugs.

Important modern rifle designers like Weatherby, Remington and Ruger in the USA and David Lloyd and Parker-Hale in England have produced variants on Mauser's M98 design, and the popular Czechoslovakian-made Brno sporting rifles also derive from this celebrated action de-

sign. Its only major competitor has been the Mannlicher-Schoenauer bolt action, developed at the Austrian gunmaking town of Steyr in 1900. This system has the large forward locking lugs of all good turn-bolt systems, and apart from some technical variations in bolt design, its most obvious distinguishing feature is the positioning of the bolt handle about half way along the length of the bolt, with the rear section of the receiver split at the top to allow its rearward movement. The Mannlicher-Schoenauer type of action is renowned for exceptionally smooth operation and clean, positive feeding of ammunition from the rotary box magazine, which is quite different from the 'staggered-column' system of most box magazines.

From the practical sporting rifleman's point of view, the bolt action has many important advantages over other systems. It is exceptionally accurate, due to the natural stiffness of the action in which a large, solid steel rod effectively seals the breech and stiffens the entire action, limiting the flexing which can reduce accuracy, especially at longer ranges. The modern bolt action has a very short-travel firing pin, and modern springs mean that the action time is exceptionally fast, which also promotes accurate firing. When allied to a well-matched box magazine of staggered-column or rotary design, and with well-machined surfaces within the receiver, a bolt action can be manipulated with great speed once the rifleman is familiar with it, and reloading and firing of subsequent shots is quick and accurate.

The receiver and action of the turn-bolt system makes it a compact extension at the rear of the rifle barrel, and the weapon can therefore be fitted with a strong, rigid, one-piece wooden stock, which adds to the total rigidity of the construction. (Synthetic materials are used by some manufacturers to avoid the warping and distortion which extreme humidity or cold can cause to wood, but synthetic stocks have not gained general acceptance and wood remains popular.)

The well-made rifle is the outcome of a happy marriage between three elements, the 'lock, stock and barrel' of the old proverb. In bolt-actioned rifles, the joining of barrel and action is a straightforward matter, and the barrel is screwed into the front of the action receiver along a heavy, deeply-cut thread an inch or more long. The rifling within the bore of the barrel must be precision-cut, with an appropriate rate of twist for the intended cartridge and weight of bullet so as to stabilize the bullet as it begins its flight after the propellant in the cartridge is detonated. Similarly, the chamber to accommodate the cartridge must be precision cut for a snug fit, with the bullet just reaching up to the cone where the rifling begins.

Most critical for accurate, consistent shooting is satisfactory 'bedding' of the action/barrel combination within the stock. The action must be evenly and snugly bedded within the enshrouding woodwork, and epoxy resin and other synthetic compounds are often used to achieve the required uniformity on all the bearing surfaces. Bedding the barrel is rather different, and various bedding techniques are used, depending on the type of stock fitted. But most conventionally half-stocked rifles now have a 'free-floating' barrel, which does not come into contact with the woodwork at any point from the breech forwards. Others are centre-bedded, the barrel bearing on a point about midway along, and front-bedding is used in fully-stocked or 'stutzen'-type rifles, which are traditional favourites in Europe.

Whatever the nature of the bedding, it must always be consistent and remain so despite the rather rough handling which is normal when hunting in the field, and despite changes in temperature and humidity. There is only one satisfactory way to check a rifle's bedding, and that is to fire it regularly at a target under controlled range conditions. Inaccuracy or inconsistency revealed then must be remedied by a competent rifle-smith before the rifle is used again for live game hunting, or a missed or (worse) a wounded animal may be the result.

Rifle barrels can be of various lengths, and a cartridge will normally develop maximum muzzle velocity, and thus maximum bullet energy, in a barrel some 24 inches long. (The longer, target-shooters' barrels are impractically long for easy use in the field.) But many lever-actioned rifles and stutzen-type rifles have 18-inch barrels, which mean a shorter, lighter rifle which can be easier to

handle in thick cover. This may more than compensate for the loss in ballistic performance which comes from a shorter barrel, and the bullet should retain adequate trajectory and energy for accurate, effective shooting at all normal sporting distances. The hill stalker and the hunter of mountain sheep may find he has to deal with targets at much longer distances than the woodland stalker and he will be better served by the longer-barrelled style.

The comparative simplicity of

the modern bolt-action makes mass production easy, and excellent production-line rifles are readily available from many popular manufacturers in Britain, Europe and the USA. A simple but highly accurate sporting centrefire rifle like the Midland 2100 marketed by Parker-Hale, or the Winchester Model 70, can be bought for the price of a cheap double-barrelled shotgun, while leaving great scope for the production and hand-finishing of top quality, custom-made rifles with

superb woodwork and fine wood-to-metal fit at much higher prices, although even the best of these will be much less expensive than a good quality London-made sidelock shotgun. Such rifles are a delight to own and use, but may not shoot any straighter than an off-the shelf model.

An important recent trend in bolt-action design has been the incorporation of safety slides to the rear of the action or on the top tang behind the bolt, replacing the old flag-type safeties of

earlier designs, In addition, bolt handles are now bent and angled into lower positions than formerly, and designers have given some thought to the ergonomics of how the rifleman handles his gun and manipulates the bolt. These modifications allow telescopic sights to be mounted very low over the receiver, placing the line of sight close to the axis of the rifle barrel's bore, and allowing the rifleman's eye to come readily into position when the rifle is brought to the shoulder.

Modern bolt actions eject spent cartridges with a sharp sideways motion, which avoids fouling the low-mounted scope sight, and an increasingly popular variation on the detachable box magazine is an integral, staggered-column magazine below the receiver, with a hinged floor-plate placed forward of the trigger guard, enabling the magazine to be charged from above and unloaded quickly from below. The traditional two-stage, military-style trigger mechanism has generally given

way to a crisp, single-stage type developed from target rifle designs, and many manufacturers now make centrefire rifles with a choice of standard weight, tapered barrels or target-quality barrels. These are heavier but can improve accuracy at long range, especially in the specialized sport of varmint hunting popular in North America.

To these many outstanding qualities must be added another great advantage of the bolt-action – its safety. By opening the bolt the rifleman can instant-

ly make the rifle safe, can visually check that the chamber and barrel are clear of cartridges or dangerous obstructions, and also check that the magazine is empty. All rifle bolts can be completely removed from the receiver by pressing a simple catch, which makes it easy to check that the bore is unobstructed and to clean the barrel and action thoroughly.

All in all, the modern bolt-action rifle is suitable for almost every form of sporting rifle shooting.

The uppermost gun shown here is a Marlin 781 .22, whose tubular magazine holds 25 short, 19 long or 17 long rifle cartridges. Below it are a Krico .308 Win, a Krico .22 Hornet with stutzen-type stock and, at the bottom, a Marlin 780 .22, whose clip holds 7 short, long or long rifle cartridges.

LEVER, PUMP & SEMIAUTOMATIC ACTION RIFLES

Despite the overwhelming predominance and popularity of the bolt-action magazine rifle among sportsmen, alternative actions are also available for repeating, single-barrelled sporting rifles. Perhaps the most familiar of these, especially for the North American sportsman, is the lever action, best exemplified by the Winchester repeating rifle familiar from countless Western movies.

The lever action is based upon the movement of a levering system pivoted below the action receiver and comprising the trigger guard and an elongated metal loop for the firer's hand, slung below the wrist of the action. The lever action works on the principle that a downward and forward thrust of the lever cocks the firing mechanism, opens the breech and ejects a spent cartridge, while the upward and rearward return of the lever feeds a fresh cartridge into the breech from the magazine and returns the rifle to the ready-to-fire state. The magazine may be of the box or rotary type similar to those used in many turn-bolt rifles, or a tubular magazine, usually placed directly beneath the single rifle barrel. The latter is typical of the Winchester-type lever action rifle.

The lever action was developed and used, with great success, primarily for short cartridges, from the .22 rimfire to the .30/30 and similar cartridges used widely in North America for hunting at short range in thick undergrowth. The original lever action design has a locking mechanism which is adequate to seal the breech and withstand the pressure of these older, 'gentler' cartridges, but modifications to the original design became necessary to accommodate the high breech pressures developed by modern cartridges like the .243 Win and the .308. For these and other long, high-pressure cartridges, Winchester developed their Model 88 lever action which has a rotating, front-locking bolt which is more similar to the tight system of locking lugs of the turn-bolt actions.

The lever action can be fast in use, and had particular appeal to the left-handed sportsman before the ready availability of

bolt-actioned rifles designed for left-handed use. However, the design can pose various problems. Tubular magazines are slow to charge, and cartridges must be loaded one at a time, which may be laborious. Fragments of grit and other obstructions can prevent the easy feeding of cartridges from the magazine tube, and it can be difficult to keep this clean. The long, spiral magazine spring is heavily compressed when the tubular magazine is fully loaded, leading to progressive weakening of the spring when only one or two rounds remain in the magazine, and this can lead to poor feeding and loading difficulties.

The lever action requires extra care for safe handling, and it is often difficult to be absolutely certain that neither the magazine nor the breech contains a live cartridge. A temporary blockage in the tubular magazine may make it possible to operate the lever action repeatedly without loading a cartridge, leading to the reasonable assumption that the gun has been cleared and is empty, even though a cartridge may remain within and be inadvertently chambered later, with potentially tragic consequences. Also, the tubular magazine prevents the use of pointed bullets, since one of the points, resting against the primer of the cartridge ahead of it, could cause that round to go off when the rifle recoils.

Nevertheless, the lever-action rifle continues to play an important part in sporting shooting, especially in North America where it remains a firm traditional favourite.

The pump action is another alternative to the bolt action, although the name is rather misleading for the action involves a sliding movement rather than a pumping one, and it is sometimes referred to as a 'trombone' style. This action is broadly similar to that of the pump-actioned shotgun: the shooter's forward hand grips a wooden fore-end or slide handle underneath the barrel, and when this is slid to the rear the breech-block is forced backwards, opening the breech and extracting and ejecting the fired case and recocking the firing mechanism. The magazine

spring raises a fresh cartridge, which is fed forward into the rifle's chamber as the slide handle is moved forward and returned to its original position, which re-engages the locking lug at the breech and prepares the rifle for firing.

The slide action is mechanically simple and physically solid, and much the same system is used for all shotgun and rifle calibres. Disadvantages of the system include occasional difficulties in extracting a jammed cartridge, for which the slide action affords little leverage. Additionally, the action can be noisy in operation and careful maintenance is required if the rifle is not to develop small rattles in the slide mechanism, which may upset the stalk and frighten the game.

Like the lever action, the slide

action may have a particular appeal for the left-handed shooter, but some pump-action rifles can be unpleasant to handle, owing to the forward weight of the slide mechanism and the consequent forward positioning of the point of balance.

Finally, there is the so-called 'semiautomatic' rifle action. This is basically a variation on the machine gun principle, and it makes use of the forces created by the firing of a cartridge to eject the spent cartridge case, recock the firing action and bring a fresh cartridge from the magazine into the breech ready for firing when the trigger is next pressed. (Unlike the fully-automatic action of the machine gun type, it is not designed to discharge successive rounds while continuous pressure is

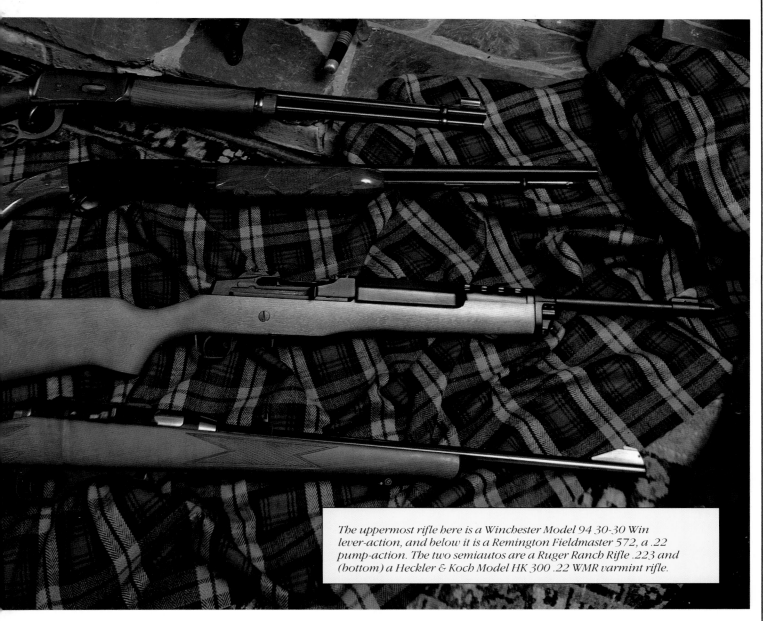

The uppermost rifle here is a Winchester Model 94 30-30 Win lever-action, and below it is a Remington Fieldmaster 572, a .22 pump-action. The two semiautos are a Ruger Ranch Rifle .223 and (bottom) a Heckler & Koch Model HK 300 .22 WMR varmint rifle.

maintained on the trigger, nor would a fully-automatic action have any place whatsoever in the sporting shooting scene.)

It is probably better to refer to the semiautomatic action as a 'self-loading' system, which is a more accurate reflection of how the mechanism has been designed: the firing of one cartridge causes the mechanical loading of the next one from the magazine. This style of action may be one of three basic designs – the blowback, the recoil-operated and the gas-operated systems.

The blowback action makes use of the simple physical laws of action and reaction. The fired cartridge is driven backwards and the head of the cartridge case presses against the face of the breech block and begins to force it backwards, although the

inertia of the breech block means that the bullet and the propellant gases leave the barrel long before the breech opens. The breech block, thus blown back, extracts the spent cartridge case and recocks the firing mechanism before returning to the forward position, chambering a fresh cartridge and sealing the breech ready for the next shot.

The recoil action, of which the best design was invented by the American firm of Browning Arms and later developed in Belgium by the FN factory, makes use of the recoil or 'kick' of the fired rifle which causes a sliding breech block or sliding bolt to travel backwards, eventually disengaging the bolt and opening the breech, sufficient time having elapsed for the bullet and the powder charge to

clear the barrel and for the initial expansion of the cartridge case to retract and free the case from the chamber wall, allowing it to be drawn to the rear and ejected. As the recoil action moves backwards, it compresses a spring which then drives the breech block forward, picking up a fresh cartridge from the magazine as it goes, feeding it into the chamber and turning the locking lugs to seal the breech in preparation for a fresh shot.

The gas-operated action makes use of a small proportion of the expanding propellant gases which explode at great speed and pressure behind the bullet when a cartridge is fired. Some of these gases are diverted into a pressure chamber, where they exert great force on a piston system which unlocks

the breech and forces the action mechanism to the rear, ejecting the spent cartridge and recocking the firing mechanism as it does so. The rearward movement of the action compresses a recoil spring, which then pushes the working parts forward to chamber another cartridge and return the rifle to the sealed-breech, ready-to-fire state.

In many countries, including Great Britain, the use of self-loading centrefire rifles for the shooting of live quarry such as deer is illegal, which restricts their use to comparatively few countries of the western world. However, the self-loading .22 rimfire (permissible for hunting in most countries) is a universally popular type of rifle, available in many attractive and well designed styles.

SCOPE SIGHTS

The telescopic sight now enjoys universal popularity among sporting riflemen, on everything from air rifles and .22 rimfire calibres up to the very heaviest big-game calibres. Almost everyone who uses a modern bolt-actioned magazine rifle will have it fitted with a telescopic sight, and they can also be mounted on self-loading, pump-action and lever-action rifles of modern design, where ejected cartridge cases are thrown out sideways, clear of the scope.

The principle of the system is simple, and the sight consists of a series of lenses within a short metal tube mounted above the rifle barrel and, very occasionally, slighly offset to one side of it. The magnifying power of good lenses makes the target appear larger and more distinct, and there is a single built-in reticle or sighting mark which can be superimposed upon the target. When securely fitted and properly zeroed, a telescopic sight enables a rifleman to see both his target and his aiming mark clearly and in the same focal plane, and there is no problem about aligning a clearly-focused foresight and rearsight with a distant target, as with open and aperture sights.

Modern scope sights with large objective (frontal) lenses and moderate power (4× to 6×) have considerable light-gathering ability, making it easier to see the target and shoot accurately in the dim light of dawn and dusk or in the gloom of dense woodland, and these are precisely the conditions deer stalkers and other sportsmen may have to face.

Telescopic sights are available in a great range of specifications and styles. Magnification power may be as little as 1½× and up to 25× or more, and the simple crosshaired reticle has many variant forms, including flat-topped posts, pointed upright markings and combinations of posts and wires, and some with graduations like the calibrations on a vernier-scaled aperture sight for target shooting.

The higher the magnification, the more it exaggerates every wobble and tremor of the rifle, and so some users opt for only a 4× or 6× power. Equally important, however, is the diameter of the objective lens, usually measured in millimetres. A scope sight designa-

tion of 6 × 40 simply means that the image is magnified six times and the sight has a 40-millimetre diameter lens at the front. The objective lens gathers the light, and, generally speaking, the larger the objective lens the greater the light-gathering power will be – an important consideration in poor light such as at dawn or dusk.

However, there are limits to the light-gathering ability of the human eye, and the pupil of the eye cannot normally dilate (expand) to more than about 7 mm across. The light and the image passing through a telescopic sight is focused on a small area known as the 'exit pupil', and if the diameter of this is much less than 7mm then the eye will receive less light than it can accommodate, which is undesirable. However, if a scope sight's exit pupil is much greater than 7mm, then the fully-dilated human pupil cannot accommodate all the light passing through the sight, which is also undesirable. Ideally, therefore, a scope sight with a magnification and an objective lens size which combine to give an exit pupil diameter of approximately 7mm will make the maximum use of the shooter's ability to get the most from the sight in conditions of poor light.

'Eye relief' is the term used to denote the critical distance which must be maintained between the firer's eye and the rear lens to make the whole field of view visible. Too much or too little eye relief will reduce the width of the sight picture which is visible. In light-recoil, small-calibre rifles eye relief may be reduced to little more than an inch or so, but such a short distance can be painful and damaging in heavy-calibre rifles with significant recoil, causing the metal rim of the scope sight to recoil violently and painfully against the firer's eyebrow area. For such rifles an eye relief of 3½ inches is more appropriate.

Scope sights of variable power are readily available, and many excellent products now enable the rifleman to move from as little as 1½× to 6× by simply rotating a 'power ring' on the sight. Other models are variable from 3× to 9×, 4× to 12× and 6× to 20×, although the very high powers are likely only to appeal to the specialized, long-range varmint shoot-

er firing from a firm rest. Most riflemen will find a fixed-power scope perfectly adequate, and a variable-power scope offering a choice of magnifications from 1½× to 6× covers most normal sporting circumstances. However, it is much more important to ensure that the exit pupil diameter is optimum, that the lenses are of the highest possible optical quality, and that the objective lens is large enough to gather sufficient light without being so big as to make it necessary to mount the scope too high above the axis of the rifle barrel for comfortable use.

The conventional, circular sight picture has now been joined by the wider 'landscape' shape, more like that of a television screen, and this can provide a wider field of view and help eliminate undesirable canting or tilting of the rifle. Reticles are available in many forms and styles, all of which can be excellent. However, very fine crosshairs become almost invisible in poor light or against a dark background, while very heavy upright and cross posts can obscure much of the target and its surroundings. While individual reticle choice is largely a

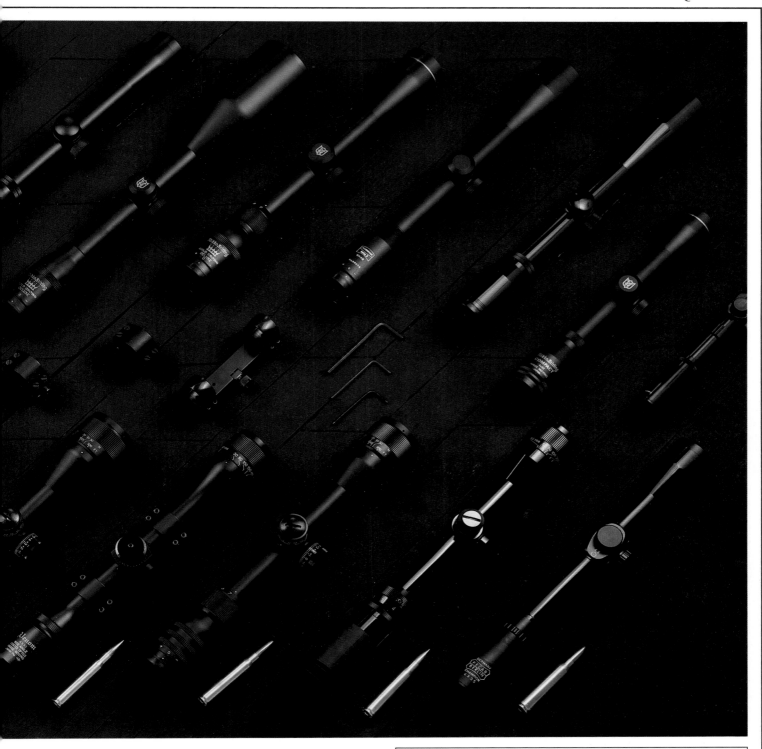

personal matter, there is a good deal to be said for choosing a 'Duplex' style of reticle where bold lines converge to fine central cross hairs.

Despite the undoubted advantages of seeing your target clearly and placing your point of aim accurately, telescopic sights can have some drawbacks. They can lead the inexperienced or over-ambitious rifleman to attempt unduly long shots, which must always be avoided. A clean, humane kill should be the object, rather than exhibitionist displays of spectacular long-range shooting. A scope sight, if

you are inexperienced, is not particularly effective in situations where you may have to swing the rifle to fire at a running target, and its special attributes are best seen when firing a steady shot at a static target, but it may, of course, occasionally be necessary to fire at a running animal, such as when a beast is wounded and must be stopped. However, rifles for shooting driven game like wild boar and the larger African species are better used shotgun-style, with simple open sights, and such rifles are usually of the double-barrelled type.

The six scopes along the bottom of the picture are, from left to right: Kassnar 3-9 × 40; Kassnar Sniper 3-9 × 40; Venom Arms 4 × 32; Kassnar 2-7 × 32; Venom Arms 2-7 × 32; and Pecar Champion 4 × 35.

The four above them on the left of the picture are, from the top: Leslie Hewett 4 × 40; Nikko Stirling Gold Crown Deluxe; Pecar Variable 4-10 × 52; and Kassnar 4 × 20.

The remainder are, from left to right: Leslie Hewett 4 × 32; Nikko Stirling Gold Crown Deluxe 6 × 56; Nikko Stirling Gold Crown Deluxe 3-9 × 40; Kassnar Beta 3-6 × 42; Vistascope 4 × 40; Nikko Stirling 4 × 32; and Leslie Hewett 4 × 20. The scope mounts in the centre are by Venom Arms.

RIFLE AMMUNITION

The rifle cartridge, like the shotgun cartridge, is a convenient package comprising four main components. The cartridge case serves as a compact container for the cordite or, more commonly nowadays, the powdered or granular nitrocellulose which, when detonated, provides the propellant gases to fire the bullet. In the head of the cartridge is located the primer or detonator, which explodes when struck by the firing pin, setting off the main powder charge within the cartridge case. (The familiar little .22 cartridge has a rimfire system, in which the firing pin strikes at a point on the rim of the cartridge base, but all other commonly-used sporting rifle cartridges are of the centrefire type, in which a detonator cap is seated centrally within the cartridge head.)

Finally, the cartridge case is sealed and the powder kept in place by the bullet, which is seated firmly within the neck of the cartridge case, completing the four-part composition of a rifle cartridge.

When you examine an individual rifle cartridge, it appears as though the cartridge case is little more than a means of holding the primer, the propellant and the bullet together, and that is indeed its only function at this stage. However, when the trigger is pulled and the firing pin strikes the detonating cap and ignites the charge contained within it, the cartridge case has another very vital task to perform. Although metallic, usually of brass or a similar alloy, the cartridge case is slightly elastic, and the pressure created by the exploding and expanding gases – up to 10 or 15 tons per square inch – causes the cartridge case to expand within the chamber so as to create a perfectly gas-tight seal within the chamber and against the breech or the face of the turn-bolt rifle action. This is vital if the propellant gases are not to blow backward into the action of the rifle, risking damage to the mechanism and possibly severe injury to the firer. It also ensures that all the propellant force of the cartridge is directed forward to bear against the rear of the bullet, driving it through the bore of the rifle and off on its way to the chosen target.

Modern, commercially-made rifle ammunition, for everything

From left to right: .404 rimless; .375 H & H Magnum; 9.3 × 74 rimless; 7mm Remington Magnum; 7 × 57 Rem Magnum; 8 × 685; .308 Win; .30 M1 Carbine; 30-06; 7 × 64; .270 Win; 6.5 × 68; 6.5 × 54 Mannlicher-Schoenauer; .243 Win; 5.6 × 52 rimless; .222 Rem; .22 Hornet; .22 high velocity.

from the little .22 rimfire up to the largest big-game calibres like the .458 Win and the massive .460 Weatherby Magnum, are accurately formed from drawn brass alloy and prepared to the fine tolerances laid down in the agreed specification for the size and length of each separate calibre. When correctly seated in the chamber of a rifle which has been made with equal care for that calibre, and in which there is no undue play or 'headspace' at the breech, the cartridge case should, when it is fired, form the perfect seal necessary for safety and accuracy in rifle shooting. (The handloader of rifle ammunition often sets even more exacting standards, preferring to use 'fireformed' cases which have already been fired once within a

particular rifle and have expanded to take on a more precise shape for the chamber of that specific rifle.)

The primer or detonating cap lies at the heart of every successful modern centrefire rifle cartridge. This tiny pill-like component contains a compound which explodes through percussion, when struck by the firing pin, and then detonates the main charge of powder. The primer comprises three basic elements: the outer container or cup, the primer detonating compound and the anvil. When the firing pin strikes the cap the contents of the cup are violently compressed, forcing the detonating compound against the anvil and causing it to explode.

Modern centrefire primers are of two types: the Boxer, in

which the anvil is contained within the primer itself; and the Berdan primer, which consists only of the container and the propellant, with the anvil forming part of the cartridge case itself, in which it can be seen as a small projection in the bottom of the pocket in which the primer cap is seated. Curiously, although the Boxer primer was invented by an English army officer, this design has always been more popular in American-made rifle ammunition, while the Berdan type, invented by an American army officer, tends to dominate the British and European rifle ammunition scene.

There are five principal types of cartridge case used in modern rifles. The rimfire, already mentioned, is virtually confined

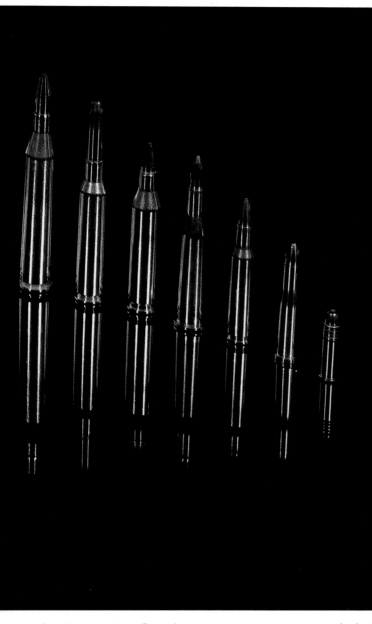

base of the bullet, just forward of the recessed rim. This is an additional aid to firm seating of the cartridge and the effective sealing of the breech as a particularly powerful powder charge explodes.

Some rifle calibres have cartridge cases which have a fairly straight profile, with straight sides tapering gently towards a narrower neck. This is clearly seen in, for example, the popular .458 Win with its long, tapered, cigarlike shape. It can also be found in some of the short cartridges designed for lever-actioned rifles, and these include the .444 Marlin, the .375 Win and the .30/30.

However, most sporting rifle calibres have a more or less pronounced neck or shoulder, where the case takes on a bottle-necked appearance, narrowing suddenly towards the neck. The .30-'06 Springfield and the .303 British cartridges have a gently sloping neck which inclines inward at an angle of approximately 17°. Heavily-loaded, medium-sized calibres like the .358 Norma Magnum, the .338 Win Magnum, the .300 Win Magnum and the 7mm Rem Magnum have a much more sharply-inclined shoulder, angling at approximately 25°.

Bullets come in many shapes, styles and designs, having evolved from early projectiles consisting of simple balls of pure lead. Forcing a pure lead projectile at high speed through the rifling of a modern style barrel would be to invite almost total melting of the bullet, massive fouling of the rifling grooves with lead deposits, and hopeless performance in the field or at targets. This problem has been overcome by coating the lead of the bullet with gilding metal, originally a cupronickel alloy and nowadays made from an alloy of copper, tin and zinc. The modern rifle bullet, whether for sporting or military purposes, is made by encasing a lead core within a coating of gilding metal, the two being swaged into the correct shape within a steel forming die.

The base of the jacketed bullet is the surface upon which the expanding propellant gases within the barrel come to bear, to drive it forward. The base may be either flat or 'boat-tailed' in shape. While the former has a simple, flat base, the boat-tailed bullet has a tapered or beveled

base which makes little difference to the propellant effect of the gases but allows the bullet to fly on its course with much reduced air drag caused by turbulence behind the bullet in its flight. Thus the boat-tailed design of bullet tends to dominate in the high-powered, flat-trajectory, long-range calibres.

Turning to the point of the bullet, rifle bullets can be divided into three broad categories: round-nosed, pointed and semipointed. The round-nosed bullet is confined mainly to calibres used at short range, in thick undergrowth or other cover or where the bullet is required to penetrate deeply into heavy, thick-skinned animals such as elephant or buffalo. They are also popular in Europe for heavy deer and wild boar at modest ranges.

The pointed or 'spitzer' bullet has the best aerodynamic shape for maintaining velocity and accuracy at long range. For target shooting and military purposes, fully-jacketed bullets of this type, with no exposed lead, are the normal choice. The sportsman's requirements are rather different, however, and he needs a bullet which will expand in a controlled fashion on impact, penetrating and expanding so as to cause a fatal wound by damaging vital internal organs, and expending the bullet's total energy within the body of the animal. This is best achieved for thin-skinned game like deer by using a semipointed type of bullet, which combines the accuracy of the pointed bullet with a design which allows some of the lead core to be exposed at the tip of the jacketed bullet, to encourage expansion on impact.

Other bullet designs have been developed to promote the controlled expansion and expenditure of bullet energy which the sportsman needs, and these include bullets with recessed or hollow points, points made from bronze or aluminium, and others which incorporate slender copper tubing. Additionally, other bullet manufacturers have experimented, with varying degrees of success, with bullets in which the lead core is divided into two or more sections by 'partitions' of gilding metal to give different degrees of expansion and, in some cases, disintegration.

to the .22 miniature rifle and its slightly larger cousin, the .22 magnum. Otherwise, the rimfire type plays little part in the sporting rifle scene. There are four other rim types to consider: rimmed, rimless, semirimmed and belted.

The rimmed cartridge case is found in some of the most long-established and best-known rifle calibres like the .303 Mark VII British and the .30-30 Win, which remains a firm favourite in North America. The head of these cartridge cases comprises a protruding rim which extends outward to form a flange around the base of the case. Rifles chambered for such cases can use very simple extractor or ejector mechanisms. Double-barrelled rifles as used for big game use an extrac-

tor or ejector system which is similar to that used in double-barrelled shotguns, which also have rimmed or flanged cartridge heads.

The rimless cartridge, best exemplified by the well known, .308 Win (7.62mm NATO), the .30-'06 Springfield and their various derivatives, has a cartridge base of the same diameter as the main cartridge case, but incorporating a deep groove just above the base, into which the extractor hooks of the rifle mechanism locate when the cartridge is chambered and the action closed behind it. This is by far the commonest rim type encountered in modern sporting rifle ammunition, but a number of large-calibre and magnum-type cartridges also have a raised band or belt at the

COMBINATION GUNS

'Combination guns' is a general term used to describe a wide range of types and designs which incorporate two or more different calibres within one firearm. Just as it was natural and desirable that the smooth-bored fowling piece developed from a single-barrelled to a double-barrelled gun, affording the sportsman an opportunity of discharging two shots in quick succession, it was logical that gunmakers should try to devise multi-barrelled firearms offering a choice of smoothbored shot barrels of differing bores, or two rifle calibres, or some combination of rifled and smoothbored barrels.

Another, more recent development has been the design of many excellent types of 'take-down' single-barrelled maga-zine rifles, in which the barrel and forestock can be quickly detached and replaced with another unit, chambered for a different cartridge but mounted and fired from the same action. The Valmet range of Finnish-made rifles is one of the best examples of this.

Combination shotguns are usually of the over-and-under type with one large-bore and one small-bore barrel. With conventional twin triggers they offer the sportsman an instant choice of, for example, a full 12-bore game load for large flying or running game and a much smaller, lighter charge for small mammals like squirrels.

For rifle/shotgun combinations, most of the development and the widest use has taken place in continental Europe.

Early examples date from the 17th century, and there has been a strong and continuing demand among European sportsmen for a single firearm capable of dealing with every-thing from gamebirds and small mammals to heavy woodland deer and wild boar. In northern and central Europe, a day's hunting may include pheasant and woodcock shooting, the culling of roe deer does and the chance of a shot at a red deer or a wild boar. To enable the hunter to cope with such a diverse range of species while carrying only one firearm, various in-genious combinations of shot and rifle barrels have been produced.

The commonest style of com-bination gun, in Europe and elsewhere, is the so-called 'drill-ing' (the German term for 'tri-plet'), comprising two smooth-bored shotgun barrels set side by side and joined with a con-ventional rib, with a third, rifled barrel positioned underneath. The 16-bore is the most popular shotgun calibre for drillings, while the rifle barrel is usually chambered for a 6.5×57mm or 7×57mm, rimmed cartridge.

All three barrels drop down as with a normal shotgun when the top lever is pushed aside, and the drilling action may be based on either the boxlock or sidelock principle. Most drill-ings have top extensions with crossbolts and side-clips at the breech which give massive strength when the action is closed and fired. An important variation in design when com-paring the drilling with a stan-

The Japanese-made Miroku rifle/shotgun combination gun has a 12-bore shotgun barrel mounted above a .308 calibre rifle barrel.

dard side-by-side shotgun is that the slide on the top tang, used as a safety catch on the shotgun, acts as a barrel selector on a drilling.

Pushing it forward engages the firing mechanism of the underslung rifle barrel and causes a folding leaf-sight to flick up above the line of the top rib. This provides a simple open sight such as is found on double-barrelled big-game rifles, but most drillings also have slots alongside the top rib to accommodate a telescopic sight with quick-detachable claw mounts. The safety catch for the firing mechanism of all three barrels consists of a sliding button on the side of the action, similar to the Greener-type side safety on certain shotguns.

The extractor and ejection mechanism and the lockwork are inevitably more complicated on drillings, and the addition of a rifle barrel to a side-by-side shotgun involves a significant increase in weight. A typical drilling will weigh well over 8 pounds, compared with the 6½ pounds of the average English-style game gun. The addition of a telescopic sight, frequently used when the rifle barrel is required for wild boar or woodland deer, adds a further 1½ pounds or more to the total weight.

Drillings also come with 12-bore barrels and larger rifle calibres, like the 8 × 57mm, and the 9.3 × 62mm calibres. There are many further permutations on the combined shot-and-rifle barrels system, and there may

be two side-by-side rifle barrels with a single, underslung shotgun barrel, and the rifle barrels need not necessarily be of the same calibre. Some of these three-barrelled weapons have a full-bore, centrefire calibre like the 8 × 57mm, alongside a .22 rimfire or a .22 Hornet barrel, giving the user a choice of two very different rifle calibres and one shotgun calibre.

The 'vierling' or four-barrelled combination gun usually comprises two side-by-side shotgun barrels, normally but not always of the same bore, with two rifle barrels beneath, usually one below the other and of different calibres. Armed with a vierling the sportsman has the equivalent of a double-barrelled shotgun and two single-shot rifles at his disposal, a formid-

able combination provided he remembers to use the right combinations of selector switches and triggers when firing.

Finally, and increasingly common, are combination guns based on the over-and-under style, with a single shotgun barrel over a rifle barrel, or two rifle barrels (which may be of the same or differing calibres) mounted one over the other. (Any double-barrelled rifle must be carefully regulated, however, to ensure that both shoot to the same point of impact at the required distance. This is a skilled process and few riflemakers now undertake it.)

Some over-and-under style drillings also occur, in which a shotgun barrel has an underslung rifle barrel of a substantial centrefire calibre like the 8 × 57mm, and an additional rifle barrel of smaller calibre like the .22 Hornet, slightly offset to one side. As with all over-and-under type actions, the barrels must be dropped down rather further than with the side-by-side type to give the full clearance necessary for cartridge ejection and reloading. Many over-and-under shotgun/rifle combinations come with a spare pair of shot barrels, which transform the gun into a straightforward over-and-under game shotgun.

Combination guns continue to have only limited appeal for sportsmen outside northern and central Europe, but the finest examples of combination gun craftsmanship from the small family gunmakers of Germany and Austria are outstandingly fine pieces of engineering and are often beautifully engraved in the characteristically heavy European style, depicting woodland animals like deer, wild boar and chamois. There are no more than a handful of regular users of drillings in Britain, partly because the British sportsman tends to draw a clear distinction between a day's shotgunning and a day's deerstalking with a rifle, and takes a separate firearm on each occasion.

However, the main obstacle to the ownership and use of combination shotgun-rifles in Britain is the important legal distinction between smooth-bored and rifled firearms, and the very stringent conditions that apply to possession and use of any firearm with a rifled barrel, especially in the larger centre-fire calibres.

REVOLVERS

The revolver is the most commonly-used hand weapon for hunting, and this is due mainly to a single factor: power. In any given calibre range, revolvers are generally capable of out-performing semiautos in this respect. Other relevant factors are reliability in field conditions, simplicity of design, and flexibility of ammunition type with regard to power and bullet design. A revolver will handle any bullet shape while a semi-auto may have difficulty in feeding the shapes most suitable for hunting.

For small game, such as rabbits, squirrels, marmots, prairie dogs and the rest of the varmint category, the most effective revolver is a .22 rimfire, either single-action or double-action.

The most commonly-used single-action revolvers (which must be cocked by hand before firing) are based on the old Colt pattern, and the only real difference between the 19th-century Peacemaker and today's plethora of copies is the number of calibres in which they are available.

The .22 revolver is extremely accurate, and although generally let down by its sights, in competent hands it is capable of taking small game out to 50 yards. Probably the best revolver of this type is the Ruger Single Six with a 6-inch barrel.

This pistol incorporates all of the traditional lines of the classic single-action, with the added bonus of modern safety features such as the transfer bar hammer safety which allows the gun to be carried with all chambers loaded without danger. In addition, it has an excellent set of adjustable sights. The 6-inch version, combined with a high velocity round such as a Remington Yellow Jacket, gives a muzzle velocity of about 1100 fps and effective expansion in small game. That power, plus the simplicity, slim shape and good ergonomics of this 32-ounce package, makes it one of the most popular of its type.

In contrast to the single-action revolvers, double-action types have many different designs and styles. The two most common are typified by the Smith and Wesson K-frame group and the Colt D-frame (Diamondback and Trooper). Superficially, these weapons appear the same, but there are some important differences.

Mechanically the S&W and the Colt are exactly opposite; for instance, the cylinder latch on the Smith is pushed forward while that on the Colt is pulled back, and the cylinder on the Smith rotates anti-clockwise while that on the Colt turns clockwise. The major difference, though, is in firing, and anyone who uses a Smith professionally will decry the Colt and vice-versa. This is due to the different feel of each type's action whilst firing: the S&W employs a roll-over system while the Colt trigger stacks up to a crisp heavy break. Many shooters prefer the S&W action because the roll-over system provides a 'plateau' which enables them to steady their aim before firing.

Probably the best weapon in the double-action category is the Smith and Wesson Model 18 with its 4-inch barrel. This 31-ounce package has far better balance than the 6-inch Model 17, and the small loss of velocity is acceptable as long as it is to be used for small game only.

For medium-sized game a larger weapon is essential. Of the guns suitable for these species the .38/.357 revolvers are the most flexible handguns available, with bullet weights varying from 90 grains, giving long, flat trajectories, up to 180 grain FMJ capable of penetrating the heavy muscle of any medium-sized animal at close range. Nevertheless, in its normal loading at around 125 to 148 grains, leaving a four- to six-inch barrel at between 1000 and 1400 fps, the .38/.357 is capable of clean kills on all species from foxes to medium deer (such as mule, whitetail, roe and fallow) and including wild boar and the smaller felines. However, it is not suitable for Scottish red deer, elk, moose or other large species.

A good choice of revolver in this category would be a 6-inch .357 Smith & Wesson 586. This handgun combines all of the attributes necessary to produce a near-perfect hunting revolver. It has a light frame which allows normal hands to fit, a heavy barrel giving a reduced recoil surge for a faster second shot and good off-hand stability, and a beefed-up cylinder able to take magnum loads without stress. If you want to take deer-sized game you need all the power you can get.

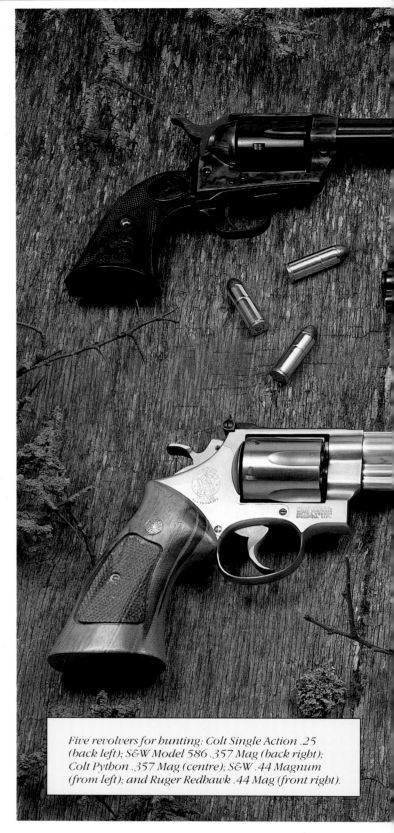

Five revolvers for hunting: Colt Single Action .25 (back left); S&W Model 586 .357 Mag (back right); Colt Python .357 Mag (centre); S&W .44 Magnum (from left); and Ruger Redhawk .44 Mag (front right).

It has been claimed that all of the dangerous game animals be killed with single shots from semi-custom-built revolvers such as the .454 Casull. However, since this operation usually requires a backup hunter with a heavy rifle, it isn't really playing the game. The whole purpose of hunting with a handgun is to pit yourself against the animal with a smaller advantage than that offered by a rifle, but still to be able to kill your quarry cleanly.

The three calibres best suited to soft-skinned large game are the .41 and .44 Magnum and the .45 Long Colt. All three have sufficient bullet weight and velocity to penetrate through to the heart or brain of the larger deer (such as the red), all of the

bears, and the felines up to and including lions.

The major problem, which incidentally is why most handgun hunters after dangerous game have a backup, is that no revolver round has sufficient energy to stop a determined lion or bear except by striking the brain or spine, so if your rushed shot isn't on the button it will take some time for the animal to lose interest in biting your head off.

One of the best revolvers for the taking of large game is the Ruger Super Blackhawk. This handgun is available in all of the suggested calibres, and in its 7½-inch version the weapon has the size and strength to handle full loads suitable for large game. At 48 ounces the Ruger isn't a small piece, but anything smaller is unlikely to produce the energy necessary to take all forms of large game. There are other long-barrelled revolvers in suitable calibres, but of all the production weapons available the Ruger is the strongest.

All of the revolvers discussed above can be scoped, and most major sight manufacturers produce pistol scopes with mounts suitable for these weapons. For instance, a 6-inch .41 Magnum Smith and Wesson can be fitted with a Leupold 2-power scope, and this weapon, using 210-grain Sierra conical hollow bullets driven by 19.5 grains of Winchester 296, is capable of 1½-inch groups at 50 yards.

AUTOLOADING PISTOLS

For hunting, autoloading (semi-automatic) pistols may be divided into three categories: the .22 rimfire for small game, the 9mm/.45 for medium game, and the 'specialist' high-power pistols suitable for large game.

For small game the .22 pistol reigns supreme. It is compact, accurate, has little recoil, is capable of rapid fire when tracking on moving game and is a pleasure to shoot. Another useful feature of the .22 is that it provides cheap practice. A day's plinking, using 300 to 400 rounds, would be expensive with a .44 but it's relatively cheap with a .22.

The best .22 semiautos for hunting are the American models rather than the European target pistols, because the American types are generally suitably shaped to fit a holster. Pistols like the High Standard Citation, now no longer made, and the Ruger Mark II are ideal. Probably the most popular .22 ever was the Colt Woodsman, sadly now long out of production; but if you can get a good one, it will be well worth having.

Autos for medium game are much more difficult to define.

The obvious choice is the 9mm Para, but due to its light weight (around 125 grains) the bullet is only capable of taking animals up to small deer such as roe or muntjac. A clean kill of whitetail or fallow is unlikely unless you are capable of perfect bullet placement. If you do go for this calibre you will find that most well-made pistols are up to the job, but unless you can stretch to a SIG 210 you will have to fit a set of decent Patridge-style sights to your choice since most 9mm pistols have either military or low-profile combat sights fitted as standard.

From the top, these pistols are the IMI Desert Eagle .44 Magnum, the Colt Gold Cup .45ACP, the Browning Hi-Power 9mm and the Colt Commander .45ACP.

Generally you will be better off if you go for a .45 ACP auto instead. There are a number to choose from besides the Colt original and some, like the Safari Arms and the AMT, come with decent sights as standard. In other cases you will have to fit your own.

The .45 will give you a 200-grain bullet pushed out at around 1000 fps, and this is capable of taking all medium game animals. However, a word of caution here: if you decide to attempt to take a bear (even a small one) with your auto, make certain that the pistol is totally reliable, as the ability to deliver a second shot may be the only way you can be sure of seeing tomorrow. Bears are inclined to become irritable if shot, and they don't always run away.

The normal tuning necessary for any hunting auto is barrel throating to your desired bullet shape, as the most common problem is the failure of the round to feed from the magazine.

Medium game autos are very suitable for scoping since the sort of game you are after tends to be found at first or at last light, both bad sighting conditions. Alternatively, they tend to appear in thick brush where they are also difficult to see. The light-gathering capabilities of a 2-power scope could make the difference between a good shot or a failure to make out the target at all. The only major problem with scoping a pistol is that it becomes bulky to carry, and will usually need a special holster.

However, if you are going to hunt dangerous game, you have the additional problem that a pistol scope upsets the handling and balance of the pistol so that it no longer points naturally, and since the scope also has a very long eye relief you will require a lot of practice before you can quickly draw a bead, especially on a moving and anti-social target which may want to bite back.

Large game autos have become the vogue in the last ten years. The first, now out of production, was the .44 Automag. This massive hand cannon was built around a .308 Win cartridge cut off at the bottle neck. It produced true magnum velocities with a heavy bullet, and was used to take African big game and even polar bears.

Once the market was proven, other companies started to develop magnum auto pistols. The next to come along was the Wildey, which was designed in 9mm and .45 magnum, the 9mm magnum being intended for small and medium game and the .45 for the rest. The 230 grain .45 bullet, travelling at around 1400 fps, is a true stopper and has been used with good effect on all manner of game. IMI (Israeli Military Industries) were next with their Desert Eagle, which differed from the other two in one major way – the ammunition. Both the Automag and the Wildey used a wildcat round which had to be produced specially for them, and consequently ammunition was not always easy to get. The Desert Eagle uses standard .357 and .44 magnum revolver rounds which are not only a lot easier to get than wildcat rounds but are also a lot cheaper.

All of the magnum autos are massive and require full-power loads simply to operate the action, so a good two-handed grip is recommended when firing them. On the plus side, however, is the the fact that their massive recoil systems take most of the punishment out of firing them.

For taking large game, the best of them is probably the Desert Eagle in .44 magnum. The power of this weapon is truly awesome. In fact, if you use the 8-inch barrelled version, the round can be hand-loaded with Hercules 240 or Winchester 296 together with a 225 grain jacketed soft-point to achieve 1600 fps, delivering about 1280 foot pounds at the muzzle. When you consider that the .45/70 rifle round, which just about everyone would consider more than suitable to take large game, has only 300 foot pounds more energy you can see that this is one hell of a handgun.

When you look at light, high-velocity rifle rounds such as the .243 you see much more impressive velocity figures, but you must also remember that such bullets have a tendency to blow up on hitting dense muscle, or to be deflected by heavy bones. The heavy, relatively slow-moving .44, however, trundles straight through, producing a good wound channel with penetration through to the major organs, giving a quick and clean kill.

HANDGUN AMMUNITION

Many years ago, the late Elmer Keith was asked why, when he hunted, he always used a heavier calibre than everyone else. His reply was, 'Son, when you want to put a hole in something, make it a hole to remember.' He was discussing rifles at the time, but his maxim is even more relevant to pistols. With very few exceptions, handguns rely on calibre rather than velocity and/or weight for their effectiveness in hunting, and as a result, when choosing a handgun for a given quarry, the first criterion is bullet diameter. For hunting game, the three basic categories of handgun are small (.22 and .32), medium (.38/.357, 9mm and .45 ACP) and large (.41 magnum and up).

Once you have chosen your calibre to suit your game, the next most important step is to select a suitable bullet type. There are at least ten different bullet shapes (not counting the modern 'fourth generation' bullets designed to kill people), and of these only three are of interest for hunting. These are, in various guises, hollow point, jacketed soft point, and semi-wadcutter in either lead or semi-jacketed form.

For small game, your choice in .22 calibre is limited to the types commercially manufactured as you cannot reload the stuff yourself. One type worth considering is the Yellow Jacket. The Yellow Jacket is not as fast as some ultra-high velocity ammunition such as the Stinger, but it has the advantage of giving controlled expansion in most media. For instance, a number of these bullets recovered from foxes were found to have formed perfect mushroom shapes of between .41 and .44 inch in diameter. Another important advantage of this bullet is that it doesn't break up on impact as do some of the really fast .22s.

The only .32 worth considering is the H & R .32 Magnum. When sufficient bullets are available for reloading, this will be an excellent calibre for taking small game, but at the moment the choice of bullets is somewhat restricted.

For medium-sized game, your options are enormously increased by the huge range of .38/.357 ammunition. Every bullet type imaginable is available in this range, so your choice will depend on what it is you want

From the left: .25ACP; .32ACP; .380ACP; 9mm; 9mm Parabellum; .45ACP; .32 S&W; .38 Special wadcutter; .38 Special lead round nose; .357 Magnum; and .357 Magnum semi-jacketed hollow point.

the bullet to do. Medium-sized game can only be stopped quickly by one of two methods: a brain or spine shot which either kills outright or produces paralysis by stopping signals from the brain from getting to the muscles down the spine, causing a massive energy dump as the bullet stops, coupled with a lot of secondary bone fragments which cause further damage to tissue.

There is a third accepted method of stopping game, and this is a heart shot. This is not so effective, however, on medium to large game when a handgun is used, because the bullet energy available is insufficient to do more than simply puncture the heart. There are thousands of recorded instances where heart-shot deer, hit by high-velocity .30 calibre bullets, have run hundreds of yards before stopping even though the heart was totally destroyed.

In spite of this, if you want to include all three target areas in

like a solid-pointed type.

For large game, such as elk, bear, moose or similar, the bullet must be robust enough to punch through heavy muscle and bone to a depth of six inches or more before it can reach any vital organ. The best bullet to use is a semi-jacketed soft-point, in a heavy calibre, such as a threequarter-jacket with a conical or round nose. This will be strong enough to get through to the animal's boiler room with the added plus that any hit on large bones will cause the point to expand.

Hollow point pistol ammunition can also be effective against large game as long as the bullet is both strong enough and heavy enough to penetrate without breaking up on the surface. In addition, it must be travelling fast enough to expand in the target, which means that it must be going at about 1500 fps.

Whatever size of game you are after, a simple rule of thumb is to work within the top 20 percent weight bracket of a suitable calibre and to use the appropriate bullet type for the job. Having chosen your bullet, the next factor to consider is the powder.

When you load hunting ammunition, it is vital to use a powder type and charge of the right sort to give you the performance you need against the animal you intend to hunt. Your round must also be accurate enough to hit your target properly. In general terms, this means that your ammunition should be capable of delivering a 2-inch group at 50 yards for small game, and a group of around 4 inches for medium and large game.

The next ingredient in building your round is power. This is a combination of factors, mainly of bullet weight, profile and velocity. Maximum velocity will only be obtained by matching your powder not only to the bullet but also to the barrel length of your pistol: basically, the longer the barrel, the slower-burning the powder should be, and in general the slower-burning powders provide more power.

One final thought. No matter how powerful your load or how effective your bullet, a gut-shot animal should be anathema to any true sportsman. If in doubt, wait; a surer shot will come along.

your hunting, the only bullet that will give you a good chance of success is the semi-wadcutter. This bullet, designed by Elmer Keith for this very purpose, will puncture brain casing, and due to its flat tip it will dump masses of energy into a bone. More importantly, the sharp front edges of the end of the ogive cause a plug of tissue to be cut out of the animal, causing a more effective wound channel which bleeds rapidly. As a consequence, a poor hit will kill the animal sooner than will a similar hit from a bullet of different design.

Hollow point bullets are not as effective because, although they expand up to twice their original diameter in .22, at larger calibres the bullet strength required to allow them to puncture the skin and muscle of medium game prevents them from expanding effectively unless a bone is hit. In fact, what often happens is that the hollow fills with tissue so the bullet acts

RELOADING

A selection of Lyman reloading tools, including an Acculine reloading press (back left), a No. 55 powder measure (front left) and a T-Mag turret reloading press (front centre), which can be mounted with up to six different reloading dies. On the right is a Universal Trimmer, with a chuck that will take all types of metal pistol or rifle cartridge cases.

Apart from the obvious reasons such as cost, accuracy and the building of a special load for a particular purpose, the feeling of satisfaction to be had from the construction of a carefully-made round, designed for your particular weapon and which kills your chosen quarry cleanly, is vastly greater than if you had used a store-bought factory round for the same purpose.

Most (but not all) types of shotgun, rifle and pistol rounds can be reloaded and, in addition to the many available books on the subject, there is a wealth of instructional material produced by the manufacturers of the bullets, shot, powder, cases, primers and tools used in reloading.

Reloading is, in principle, a fairly straightforward process. For instance, reloading a typical shotgun shell involves some seven basic stages. Starting with a clean, sound case, the first step is to remove the old primer cap, and then the new one is inserted. Next, the shell is charged with a precisely-measured amount of powder, the seating wads are fitted on top of the powder, the shot charge is added, and then the shell is crimped and resized. However, as with any activity involving propellants, reloading can be dangerous unless you follow the instructions carefully and observe *all* the recommended safety precautions.

For the rifle or pistol shooter, there is enormous scope for individual experimentation with different bullet types and designs, and the enthusiastic hand-loader who chooses to reload his own cartridges can experiment with many permutations of primer/powder/bullet com-

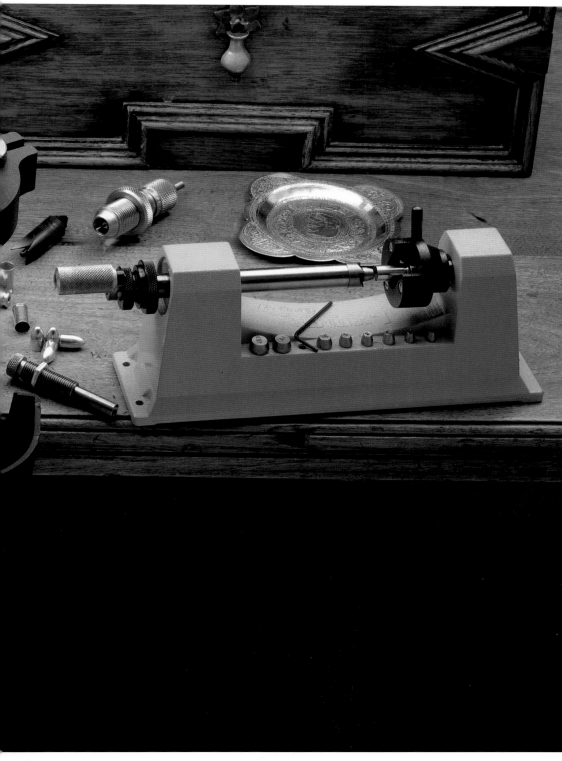

due to the number of accidents which occur each year, deserve special care – the choice of bullet and the choice of powder.

Most loading charts give between three and six different bullet weights for a given calibre and, to the uninitiated, there is an apparently illogical relationship between bullet weight, powder weight and velocity. This is due to two factors. The first is the bullet material: the frictional coefficient of a jacketed bullet is much lower than that of a similar bullet made entirely of lead. The second factor is the bearing surface of the bullet, that is, the area of the bullet in contact with the bore. Two bullets of the same weight (such as a full wadcutter and a long-ogive round nose) can have vastly different bearing surface areas, and the larger the bearing surface, the greater the friction. As a result, a bullet with a high coefficient of friction and a large bearing surface will produce a higher velocity and pressure than a bullet of the same weight but a low coefficient of friction and a smaller bearing surface, and this accounts for the apparent illogicalities in the data given in the loading charts.

As for the powder, there are over fifty different types available to the loader for pistol ammunition alone, but a given loading chart may only list six or seven of them. Until you either have sufficient knowledge or you can consult a *real* expert (not the armchair variety), use only the powders listed; never make the mistake of using a powder whose characteristics you do not know.

Another mistake to avoid is the all-too-common one of underloading. Some people think that if a 4-grain load is safe, then a 2-grain load will be twice as safe, but this is a dangerous fallacy. The propellant in a round of ammunition is designed to burn from the base of the case towards the bullet. If the combustion chamber (the space behind the bullet) is less than half full, it is possible to get a flashover – the powder is ignited at both the front and the back of the case at the same time, producing two pressure waves which meet in the middle at twice the normal velocity. This effect is called detonation, and it occasionally detonates guns.

binations. The skilled handloader, using carefully-selected and well-matched components, can achieve remarkable and pleasing results.

Setting aside the satisfaction element, one of the most important reasons for reloading is the production of a round of ammunition suitable for the task in hand. For pistol ammunition, for example, your main requirements might be any or all of the following: power, velocity (not necessarily the same as power), accuracy, low recoil, bullet effect or cost. Once you have decided what you want from your ammunition, you can work out a detailed specification for it and then go ahead and load it.

All of the major propellant manufacturers produce loading lists, which provide invaluable data and are a useful starting point when you're planning your load. However, remember that the propellant manufacturer can only control the quality of his powder: he cannot control the use you make of it, or the condition of either your firearm or your cases. For example, using magnum loads in tired cases, in a loose, light-framed pistol, is asking for trouble.

Even if your gun and all other components are in good condition there are two areas which,

ACCESSORIES

The range of shooting accessories is vast, as a visit to any gunshop will quickly confirm. Every accessory on view will serve some purpose, but not all will be appropriate to the requirements of an individual shooter. In the first instance, it is essential to obtain extras actually *needed* in order to undertake the chosen form of shooting successfully. Once basic equipment is assembled, additional accessories become a matter of personal preference – though it is worth observing that many items are designed more to catch the eye of a prospective purchaser than to offer a practical benefit.

Having aquired an expensive weapon – or weapons – it makes sound sense to look after the investment. An uncovered gun is easily knocked, and is always vulnerable to water or condensation damage. A hard gun case which takes the disassembled gun is ideal for use in a vehicle, while outside, a soft gun slip allows an assembled gun to be carried safely, and protected from the weather if necessary. Pistol shooters will need the equivalent fitted carrying case or holster.

There are a number of accessories associated with the weapon itself, which may be required according to circumstances: dummy 'snap' cartridges that permit dry firing without damage to firing pins; anti-recoil and stock extension pads; muzzle stoppers to prevent water entering barrels; cartridge extractors for removing swollen rounds jammed in the breech; handguards to extend the fore-end for those with long arms, which also give relief from hot barrels; and converters that allow the firing of smaller-calibre ammunition or blank rounds.

All guns must be cleaned regularly, and this can be a satisfying ritual if the right tools are employed. There are purpose-designed cleaning kits for every sort of weapon, and it is sensible to purchase one complete, although, of course, a kit can be assembled piecemeal. Jointed or single rods for the insides of barrels come with a variety of brushes, from phosphor bronze wire (for scrubbing off lead fouling) to wool fabric (for removing burnt powder deposits). Full-length barrel mops are also available, and special brushes are made for awkward jobs like cleaning chambers. Various oils are produced for particular uses – including spray-on water repellant that may be applied before taking the gun out, or when shooting. Vegetable products like walnut oil are marketed for use on woodwork, which should never be treated with mineral oil.

The storage and security of guns is an important consideration. Gun racks come in many shapes and sizes, and it is wise to choose one that has a lockable cable which can be threaded through trigger guards to secure the contents. For those who do not wish to display their collection, gun safes and security cabinets – some of which come disguised as attractive pieces of furniture – are preferable. There are even locks for use on individual weapons, and these locks are fitted to the breech to prevent the gun from being fired.

Many shooters elect to load their own ammunition at home, for reasons of cost, for pleasure, or because they require special loads which are not available commercially. This interest is amply served, with a good range of home loading equipment on offer, from tools which turn out single rounds to automatic presses. However obtained, ammunition must be carried – sometimes in large quantities – and be available to hand during shooting. Cartridge boxes enable 250 rounds or more to be transported from place to place with ease. For field use, a leather or canvas bag with shoulder strap will carry up to 100 12-bore rounds, while belts with individual sockets for 25 to 30 cartridges are convenient for the shooter who does not expect to fire more rounds than that during a day.

Shot game must be carried, too. A game bag of suitable size (preferably with a washable lining) is the most effective answer, but there are alternatives, from simple wire loops that fasten onto clothing, to frame carriers with wire slides that will carry a dozen birds by the neck.

Sportsmen usually feel naked without a knife, and as a result there are many brands available. These are divided into two main types: folding pocket knives, and fixed blade hunting knives carried on the belt. Folding knives should lock open to avoid accidents in use. Cheap knives, of which there are many, often look very attractive but the sportsman should always buy the best the budget will stand. Good quality steel performs well, and lasts a lifetime.

If sportsmen usually feel naked without a knife, they always feel naked without clothes, but they should never dress for hunting on these grounds alone. An uncomfortable shooter is likely to shoot badly, so the correct choice of clothing is vital. While the variety of clothing is infinite, there are some helpful guidelines in this area. Clothes should be loose rather

The accessories shown here include knives from Browning; cleaning kit, gun case, cartridge bag (on chair), cartridge belts (over chair), place finder and game book from Holland & Holland; spotting scope, game bag, hearing protectors and game carrier from Parker-Hale; and glasses, skeet vest, cartridge belt (on nail) and cartridge bag from Leslie Hewett. When buying accessories, just as when choosing a gun, it pays to opt for the best that you can afford. Good-quality equipment is well-made, reliable and a pleasure to use, and should give you years of service.

than tight, and have no features that might interfere with clean shooting – a protruding breast pocket, for example. The shooter should dress to be warm, comfortable and above all *dry* in the prevailing or anticipated weather conditions, but never hot. Clothing should be drab rather than bright, to avoid

startling the quarry, except in situations where safety considerations apply, for instance when deer hunting in company. Appropriate footwear must never be neglected, because unlike an army, a shooting party marches on its feet. It is sensible to ascertain the accepted dress style before shooting with stran-

gers, as it can be extremely disconcerting for all concerned if someone turns up for a shoot in camouflaged flak jacket and trousers, to find everyone else wearing thornproofs and breeks.

Lastly, the accessory market offers welcome hope to the shooter who has more bad days

than good, missing more than he hits; to the hunter who rarely finds a deer; and to the man who sees his dog vanishing over the horizon with monotonous regularity. A wealth of detailed instructional material is produced by experts, and available on video and in print, to help improve performance.

GUNDOGS

In this section we look at most breeds of sporting dogs commonly used nowadays by sporting shooters in Britain, Europe and North America. They have been grouped according to the distinctive ways in which they work in the field and the various skills, specialized or multipurpose, which they can provide to enhance the effectiveness of a day's shooting, and thus to increase the sportsman's sense of pleasure and satisfaction.

All dogs, from the tiniest chihuahua to the biggest Irish wolfhound, and, among sporting breeds, from the smallest spaniels to the biggest retrievers and hounds, belong to the genus *Canis*, and will readily interbreed. Similarly, any breed of domestic dog may interbreed with wolves, jackals and dingoes, and all these types of wild and domestic dog-like creatures probably go back to a common ancestral type. They share other characteristics, including a tendency to live by a combination of hunting and carrion feeding; to live and hunt in packs, within which there are dominant and subordinate individuals; and all are easy to rear and tame in captivity, especially from the young puppy stage. The first domesticated dogs probably originated from the young puppies of wolves or jackals found by chance and reared in close contact with human beings. In the absence of a natural parent or a pack leader, the puppy's human master assumes the dominant role and becomes the source of guidance and authority which all dogs look for. From these first points of contact man and dog gradually developed an intimate working relationship in a co-operative hunting partnership.

The earliest accurately-dated evidence about domestic dogs comes from Mesolithic remains stretching from the eastern Mediterranean into northern Europe, and it seems likely that the first domesticated dogs, which were probably used for hunting and also for guarding livestock, evolved in the Middle East and spread northwestwards as the last great glacial ice-sheet gradually retreated and opened up central and northern Europe to human settlement and to colonization by many species of birds and mammals. By about 7000 BC two types of domestic dog were in existence in the part of northwest Europe we now call Denmark.

Leaping forward several thousand years, today's gundog breeds owe their origins to hunting for food and for sport as it was practised before the development of gunpowder and sporting firearms. In late medieval Europe large game was caught mainly by pursuing it with fast 'gazehounds', the ancestors of the modern large breeds like the Borzoi or Russian wolfhound and the Great Dane or boarhound, or by relentless pursuit by scenting hounds, the forebears of modern staghounds, harriers and foxhounds. The gundog breeds, however, began in a different role, as the companions of the falconer and the 'fowler'.

Falconry or hawking, which involves using a trained broad-winged hawk or a long-winged falcon to catch and kill birds and small mammals on the wing or on foot, was both a means of catching food and a highly satisfying sport in its own right, especially popular among the higher social classes of feudal Europe, for whom it was an elegant and important ritual activity. All forms of falconry were made easier by dogs trained to find game for the hawks. This was achieved by using dogs to flush or spring game from cover, which is the origin of today's flushing breeds like spaniels. Other dogs were kept and bred for their special ability to locate game by detecting its air-scent and pointing or setting to indicate its whereabouts, so that the falconers with their birds could manoeuvre into position before the game was flushed. Thus the basis was laid for our modern pointers and setters, and for many of the multipurpose 'hunt, point and retrieve' gundog breeds.

The development of sporting firearms in Europe was slow but steady from the 16th century onwards, and it was not until the 18th century that sportsmen had general access to fowling pieces which were capable of accurate use against fast-flying or fast-running game. Until the 1760s most quarry was shot while perching, sitting or squatting.

Subsequently the flintlock muzzle-loading shotgun and rifle evolved through the era of the more reliable percussion-capped system and finally reached their present peak of development with the various types of breech-loading shotguns and sporting rifles now in universal use. As the skills of the sporting shotgunner and rifleman have developed the importance of the dog remains undiminished. In many respects, indeed, it has increased. This is particularly true of the retrieving breeds, without which many forms of sporting shotgun shooting would be both inefficient and inhumane. The pointing and setting breeds have retained their importance, especially in areas where game is thinly distributed and wide questing is necessary, while flushing dogs like the springer spaniel have achieved worldwide popularity. And many a modern deer stalker has had good cause to be grateful for the services of a steady, reliable dog to help locate a dead animal fallen in thick cover, or to follow up and locate a wounded animal which might otherwise be lost and suffer accordingly.

The wide variety of sporting shooting tactics, terrain, quarry and local preferences, both personal and national, to be found in the world of modern sporting shooting has led to the development of a bewilderingly wide range of gundog breeds. In the pages which follow we introduce them to you, individually and in groups, with all their many differing skills, styles and personalities. We also offer some basic guidance on choosing your gundog puppy, rearing it, caring for it and training it to the point where it will become your most loyal sporting companion and your most valuable sporting ally.

CHOOSING A DOG

Dogs play a central role in the sporting shooting of live quarry of almost every species. And just as there is a wide range of quarry species for the sportsman to pursue, there is a large and sometimes bewildering array of sporting dog breeds. Making your choice of a sporting dog from among these can be greatly simplified if you first define what qualities and working abilities you need in a sporting dog, and, equally importantly, by considering your own temperament, domestic circumstances and way of life.

Of course, you may not need a dog at all. In stalking red deer on the hill in Scotland, or chamois in high mountains, dogs play no part in the sport. Similarly, the more organized forms of game bird shooting may mean that sufficient dogs are provided by beaters and pickers-up. If you stand as one of a line of of guns shooting partridge or pheasants, or waiting in a butt for driven

grouse, you may find you require all your concentration to shoot quickly and accurately during the drives, while the flushing and retrieving of game is carried out by the line of beaters and by the pickers-up waiting behind you.

At most, on a big driven shoot, you may only be able to use your dog briefly to pick up those birds which have fallen immediately around your stand or butt before you have to move off to the next drive. Under these circumstances dog-work is best left to to others, and those who shoot driven birds on a large scale tend to find they shoot better when they do not have to worry about handling and working a gundog at the same time.

Although examples like these show that the individual shooter may not always need or want a dog, they are exceptions to the general rule. Most sporting shooting is made more enjoy-

able, effective and humane if the individual shooter is accompanied by a good dog, well trained and properly prepared for working under the prevailing conditions.

Sporting breeds which have a part to play in live quarry shooting can be considered in three broad groups. First are the hounds, by which are meant breeds which hunt slowly, following their quarry by scent, and which are principally used for mammals. Hounds play an important part in raccoon hunting in North America, to find the trail of an animal, to pursue it and, eventually, to make it climb a tree. Various breeds of hunting hound have been developed for this, including the Walker hound and the Plott hound, both derived from ancient European harrier- and beagle-type dogs.

In France, Belgium and the Scandinavian countries, hounds of this type are often used to

hunt other mammals like hares and roe deer, and also elk, using the specially-bred Scandinavian elk hound, to find the quarry and move it to within range of the solitary sportsman/dog handler with his shotgun or rifle, or perhaps a line of sportsmen waiting with rifles for the larger species like elk.

Secondly, the British and Irish woodland deer stalker is increasingly aware of the benefits of stalking with a trained dog, which may either accompany him on foot, sit with him in a high seat or be kept in readiness in a vehicle nearby. Almost any breed of dog can be trained to follow a blood trail and locate a deer carcase, and many household pets and crossbred dogs have been used successfully for this. But greater versatility and

---

When you've decided what dog you want, choose a puppy that comes from good working stock, not from show-bred parents.

effectiveness can be achieved by using a purpose-bred continental breed, such as the working *Tekel* or dachshund of northern Europe, the beagle-like Danish hound, and working-bred varieties of schnauzer and griffon. These can be trained to walk silently with the stalker, to remain quiet and still for long periods with a rifleman in a high seat, and can track and locate dead and wounded deer from scent and blood trails which may be many hours old.

Several of the all-purpose gundog breeds, often known as 'hunt, point and retrieve' (HPR) dogs, are magnificent stalkers' dogs. The German wirehaired pointer (*Draathaar*), the German shorthaired pointer (GSP), the large Münsterlander and the German longhaired pointer are used to track and locate dead and wounded deer, and also to move deer at a measured pace through blocks of woodland towards riflemen stationed at strategic points. This is a most effective form of deer culling, especially for shooting the females and yearlings on the short days and in the bad weather of winter.

Thirdly, there are the 'true gundog' breeds, and it is from these that the sporting shotgunner will usually make his choice. The bird dog breeds, like the English pointer and the various types of setter, are highly specialized for finding game in open country and in woodland where ground cover is not too thick. Their chief task is to run hard and fast, covering many miles in a shooting day, and indicating the presence of game, which may be either birds or small mammals, by freezing on a fixed point or 'set'.

While they may be required to retrieve, the finding and flushing of game is their main purpose, and they are best suited to working for not more than two or three guns, and for questing widely over rough and open country. In Britain, this means they are rarely found working away from the wilder and more open country of northern and western areas, and there is little or no scope for their special working skills in modern woodland or farmland game shooting in Britain today.

Those whose sport consists primarily of driven game will do well to look carefully at the various retriever breeds, of which the labrador is the most popular. The golden retriever, the flatcoated retriever and the curlycoated retriever are all variations on the common theme of a large, powerful dog, bred primarily for its ability to find dead and wounded game using not only its nose, but also its eyes to mark the fall of shot birds, and sometimes its ears to hear a running bird move in thick cover.

If properly bred, and provided that their training and handling has been carefully developed, all these breeds should be content to stay steadily and quietly to heel until they are sent out on a retrieve, and they should display great energy and drive in searching for lost game, and firmness and gentleness in retrieving it to hand.

The retrieving breeds have a strong natural hunting instinct, and many are also used as flushing dogs, especially on informal shoots and rough shooting days, although care must be taken that this does not affect their steadiness when used as 'no-slip' retrievers on driven shoots.

The wildfowler, whether on inland waters or along the coast, requires a powerful retrieving dog which is able to endure the long hours of cold and wetness which waterfowl hunting entails, with the additional harshness of ice and snow in late winter. The thick, oily coats of the Irish water spaniel and the curlycoated retriever make these ideal water dogs, although the majority of wildfowlers prefer the more tractable labrador or the golden retriever, or one of the large-type English springer spaniels.

Finally, which dog best suits the all-round sportsman, whose shooting season may include rough shooting, upland game bird hunting and wildfowling? The English springer spaniel is one contender, and it has a good claim to be regarded as the finest all-rounder among modern British gundog breeds, and its enormous popularity reflects its ability to fulfil many roles in the shooting field.

However, other breeds have their enthusiastic advocates, too, and some of the continental HPR dogs can combine a great range of working abilities in one animal. The German shorthaired pointer and, increasingly, the German wirehaired

TYPE	BREED	SPORTING USE
Pointers & setters	English pointer Irish setter English setter Gordon setter	Finding, pointing and flushing game, 'pointing dead' and sometimes retrieving.
Multipurpose dogs	German shorthaired pointer German wirehaired pointer Münsterlanders Vizsla Weimaraner Spinone German longhaired pointer Brittany spaniel	As for pointers and setters, but working closer to the guns, and usually retrieving from land or water; also tracking deer.
Flushing dogs	Springer spaniel Cocker spaniel Welsh springer Sussex spaniel Field spaniel Clumber spaniel American springer Brittany	Beating out thick cover, finding and flushing game, retrieving shot game from land and water.
Retrievers	Labrador retriever Golden retriever Curlycoated retriever Flatcoated retriever Chesapeake Bay retriever Irish water spaniel	Primarily retrieving dead and wounded game from land and water. Sometimes used as flushing dogs, and for tracking and finding wounded deer.
Hounds	Walker hound Plott hound Elkhound Griffon Coonhound	For finding and hunting small and large mammals, and treeing them or bringing them to bay.

pointer, are to be found in every form of shooting, and a well-trained individual should be capable of acting as a pointer, flushing dog and retriever as the occasion demands. The large Münsterlander, the Weimaraner, the Hungarian Vizsla and the Italian Spinone work in much the same way, and the small Münsterlander and the Britanny spaniel may appeal to those who prefer a spaniel-sized dog with natural pointing ability. These HPR breeds can, if correctly trained and handled, be ideal in almost every shooting situation, although few will have the complete steadiness and silence required of a dog on driven shooting days.

In making his choice, the sportsman should consider the various breeds' qualities carefully, and also give some thought as to how a particular breed is likely to fit in with his house, his family arrangements, his type of shooting and, not least, his own personality and temperament. Some dog handlers fare well with tough, wilful breeds, while others can achieve little with a dog that is not gentle, biddable and willing to please. A slow, pottering style of hunting may not suit an athletic young sportsman who aims to cover miles of rough country in a shooting day. Nor will a fast and active dog suit an elderly or sedentary sportsman, or one who does most of his shooting standing at a peg or in a butt.

The cardinal rule in choosing a sporting dog, of whatever breed, is to ensure that it comes from proven working stock. Only in this way can you be sure that a puppy will have the instinctive working ability that is the raw material which training and experience later mould into the finished working gundog.

Many sporting breeds are also popular on the show bench, where natural instinct and working ability are less important than conformation and appearance. As a general rule, it is advisable not to expect top-class working ability from any puppy which has even a small amount of show-bred blood.

TRAINING GUNDOGS

Training a working gundog begins, in a sense, before it is born, and even before it is conceived. Unless both parents are from proven working stock and themselves display evident natural working ability, it is unlikely that their progeny will have the innate tendencies to hunt, retrieve and point which, individually or collectively, are the most important qualities of the working gundog breeds. The gundog puppy, of whatever breed, should therefore be chosen with one eye on the pedigree and the working performance of its ancestors, and the other on the behaviour and appearance of the puppy itself, and also of its dam and sire.

Personal preferences play an important part, too, not least in deciding whether to choose a

dog puppy or a bitch, and in the eventual choice of one individual from among its litter of brothers and sisters. Bitches tend to be quieter, less headstrong and gentler than dogs, although they present their owners with the regular problem, usually every six months, of coming into season, which generally means they must be withdrawn from work and kept secure from the attentions of any male dog for about three weeks.

Spaying a bitch will prevent unwanted puppies, but may cause behavioural problems and a tendency for the bitch to put on too much weight. In addition, many gundog owners have had their bitches spayed only to regret it later, when they would like to have bred from an

outstanding working bitch. Castration may reduce a male dog's libido and aggression, but also rules out breeding and may cause a tendency to obesity and a lack of drive. Neither spaying or castration should be done without careful thought.

Although training techniques for retrievers, flushing dogs like spaniels, and bird dogs take very different forms, especially at the advanced stages, the initial training of every gundog puppy follows much the same pattern. Training is aimed at disciplining, heightening and refining the growing puppy's natural working ability. At the same time, it also ensures that the dog is healthy and happy, and thoroughly 'humanized' so that it becomes a good companion, acceptable in other human and

Teaching a dog to find and fetch a thrown dummy will encourage and develop its natural retrieving instincts.

canine company, and able to travel in cars and, if need be, to come into the house without being a nuisance to others or becoming unhappy or distressed itself.

Dogs are pack animals, like the wolves which are their wild cousins. They therefore respect and respond positively to the presence of a 'pack leader', which in the case of a gundog is its trainer and handler. Having quietly but firmly established your position as pack leader from the outset, all training is aimed at drawing out and developing natural working ability, through praise and punishment when appropriate. Most dogs are attentive to their owners and are eager to please and be praised. Thus praise should always follow obedience, hard work and good behaviour, and punishment should always follow when a dog does wrong.

Punishment should be appropriate to the misdemeanour and also to the individual dog. A sensitive puppy calls for a different approach to a tough, wilful one. Punishment must also follow immediately after the crime, and preferably be carried out at the place where the puppy did something wrong. In this way punishment is directly associated in the puppy's mind with its action. It is worse than useless to punish a dog when it cannot realize why it is being punished. Whipping is a thing of the past, and no dog should be beaten with a heavy stick or anything else which can cause bruising or internal injury.

Successful gundog training means making haste slowly, and at a pace appropriate to the individual character and ability of the puppy. Simple obedience is an essential preliminary to training for the shooting field. Every puppy must quicky learn the meaning of the word 'No!', and be taught to come when it is called, to sit when told to do so, and to remain sitting until it is ordered to move. This can begin very simply, with the handler gently pressing the young puppy into a sitting position and encouraging it to remain there while he moves a few paces away. Extravagant praise encourages obedience, and gradually the physical distance and the length of time involved can be increased, until a point is reached where the puppy will sit and stay for long periods of time and at a considerable distance from the handler.

Another essential in early training is teaching the growing gundog to stop on command. To attempt to train any dog without being able to make it sit or drop belly-flat on command is as unwise as trying to drive a car without brakes. Every puppy should learn to drop into a sitting or belly-flat position instantly, on word of command, or

by a particular whistle call or hand signal, and it is best to accustom every dog to dropping to any one of these three. (This can later be extended to dropping when game flushes or runs, and some trainers also like a dog to drop when a gun is mounted to the shoulder.)

More advanced training takes different forms for different gundog breeds. Bird dogs must be encouraged to hunt widely from an early age, and most will do so instinctively, taking a crosswind, quartering line. This should be encouraged, and the puppy should turn instantly to a single note on the handler's whistle, turning into the wind and running back on a parallel beat. Bird dogs must also come in to their handler's side at a gallop when called, usually with a series of short, quickly repeated whistle notes. Above all, every bird dog must learn to drop or 'down charge' when a long whistle note is blown, or when the handler raises his hand to give the 'hup' signal, and also the moment a bird flushes.

Bird dog breeds will point instinctively, although setters tend to mature more slowly than the English pointer in this respect. A steady, promising puppy may be introduced to live game when it is six or seven months old, and many trainers use dovecote pigeons and aviary quail for this. In Europe, perhaps the best wild game species for the young bird dog puppy is the snipe, especially if these can be found in small,

rushy fields not far from home. Snipe have a powerful scent, disproportionately so for their small size, and they often lie well to a pointing dog.

Retrievers and spaniels should not be introduced to live game until they have proved their ability and steadiness in various other ways, of which the most important are connected with finding and retrieving dummies. Hunting and retrieving should be natural instincts, and these are best developed by playing an educational game, encouraging the puppy to hunt for something which is hidden and also to retrieve dummies thrown at at distance.

Spaniels must alway be urged to hunt thoroughly while remaining close at hand, and their working pattern must be established so that they are always within no more than 25 yards of the handler, otherwise game will be flushed out of gunshot. Retrievers used as flushing dogs should also be trained to work close, although retriever and spaniel breeds will eventually be expected to mark, find and retrieve game which has fallen or run a long way off.

An important part of every spaniel's training involves teaching steadiness when hunted game flushes or runs. Traditionally, a pen enclosing rabbits is used as a training aid here, and the puppy is encouraged to find and bolt a rabbit, whereupon it should sit or drop instantly, although all its instincts may be to give chase. A similar training technique is

also useful for retrievers, which must always be steady in the field, whatever the temptation.

Retrieving dummies thrown in the open must be followed by an introduction to unseen retrieves, where the dog is encouraged to quest in a given direction or area for a concealed dummy, and also learns to use its memory to retrieve a dummy it has seen thrown some time ago.

Every retriever and spaniel is expected to work well in water, and most working-bred gundogs will readily do so. Their introduction to water must be made thoughtfully, however, and it may be best if the handler chooses a warm day and wades into the water with the dog. Begin in the shallows, where the dog is not out of its depth, and it will gradually gain confidence and be able to tackle deeper water by swimming.

Few dogs from proven shooting stock are gun-shy, and fear of gunshots is invariably caused by the handler's thoughtlessness. Begin simply, accustoming the puppy to sharp, loud noises, for instance a quick, resonant handclap. If these noises are heard at feeding time, so much the better, as the puppy may then associate them with something pleasurable. Then let the pupil hear a few shotgun shots fired at a distance, and only gradually move towards the day when the puppy hears a shotgun fired close by. (Even a steady, experienced gundog may be made gunshy if shots are fired too close to its sensitive ears.)

A good handler is aware of his dog's strengths and failings, and will always reward good work with praise.

GUNDOG CARE

It is an old (and wise) saying that you can criticize a person's shooting, but you should never criticize their dog. Even so, it's probably true that nothing can cause an individual more frustration in the shooting field than the poor performance of his gun dog. Unfortunately, many sportsmen endow shooting dogs with abilities far beyond reasonable expectation. Worse, they lose sight of the fact that any working dog will invariably reflect the effort (or lack of it) put in by the handler week in, week out.

In order to deliver optimum performance in the field, a gun dog needs consistent attention 365 days a year. Vital though basic training may be, it's a serious error to sit back when training is complete in the mistaken belief that the job is done. The sportsman who leaves his dog idle for months, before bringing it out on the first day of a new season expecting a flawless effort, will surely be disappointed. The animal is likely to become over-excited and unruly, before tiring quickly and

eventually losing interest.

It is necessary to maintain physical fitness and mental alertness through regular exercise, even when the dog is not required for work. This programme must include skill sharpening, with the tempo increasing to ensure peak fitness as the season approaches. The key to success is regularity: 15 minutes every day will achieve far more than one extended session on Saturday or Sunday. And, of course, no newly-trained gundog should begin its working life with a full day in the field. Half an hour may be enough first time, and stamina, experience and maturity will follow.

Diet makes an important contribution to fitness, and so a balanced diet that includes carbohydrates, protein, vitamins and minerals is essential. Feed an adult animal twice per day, giving it a light breakfast of biscuit or cereal, with the main high-protein meal in the evening, and be sure to vary the diet because dogs, like people, get bored if the same menu is con-

stantly being repeated.

With the exception of any starchy foods, kitchen leftovers can make a useful contribution, as can well-chopped raw vegetables. Toasted wholemeal bread, broken dog biscuit and brown rusks can be used alone or soaked in milk, egg or gravy. Canned dog meat is very acceptable, as are the better brands of 'complete' dry food, if served according to maker's instructions. Boiled rabbit, squirrel or sheep's head will provide variety, and offal such as raw green tripe is much appreciated and highly nutritious. The addition of a mineral/vitamin supplement can do no harm, and will cover accidental diet deficiencies. Clean, fresh water should, of course, be available to the dog at all times, especially after work on a hot day, so always carry a supply in your vehicle if you are travelling any distance to shoot.

Some authorities recommend that working dogs should be fasted for one day in seven to improve coat quality and avoid sluggishness, though this is a matter of individual preference. However, you should never feed a dog before exercise or a shooting trip.

If a dog is kennelled, the quarters should be warm and dry but well ventilated. There must be a sleeping platform above floor level, out of draughts, and the run should be large enough to permit considerable freedom of movement. A kennel dog should be admitted to the house regularly, or it may prove nervous in the company of people – hardly a recommendation in a shooting dog.

All dogs should be wormed as puppies and inoculated against the prevalent canine diseases, and the inoculations should be boosted annually. A trained gun dog represents a substantial investment, and cannot easily, swiftly or cheaply be replaced. Likewise, while ordinary cuts sustained in the field usually heal easily and well, in the case of larger gashes or any hint of infection, professional veterinary advice should be sought. The same precaution should be taken if the dog manifests unusual behaviour that might suggest hidden injury, or shows any symptoms of illness.

It is, of course, unacceptable to take a bitch on heat into the

DEW CLAWS *The dew claw is a rudimentary, functionless inner claw on the foot of some dogs, which some owners have removed to prevent it snagging when the dog is working.*

DOCKING TAILS *Tail docking, although controversial, is in fact essential for any dog which is going to be working through thick cover. An undocked tail will split, and it will be slow to heal.*

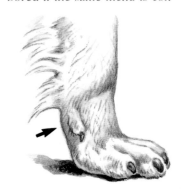

If a dog gets wet during a day's shooting, it should be dried as soon as possible, preferably by towelling it.

field. However, a well-timed course of injections allows the owner to delay a bitch's season so she will be available for work when needed. If a bitch is not wanted for breeding, or should not be bred from because of a defect, she can be spayed. The benefit is obvious, the only negative aspect a tendency to put on weight after the operation. Simply reducing the amount of food given counteracts this.

One issue that has become controversial in some parts of the world is the docking of tails and taking of dew claws. While there is no evidence to suggest the removal of dew claws is advantageous, it is certainly essential to dock the tail of any dog expected to work thick cover. This procedure is straightforward and painless when conducted four days after birth, but if the tail is left undocked, the end of it will split when the dog starts working and the wound will remain open all season. Two thirds of the tail must be left to assist during water work.

After a day's shooting, the sportsman's first thought should be for his companion. If wet, the dog should be dried at once, either by towelling or placing in a sack with a draw-string top, which may be loosely secured round the dog's neck to prevent escape. Concentrated body heat will soon dry him off. At home the dog's ears, coat and paws should be checked for foreign bodies, and these removed before the animal is fed and bedded down.

Regular grooming will maintain the coat in top condition, and provide warning of parasite infestation during summer months. When fleas or lice are discovered, treat immediately. Most dogs dislike sprays and powders, so a bath with flea shampoo is often the best solution, repeated until the infestation is completely cleared.

Thoughtful and consistent caring for a dog's general wellbeing will return handsome dividends, and while a neglected, discontented animal is indeed frustrating, there can be no greater satisfaction than shooting in company with a fit, alert and happy gundog.

RETRIEVING DOGS

The duties of a retrieving gundog are, by definition, to find and bring back what has been shot. The retrieving dog's ability to perform these duties has been achieved by choosing and breeding selectively from individual dogs which have shown the most desirable retriever characteristics. These are a fondness for carrying things gently, and an ability to use their eyes, nose and sometimes their ears to find dead and wounded quarry, pick it up and trot or swim back with it to their handlers, delivering it securely but gently into the hand.

The labrador retriever is undoubtedly the most popular and important retriever breed today throughout the British Isles and North America. They have become enormously popular, both as gundogs and also for show and as pets, in the postwar period, having taken over in importance from the once-dominant flatcoat retriever and the curlycoat retriever.

The labrador is a medium-sized, smooth-coated dog, standing 22 to 24 inches at the shoulder. It should be compact in build and also fast and stylish, with a powerful, otterlike tail and a broad head with neat, triangular ears. Most labradors are either black or yellow, and the latter term covers a wide range from pale cream to a rich yellowish-ginger. Both black and yellow puppies will occur in the same litter. There is also a solid liver or chocolate-coloured strain of labrador retriever, which has a small but enthusiastic following among sportsmen and showing circles.

Temperamentally, the working labrador tends to be friendly and docile and these qualities, combined with its short, tidy coat, have endeared it to those who like to have their gundogs with them in the house rather than being kennelled outside. As regards working qualities, few well-bred labradors are not natural retrievers from an early age. This, combined with a general desire to please and a willingness to be trained at an early age, has made them particularly popular with modern sportsmen for formal driven game shooting, rough shooting and wildfowling.

Some retrievers are trained and worked on a strictly 'no-slip' basis, which entails staying to heel at all times until they are specifically sent out for a retrieve. This style of working is best suited to formal shooting, such as when guns take up their positions at individual pegs or butts for shooting driven partridges, pheasants or grouse. Under these conditions, absolute steadiness and silence is required, if an unruly dog is not to upset the smooth running of an important and carefully planned drive.

The inland duck shooter, the coastal wildfowler and the solitary pigeon shooter also appreciate the labrador's willingness to sit quietly in a hide or a boat, often for long periods. A good labrador learns to watch and listen for approaching birds, to mark the fall of dead and wounded game accurately, and to make a swift, effective pickup when commanded to do so.

The modern, working-bred labrador has an exceptional nose, great drive and energy in pursuing scent, and a notable reputation as a supremely effective retriever from thick cover and from water. It will also follow the trail of a 'runner' or other wounded game, often for long distances, and labrador retrievers are finding increasing

Both golden retrievers (above left) and labradors (left) are excellent at finding and retrieving game, whether on land or in water.

popularity with woodland deer stalkers, owing to their ability to find a dead animal or follow the trail of a wounded one.

The closest rival to the labrador among retrieving breeds is the golden retriever, a breed which has become very popular since the 1940s. Similar in size to the labrador retriever, the golden retriever has a longer coat, golden-yellow in colour, although individual shades vary from fairly light to quite dark. They have large, broad heads and a solid physique, and are temperamentally docile, affectionate and biddable.

Although their long coats may hold more dirt and debris and require more attention than the short-coated labrador retrievers, golden retrievers are also suitable gundogs to keep in the house. Breeders have made a special effort to maintain the golden retriever's attractive appearance and its natural working ability side by side, so as to produce a genuinely dual-purpose dog, and there is a less sharp distinction between working-bred and show-bred strains of golden retriever than in most other gundog breeds.

Although they lack the speed and dash of the labrador, golden retrievers have their own elegant style when at work, and they have proved their ability as effective game-finders and excellent retrievers from water.

Their coats give them good protection from rough cover, water and cold conditions, and they share the 'trainability' of the labrador retriever. This makes them a good choice for the sportsman who wishes to acquire a puppy and train and handle his own gundog on shooting days. Golden retrievers have a large and growing following, especially in Great Britain, and have achieved some notable results at field trials.

The current pre-eminence of the labrador and the golden retriever is a relatively recent phenomenon, and a century ago flatcoated retrievers and curly-coated retrievers were seen much more commonly in the shooting field.

The flatcoated retriever reached its peak of popularity in the 1890s, which was the era of some of the biggest and most extravagantly organized covert shoots in Britain. This breed is similar in size to the labrador retriever, but has a longer, slightly feathered coat and a more slender, racy build which is somewhat reminiscent of the setter breeds. The flatcoat's head is longer and more slender, with a less pronounced step or 'stop' between forehead and muzzle. They share the tendency of most retriever breeds to be docile and kindly by nature, but they are often slower to mature and take longer to train. While a

labrador retriever may be undertaking regular, difficult work in the field from the age of 18 months, few flatcoated retrievers will have reached this stage until they are another year or more older.

Carefully trained, flatcoated retrievers work exceptionally well, with an excellent nose and considerable game-finding ability on land and water. However, they lack the agreeable working style of the golden retriever and the dash and pace of the labrador, and it is increasingly uncommon to see a well-trained flatcoated retriever in the shooting field, which is rather a pity in view of the breed's history.

The curlycoated retriever, like the flatcoat, was enormously popular in the last century, particularly where covert shooting was combined with upland grouse shooting, duck and snipe shooting on inland marshes, and coastal wildfowling. Their dense, tightly-curled coats are similar to those of the Irish water spaniel, which makes them excellent for work in cold water during the winter months, and their long legs were regarded as an asset when working in rushes or deep heather.

Mature curlycoated retrievers are large, heavily-built dogs with heads which are both broad and long, and with less of a stop than the labrador retriever and golden retriever.

The Chesapeake Bay retriever is an excellent working dog, but it can be stubborn and is often aggressive.

Like the Irish water spaniel they tend to be slow developers, with a wilful and selfish streak which can make them slow and difficult to train. Some individuals have tended to be hard-mouthed, damaging the game they retrieve, and this has also given the breed something of a bad press in recent times. The curlycoated retriever nevertheless has a small but keen following in the sporting world, and while it is unlikely ever again to rival the labrador or the golden retriever in popularity, its working qualities are not threatened by excessive breeding for the show bench.

Finally, the Chesapeake Bay retriever is an important North American breed of water retriever, which is gradually gaining a small band of supporters in Britain and Europe. These are large, bold dogs with something of the build of a large labrador retriever and a slightly curly, oily coat which is an asset for dogs which work a lot in water. They are similar in many ways to the curlycoated retriever, and the popularity of this breed in Britain appears to be limited only by the availability of good working-bred dogs from imported stock.

POINTERS & SETTERS

Pointers and setters are probably the oldest and best established gundog breeds in Britain, Europe and North America, and they continue to play a key role in game shooting in most countries. Care must be taken to distinguish them from the 'hunt, point and retrieve' (HPR) breeds of continental Europe, which are multipurpose gundogs for whom pointing is but one of their various skills.

Pointers and setters can work effectively in scrubland, as when pheasants, woodcock or bobwhite quail are the quarry, and even in quite thick woodlands, when the woodland grouse of North America and the forest-loving woodcock and pheasants of Europe are sought. However, the modern pointing breeds (both pointers and setters) have all been principally developed in Britain and Ireland, where their work is usually in open country.

The very appearance of these breeds gives a good indication of the manner in which they work. They tend to be tallish in stature, although some strains of English setter may be no higher than a springer spaniel at the shoulder, but their carriage is generally erect and their appearance long-legged, with head held high, and all these are common attributes of dogs which work at a fast pace, covering many miles of ground in an ordinary day's shooting and, most importantly, locating their game by detecting its live scent carried on the breeze.

Air scent is detected by dogs which range with their heads held high and working across or into the wind, while retrievers and flushing dogs work from the scent of game which is rising from or close to the ground, and which is also often a blood scent or a dead game scent.

Retrievers, spaniels and many other non-sporting breeds often make a quick 'flash point' before dashing forward to investigate scents of various kinds. Pointing breeds should stop abruptly, freezing from a full gallop into statuesque immobility when they wind game, and holding that position for as long as the game remains where it is and the scent persists. On a grouse moor, for example, a setter or pointer may find a covey of grouse several hundred yards away from the guns, who may have a slow and difficult approach. It is not uncommon, therefore, for them to have to hold their point for 10 or 15 minutes, and sometimes much longer.

Pointing styles vary from breed to breed, and the racy English pointer has a particularly elegant stance on point, often leaning forward intently with head, neck, back and tail forming a nearly straight line directed towards the game, which may be anything from a solitary woodcock to a large covey of partridge or grouse.

Setters often behave differently, and the English, Irish and Gordon setter breeds were all developed from early strains of

spaniel-like dog, and comparison with the appearance of most spaniel breeds clearly indicates this strong common ancestry. Their role, in the days before the widespread use of firearms and 'shooting flying', was to find birds for falconers and bird netters, both of whom preferred a dog which squatted or sat ('set') when it winded game. Although modern sportsmen shooting over setters do not require their dogs to adopt a crouching or belly-flat position, this trait still lingers in many individual dogs, and a setter on point will often hold itself in a semi-crouching position, very different from that of the English pointer but just as stylish in its own way.

The pointing breeds are often referred to in North America as 'bird dogs', which is a useful term and one which indicates that they are used mainly to hunt game birds, especially those which tend to squat in cover and which are not easily found by a gun or guns walking-up without dogs. They are particularly useful and important in areas where game tends to be thinly and widely scattered, and much upland gamebird hunting in North America and grouse shooting on many thinly populated moors in the British Isles, especially in western Scotland and in Ireland, could not easily take place without them. Their wide-ranging habits mean that two or three guns shooting over a pair of pointers or setters can effectively cover many times more ground in one day than would be possible with any other gundog breed.

In Britain and Ireland the pointing breeds tend, through a combination of selective breeding and individual training, to work by quartering very precisely, galloping freely to and fro across the wind on a wide beat which may be as much as three or four hundred yards from end to end. At the end of its beat, each dog turns upwind and swings back across the wind about twenty or thirty yards ahead of the last cross-wind beat it took. Advancing in this way, especially across relatively flat grassland and moorland, means that the dog should detect any

game lying within the wide sweep which it covers, and in this way one or two guns can effectively comb an area which could otherwise only be hunted by an extended line of 10 or 12 sportsmen advancing in line abreast, with flushing dogs like spaniels working within gunshot.

Though staunch on point, the bird dog is also trained to work forward or 'road in' on command (often indicated by a click of the handler's fingers), and to flush the bird or mammal which it has been pointing. When game takes wing, runs off or moves in any way, a well-trained bird dog will drop instantly and remain belly-flat. This not only encourages steadiness but also ensures that the dog is safely down out of the line of fire, for the guns may have to fire comparatively low shots at game which flushes or runs away close in front.

In Britain and Ireland, bird dogs are generally never used for retrieving, although they are often useful in 'pointing dead' when a wounded bird has gone ahead and collapsed at some distance. By modern convention, retrievers or spaniels are invariably used to collect shot game. Consequently, bird dogs in Britain and Ireland are not bred with their retrieving ability or softness of mouth in mind, although many individuals, especially setters, will show a readiness to retrieve, and some individuals can be most proficient at it, making them very talented multipurpose rough shooting dogs.

In North America and continental Europe, however, pointers and setters are trained and used somewhat differently. Precise, cross-wind quartering is not regarded as so important, nor is it always appropriate for the terrain being hunted. Quail-hunting pointers in the southern states of the USA, for example, have a much less regular hunting pattern than their British counterparts, and are often followed by hunters on horseback, who rein in and dismount when the bird dogs come on point. Often they remain so, a 'quirt' or flushing whip being used to flush the birds while the dogs remain steady, standing or dropping when the birds flush and not moving until ordered in to retrieve. A soft mouth is therefore

The two best-known blood lines of English setter are the Laverack and the Llewellin; this is one of the Llewellin type.

a desirable quality in bird dogs as they are used in North America.

The English pointer is probably the best-known bird dog, a classically elegant, shorthaired breed, predominantly white with markings which may be yellow, liver, black or lemon, or some combination of these which may take the form of large spots, splashes or ticks. It is a lightly-built but robust dog, with the long legs, deep ribcage and racy looks of the true bird dog.

If well bred, the English pointer's game-finding and pointing instinct is firmly ingrained, and even quite young puppies will often point staunchly. They are generally quick to mature, and rather easier to train to the point where their shooting careers can begin than is the case with the setter breeds. The English pointer is believed to be descended from Spanish bird dog stock, but its modern descendants are fast-paced and fine-boned compared to the ponderous, slow-working Spanish pointers described and depicted in old books and prints.

The English setter is one of the most popular bird dog breeds throughout Europe and North America, and the two best-known blood lines are Laverack and Llewellin, names derived from two important 19th-century breeders. English setters from working stock are often very small and lightly-built, quite different from the large strain which has been developed for the show bench. Predominantly white, English setters can be spotted or ticked with black, and tan or yellow also occur, while some individuals have tricolour markings.

The Irish setter is a familiar and popular breed, especially as a household pet in and in the show ring. The working-bred Irish setter, however, is smaller and has a rather broader head than his show-bench counterpart. He may also have a lighter, foxy-red coat rather than the deep mahogany of the show dog, and is usually less extravagantly feathered on legs and tail. The Irish red setter has been selectively bred from the old red-and-white strains, which had a background of white with prominent, rich red spotting and blotching. Some Irish setters also have a 'shower of hail' ticking of white against a red background, and others may have conspicuous blotches of white, especially on the chest.

The English pointer is a well-proportioned and fast-paced dog with a deeply ingrained finding and pointing instinct.

The Gordon setter (so called because of the breed's historic association with the Dukes of Gordon) is a big, heavy-boned dog by comparison with the Irish and English setters. Predominantly black with tan facings, they are generally acknowledged to have wonderful noses and a very staunch disposition on point. They lack the fast pace of the English pointer and the English and Irish setters, but they share the latter breed's ability to withstand harsh weather and rough going, and they are said to be generally more biddable and slightly easier to train than other setter breeds.

MULTIPURPOSE DOGS

The origins of the development of multipurpose hunting dogs, also known as HPR (hunt, point and retrieve) dogs, lie in mid-19th-century Germany. One of the effects of the revolution there in 1848 was that for the first time the common man was permitted to hunt game on his own land, and as a result the number of hunters in Germany was greatly increased.

This was also an age when great advances were being made in the scientific breeding of domestic animals, including dogs. British breeders had striven, with great success, to improve the working performance of their pointer and setter breeds, turning them into highly specialized, ultra-efficient game finders, possessed of style and endurance and well able to deal with an abundance of feathered game. They were no longer expected to retrieve, as this was now done by the rapidly-evolving retriever breeds.

German hunters were desirous of improving the old German pointer which, although possessed of an excellent nose, was slow and heavy and lacked pace and endurance. They had no wish to produce a specialized breed, and so the concept of the versatile hunting dog was born. Their ideal was a medium-sized dog (21 to 26 inches high) which was an effective all-rounder, capable of dealing with a variety of game species: able to find, point and retrieve game from both land and water;

Multipurpose or hunt, point and retrieve dogs are versatile breeds which are widely used in continental Europe. They were first developed in Germany, in the mid-19th century.

able to track and trail and to work equally well on upland gamebirds, waterfowl, hares, deer, foxes and wild boar; able to give assistance when dealing with poachers; and not far removed in its abilities from the English pointer.

The large Münsterlander (above left) is a popular German multipurpose breed, while the Vizsla (left) is of Hungarian origin.

The Brittany or Brittany spaniel (above) originated in France as a multipurpose breed, but is now the most popular working spaniel in the USA.

Groups of enthusiasts tried various breeding combinations in their search for their ideal dog. Those who desired a smooth-coated dog crossed the old German pointer with a bloodhound, the Hanoverian Schweisshund and the English pointer, and came up with the German shorthaired pointer or Kurzhaar, a liver-and-white, solid liver, black-and-white or all-black breed.

Others considered that the new breed should possess, for protection against thick covert and cold water, a thick, wiry coat with a soft, waterproof undercoat, and in their experimenting several breeds were created.

The standard poodle, chosen for its intelligence and retrieving abilities on land and water, was crossed with the English pointer, resulting in the Pudel pointer, a solid liver breed. The Stichelhaar, a liver-and-white or solid liver breed, was derived from the breeding of German rough-coated pointing dogs with the English foxhound, for stamina and nose, and the relatively unknown Polish water dog, for its aquatic abilities.

A Dutchman, Edouard Korthals, created (in Germany) the grey-brown wirehaired pointing griffon from an amalgam of rough-coated pointers: 'griffons' from Holland, Belgium and France, crossed with setter, spaniel and otterhound. Other breeders combined these breeds to produce the liver-and-white, solid liver or black-and-white German wirehaired pointer (the Drahthaar), now one of the most numerous and successful of all German gundog breeds and one which is still evolving.

At the same time, breeders in other European countries were also developing versatile hunting breeds. In Hungary the Vizsla, a golden-red breed, was produced from crossing local red-yellow hunting dogs with German shorthaired pointers and pointers, and later a wirehaired variety was produced from a cross with the German wirehaired pointer.

The Cêzký Fousek ('Czech whiskers') of Czechoslovakia was derived from Korthals' griffon and the German wirehaired pointer. In France, the Brittany was developed from crossing the English setter with a local spaniel breed with outcrosses to two pointers, the Italian Bracco and the Braque du Bourbonnais, resulting in a spaniel-sized, liver-and-white or orange-and-white breed.

There are a number of other breeds which come into the HPR category and which are relatively unimproved, approximating more to ancient types. In Germany, there is the smooth-coated Weimaraner, a large grey breed developed in 18th-century Thuringia which has a great deal of hound in its make-up, and there are breeds developed from the widely-distributed setter or 'great land spaniel', including the German longhaired pointer, a liver-and-white or solid liver breed to which the black-and-white large Münsterlander is closely related. The slightly smaller liver-and-white Kleiner (small) Münsterlander is similar to the English setter. Holland possesses a similar breed to the large Münsterlander in the Drentse partridge dog.

The Spinone, a large, rough-coated, white or liver-and-white breed, comes from Piedmont in Italy. This dog is a modern representative of an ancient breed that was once distributed widely throughout western Europe and was first mentioned in 13th-century manuscripts. In Victorian England, the Spinone was known erroneously as the 'Russian setter'.

All of these breeds, with the exception of the German longhaired pointer, the Münsterlanders and the Drentse partridge dog, are tail-docked. This is the only way to avoid injury to the tail when the dog is working in thick covert.

These pointer-retriever breeds fit the requirements of the sportsman or sportswoman who indulges in a variety of field sports but is only able to own a single dog. When well bred and properly trained, the same dog can be used successfully for game shooting, wildfowling, falconry and tracking lost or wounded deer.

FLUSHING DOGS

Many species of sporting birds and small mammals live in thick cover or take refuge there when danger threatens. To deal with game under these conditions, various breeds of gundog have been developed whose primary role is to locate game in cover and flush it – make it run off or take wing – within range of walking or standing guns. In addition, these flushing breeds are also capable of finding and retrieving wounded or dead game on land and water.

This work requires dogs which have a good nose, especially for scent on the ground or close to ground level. They must be active, willing hunters, able to cover ground thoroughly and to restrict their working range so as not to flush game out of shot. Thick cover also demands dogs which are courageous in tackling thorns, brambles and other tough vegetation, so the flushing breeds tend to be thick-skinned with thick protective coats. To minimize the risk of injury to the thinner and relatively unprotected skin of the end of their tails, most breeds of flushing dog are docked as young puppies.

The various spaniel breeds are the main gundogs used for flushing, and most have their origins in the 17th and 18th centuries. Falconers, and later sportsmen with fowling pieces, required dogs which would work steadily and methodically through thick cover to flush woodland species like pheasants and woodcock. This was particularly important in late autumn and winter when sportsmen abandoned the open fields and moorlands and sought their sport in copses and woodlands, which were bare of most of their leaves and thus more manageable from a sporting point of view. The springer and cocker spaniels take their names from the way in which they were expected to work – respectively to 'spring' game from its resting place, and to beat out the coverts for woodcock.

Among modern sporting spaniel breeds the English springer is pre-eminent in Britain and also very popular in North America. It is widely regarded as the ideal rough-shooter's dog, an all-rounder which can be used effectively in almost every form of sporting shooting. Basically white in colour, English

Although the Clumber spaniel is a heavily-built and slow-paced dog, it is an effective and reliable worker.

springers may be marked with black, liver or yellow blotching, spotting and ticking, and occasional tricoloured individuals occur. They have the broad heads and longish, rounded ears characteristic of all spaniels, and there is considerable individual variation in size.

Some excellent working springers may stand as tall as a medium-sized labrador retriever, while others may be little larger than a small hunt terrier. On average, however, a springer spaniel will stand about 15 inches at the shoulder, and have a solid, muscular and compact appearance. When working they give an impression of speed, liveliness and merriment with a rapid action from that shortened, docked tail, and a busy, nose-down way of searching for game. A springer spaniel, bred from good working stock, will have a natural hunting instinct and will require little persuasion to drive hard, even through the thickest cover, and also to enter water. Their retrieving instinct and ability, though not so highly developed as the specialist retriever breeds, helps to give them a range of skills useful in many shooting situations.

The working cocker spaniel is a very different dog from the more familiar show-bred cocker, with its exaggeratedly long, heavy ears. Usually smaller than the English springer spaniel,

cockers tend to have similar colouring, with black and white and liver and white predominating, although some individuals may be almost pure white, or sometimes solid liver or nearly pure black.

These are energetic, lively little spaniels and their small size makes it possible for them to work in tight cover which might defeat other dogs. However, it also restricts the size of game they can retrieve. But this is more than compensated for by their eagerness to work, and their excellent nose for finding game. They are said to be rather more difficult to train than springer spaniels, with a less obvious desire to please their masters, but sensitive handling and careful training can overcome this.

The English springer and cocker spaniels dominate the flushing breeds of gundog, but the spaniel family of gundogs has five additional representatives, each of which has its attractions and enjoys a small but devoted following among sportsmen and dog fanciers.

The Welsh springer spaniel is comparable in size to the larger type of English springer, but this breed does not display the springer's variety of coloration, being always reddish-brown and white. Like all working spaniels, the Welsh springer has an excellent nose and will work dense cover effectively, and also retrieve from water, although in both of these it may lack the confidence and dash of the English springer. Most Welsh springers will make reliable re-

trieving dogs, although the retrieving instinct may require a good deal of encouragement during training as it is often less well-developed than with the English springer or cocker.

While the Welsh springer is a popular and successful sporting breed, its reputation has suffered from the tendency of many individuals to whimper or bark when hunting, especially when on a strong scent, although great efforts have been made to reduce and eliminate this undesirable trait by careful, selective breeding.

The field spaniel is an ancient and well-established breed of British sporting spaniel which has declined greatly in popularity as a sporting breed since the 1940s. At its best, a field spaniel can work as diligently and effectively as any English springer, and there are some fine working strains in the hands of some of the breed's remaining supporters. However, field spaniels have been bred increasingly for the show bench rather than for work, which has seriously damaged the breed's reputation as a practical gundog.

The Sussex spaniel is another of the minority spaniel breeds, which has declined greatly in popularity since its heyday in the 1890s. Predominantly liver or black in colour, these little spaniels have something of the appearance of a slower and more heavily-built cocker spaniel, and they are acknowledged to have a good nose and a willingness to please. However, dwindling popularity and the influence of show breeding have combined to reduce the natural working ability of the Sussex spaniel, although several strains of genuine working stock still remain in the hands of a few breeders. Since the 1960s an effort has been made to promote and popularize this breed, but with limited success.

The Clumber spaniel takes its name from Clumber Park, seat of the Dukes of Newcastle, with whom the breed is closely associated in Britain. One of the dukes is said to have imported the first of this spaniel strain from France in the 18th century, and the breed was carefully developed and jealously treasured by the Newcastle family.

Clumber spaniels are heavily-built, chunky dogs with wide, generous heads, deep in the body and with a robust, plodding action. The Clumber stands about 18 inches at the shoulder and may weigh 55 to 70 pounds.

Unlike most other spaniel breeds, which are often inclined to over-excitability and well-meaning unruliness, the Clumber has a reputation for being docile and easy to handle, and for finding game most effectively, although its natural working pace is much slower than the modern cocker or English springer spaniel.

The Clumber spaniel still has

The English springer is the dominant sporting spaniel in Britain, but in the USA the Brittany, which originated in France, is more popular.

a good reputation as a reliable worker, especially where game sits very tight and scent may be poor, and it can usually be relied upon to work close to the guns. Traditionally, Clumber enthusiasts try to work their spaniels in small teams of three or four together.

Finally, there is the Irish water spaniel. This is an unusual dog in many respects, not least because there is great uncertainty in the gundog world about whether it should be regarded primarily as a spaniel or as a retriever.

The Irish water spaniel is a large, solidly-built dog, similar in size to a retriever, and with an unmistakable appearance. It has

the broad head and hanging ears of the typical spaniel, but the coat is a solid liver colour, lying in thick, oily curls which extend from the prominent poodle-like topknot on its head to the base of its tail. This is powerful, whiplike and sparsely covered with flat hair, and it is not customarily docked.

A willing and energetic worker, the Irish water spaniel is slower than the English springer or the working cocker, and his thick coat can cause him to become entangled in rough cover, which limits his hunting ability, makes the dog uncomfortable because of the thorns and burrs which it collects, and presents the owner or handler

with a major combing-out routine at the end of the day.

However, the Irish water spaniel is, as its name suggests, an outstanding dog in water, and the breed is a firm favourite with many wildfowlers. In open country, it can perform well as a good general purpose retriever, but it has a reputation for being slow to mature, wilful, and difficult to train. A good specimen, well trained and handled, can hold its own with most other gundogs and is a quite outstanding dog for inland marsh shooting and coastal wildfowling. Its unusual (and slightly comic) appearance makes this breed an uncommon but interesting sight in the shooting field.

HOUNDS

Well over a hundred separate breeds of hound are recognized around the world. They were the first dogs to be used by man and were bred exclusively for the hunting field. Different methods of acquiring game and a multiplicity of quarry species have led to the breeding of a wide range of hounds.

They vary in shape and size between the dachshund and the wolfhound, although the most obvious characteristic of many is their long legs. Built for speed, most types of hound are expected to pursue game, either running down their quarry or holding it at bay until the hunter catches up. Many of these breeds predate the use of firearms for sporting purposes. The greyhound, for example, was first introduced into Britain by the Celts. Then, as now, this hound was employed as a hare-seeking missile, and very exciting it is to watch.

Nevertheless, the original use of hunting dogs, all those thousands of years ago, was to hold quarry at bay. Those last two words are important: after cornering the animal, hounds were expected to bay loudly. They were not only shouting it into submission, but at the same time were informing their handlers of where they had brought the quarry to a stop.

This basic precept had become highly ritualized by the seventeenth century in Europe. Packs of hounds were followed by a retinue of noblemen, gentry and hunt servants mounted on horseback. Some packs hunted deer, others chased wild boar, and in England in particular, foxhunting became popular with practically every rural community.

Long before this, however, primitive man had relied on hounds to hold at bay a wide variety of wild animals, and in those days rocks and clubs were used to administer the coup de grace. Later on, spears were used for this purpose, but nowadays a shotgun or rifle is the preferred weapon.

The huntsman learns to read the voice of his hounds. Excited yelps tell him when quarry has been scented, and more concentrated baying is the sign that

the trail is warm and informs him of the direction in which his quarry is travelling. Frantic baying is a sure sign that the animal has been cornered. Not all hounds are hunted in packs, and very often nowadays the hunter takes maybe only two or three dogs out with him. Depending on locality, his quarry could be wild boar, elk, deer, raccoon, opossum, lynx, or cougar.

While greyhounds and their like hunt by sight, most of the hounds that bring quarry to bay rely on scent to do so. All of the pack-hounds have a famous ancestor – the Chien de Saint Hubert. It was with these that St Hubert, the patron saint of deer hunters, hunted in France during the seventh century. This breed was introduced into England in 1066 by William the Conquerer and is now known as the bloodhound, this name being said to mean that the breed has pure blood. Early in the seventeenth century, bloodhounds were shipped by the English to their first American colony, Virginia, to protect the settlers from attacks by the native Americans.

Besides acting as guard dogs, bloodhounds proved apt for hunting racoon and opossum. This generally involves chasing the quarry through thick cover where the dog's nose is invaluable. In fact, this hound is considered to have the best scenting

The deerhound, one of the more ancient breeds of hound, is said to have been brought to Britain by Phoenician traders.

The Scandinavian elkhound (above), very much a spitz type of hound, is used for hunting European elk.

The bloodhound (below) is an ancient breed of hound from which many other breeds have been developed.

grey and they should be at least 30 inches tall.

The Irish wolfhound is similar in shape and size to the deerhound, but its colour varies between black, white, red, fawn or brindle. The breed almost became extinct along with the wolf in Ireland, but was rescued from oblivion by breeders. Originally it also hunted bears, red deer and the very large Irish elk.

In Scandinavia, three breeds of elkhound still retain their popularity. Grey and black varieties are to be found in Norway, while in Sweden the Jamthund has been bred to a standard of 24 inches – a little taller than the Norwegian breeds.

Another variety, the grahund, is also popular in Scandinavia and looks similar to the elkhound. These dogs are used primarily to hunt elk although they are willing to tackle other big game like boar. However, separate breeds exist for this purpose: the griffon, of which one variety is fawn, the other wolf grey, is popular in France for this type of work, and south of the Pyrenees, in Spain, the Alano is favourite. This breed is most frequently hunted in packs, and at 21 inches high, it is a fraction smaller than the shaggy-haired griffons. The Alano is a handsome breed, having a shiny, short black coat with brown markings on its face and feet and a white tip to its tail.

In Finland, the Karelian bear dog is as quarrelsome and ill-natured a dog as any hunter could wish to handle. Nevertheless, it is a tough, courageous breed and is used to hunt bears, elk and lynx. It stands 24 inches tall, has a brownish-black coat with white patches and is also of the spitz type of hound.

Another breed, the Transylvanian hound, was used by the noblemen of eastern Hungary to hunt bears and wolves in the mountains. The breed is still popular, although nowadays it is used more as a guard dog than to bug bears.

One important point to remember with any of these hounds is that they have been bred for specific quarry – often with particular terrain in mind. Thus the Argentinian mastiff hunts boar and puma in thick cover while the Walker hound is frequently used to corner cougars in North America. Appropriately enough, the blood line that St. Hubert established still predominates in many of them to this day.

powers of any breed. Over the course of years, the original bloodhound shape was streamlined by cross-breading, creating the coonhound. At least, this is the only bloodline that is recognized by the American Kennel Club.

Nevertheless, an abundant variety of mongrels go by the name of coondog. Early settlers and, later, plantation workers, were more interested in having a dog which could tree a racoon, frighten off strangers, and fulfil the role of family pet. Suitability rather than pedigree is still the main criterion that governs this breed.

The deerhound is one of the more ancient breeds, said to have been introduced into Britain by the Phoenicians. (In Perthshire, in Scotland, pre-Christian cave paintings show rough-haired dogs hunting deer and wolves and holding them at bay.) Their general colour is

GAME SPECIES

When man's hunting activities were a matter of necessity and survival, his forays with spear, net and bow were constrained by three principal factors – the game which was most readily available, the species which were easiest to catch and kill and, quite naturally, those which made the best eating. For the modern sporting shooter there remains great satisfaction in cooking and eating quarry which you have found, stalked and bagged through your own efforts, skills and hunting abilities. But whereas our primitive ancestors hunted for food, ours is just as likely to be bought off the shelves of a supermarket, and we are unlikely to go hungry if we have been unlucky and had a blank day's shooting.

Nevertheless, the game and other quarry species which represent the focus for our activities are still chosen for many of the qualities which first brought them to the attention of primitive man. Availability is, of course, all-important, which is why our shooting usually takes us away from towns and cities into natural habitats where wild creatures live. And that habitat must be the correct one for the species we have in mind. It is as pointless to go looking for chamois among tidal mudflats and marshes as it would be to set off into high mountains for an evening's wildfowl flighting.

Another criterion has changed with the evolution of sporting shooting as a recreational activity. Satisfaction comes not from bagging quarry which is easily available. We prefer the elusive, the furtive, the fast and the truly wild, all of which test our skills in fieldcraft and our performance with whatever guns, handguns and rifles we use. The more testing the hunting and the more demanding the shooting, the greater our satisfaction when we are successful.

Most sporting mammals, from the often under-estimated rabbit to the largest woodland deer, provide excellent, nutritious meat. It varies enormously from species to species, from the bland taste and pale colour of rabbit flesh to the dark, heavy meat of the brown hare, and the tender venison from a yearling deer cannot be compared to the rank toughness of a mature stag shot at the end of the autumn rut. The individual sportsman's tastes in game will vary, but the bag should never be wasted. One of the cardinal rules of good sportsmanship is that the hunter eats what he kills, and that there should be no unnecessary waste.

The responsible sportsman is always an active conservationist. Nowhere is practical concern for game more apparent than among the sporting community, although this is an apparent contradiction which many anti-shooting people fail to understand. The sportsman will be the first to notice if game populations expand or dwindle and he will take a carefully regulated harvest as appropriate, always ensuring that an adequate breeding nucleus remains in reserve as the 'seed corn' for the future.

The modern, well-informed sportsman is also an ecologist, and realizes that no species exists in isolation. Systems of living organisms interact, and this has led to a widespread use of a familiar term – 'the balance of Nature'. This is a convenient but misleading expression, for Nature is constantly changing and evolving, and continues in a state of unstable equilibrium rather than of balance. But experience among sportsmen and wildlife managers everywhere has demonstrated that where land is managed sensitively for wildlife, healthy game populations will thrive alongside countless other species of insects, plants, animals and birds. Often, too, game and the vested interests of the sportsman have provided the motivation, the impetus and the input of human effort and financial resources to ensure that areas of land, whether privately owned or state controlled, are set aside for game management. There, where predation is controlled, where populations of gamebirds, sporting mammals and many other species which share the same habitats are regularly monitored, the best conditions exist to promote a natural environment which benefits wildlife in all its forms. This is equally true of woodlands managed for pheasants, of marshlands set aside for wildfowl and waders, or vast areas of wilderness forests and high mountains where elk, wild boar, wild sheep and similar species live.

Large or small, exotic or common, bird or mammal – the twentieth century sporting shooter still has an enormously wide and varied range of game and quarry species from which to choose, however limited and restricted it might appear when compared with the comparative freedoms of earlier generations. Inevitably, through personal inclination and local opportunities, we tend to concentrate our sporting efforts on just a few species, and many of us find that we develop particularly close affection for and intense interest in perhaps just one or two species. This is how the quail enthusiast, the woodcock specialist, the snipe devotee, the pheasant fanatic and the enthusiastic deer stalker evolve.

But there can be few sporting shooters imbued with a genuine sporting instinct who do not aspire to test their skills on a wide range of quarry, when time, money and opportunity permit. Even if we spend all our lives enjoying excellent shooting almost in our own back yards, we never cease to learn more about our sport and the creatures which we pursue. There is even more to learn if we make the effort to join other sportsmen in pursuit of other quarry, perhaps in distant countries where we find ourselves confronted with unfamiliar species of animals, novel shooting techniques and a totally new sporting tradition.

● The Game Species section is divided into four main categories – Game Birds, Wild Fowl, Deer and Game Animals – showing the birds and animals and details of their natural lives.

NOTE. The illustrations use the scientific symbols ♂ for male and ♀ for female.

CHOICE OF GAME

The shooting sportsman makes his choice of quarry species from a bewilderingly large and diverse selection of animals and birds. The sheer scope and range of choice available becomes apparent when you read the pages which follow in the 'Species' section of this book.

Very few sportsmen will ever attempt to bag more than a relatively small proportion of the total range of legitimate sporting quarry species available in Britain, Europe and North America. To do so would involve extensive travel, unlimited time for sport, and an inexhaustible bank account to fund it. In fact, most sporting shooters spend their entire careers deriving great sporting satisfaction from just a handful of species, which is not to imply that their sport is in any way impoverished as a result. It can take a lifetime to learn the ways of just one or two species.

If your personal preference is for sport with a shotgun, you have additional decisions to make. Do you like to shoot on your own, accompanied only by a favourite dog? Or do you prefer to be one of a small group, finding varied sport on tough shooting outings? Or is your preference for the more elaborate and formal types of shooting which may involve parties of eight or ten shooters, with many additional personnel also involved, in the form of gamekeepers, beaters, 'stops' flagmen, dog-handlers, loaders and pickers-up?

In North America, and parts of Europe, the shotgun enthusiast may find he has even greater scope than his British counterpart. While the use of shotguns for shooting deer is generally discouraged in Britan, and is subject to severe legal restrictions, the use of shotguns firing rifled slugs and heavy buckshot for large sporting mammals is the traditional form of shooting in various other countries, and the sporting shotgunner may conceivably be able to use one gun to pursue everything from quail to bears.

Sporting riflemen find their sport almost entirely from shooting mammals, since the rifle's single projectile is inappropriate for fast-flying winged quarry, although there is skill and excitement in successfully stalking and shooting some wary species while they are roosting. The not-so-humble rabbit is an abundant and very challenging quarry for the sporting air-rifle shooter, and also for those using the universally popular .22 rimfire rifle, which is suitable for mammals up to the size of hares and foxes. Humane pursuit of larger mammals like deer calls for larger calibre rifles, and the very largest species of mammals like the great woodland deer and wild boar demand expertise with a rifle firing a very substantial cartridge.

WHITETAIL BUCK

CANADA GOOSE

GUNS FOR GAME

Small mammals (eg rabbits, hares): .22 or .25 air rifle; .22 rimfire rifle; shotgun with medium game load of 4-6 shot.

Larger Mammals: Roe deer: .222 centrefire rifle or larger; shotgun with AAA shot or larger, or rifled slug

Other deer, wild sheep & wild boar: .243 centrefire rifle or larger calibre; shotgun with SSG shot or rifled slug; .38, .357Mag and .44Mag handgun

Gamebirds & wildfowl: Shotgun (side-by-side, over-and-under, pump-actioned, semiautomatic or single-barrelled), .410 or 20-bore up to 8-bore

Small gamebirds, doves, quail: 20-bore or 12-bore shotgun, open bored with 1-1⅛ ounce load of shot size 5-8

Medium-sized gamebirds, including pheasants: 12-bore, moderately choked, 1-1¼ ounce load of shot size 6 or 7

Duck: 12-bore or 10-bore shotgun, moderately to tightly choked, with 1⅛-1½ ounce load of shot size 4 or 5

Geese, capercaillie, wild turkey: 12-bore to 8-bore shotgun, tightly choked, with 1¼-2 ounce load of shot size 4-1 and BB.

ROE DEER RUNNING FOR COVER

MOUNTAIN COTTONTAIL

PHEASANT ON THE ALERT

WIGEON IN FLIGHT

QUAILS

Most members of the Phasianidae (pheasant) family are sought-after game birds – including many species of quail. Quails may be divided into two distinct groups, of which the uniquely American species (Odontophorinae) are the most striking. There are 36 American species, distributed from Canada to Brazil. They have characteristics not found in other Phasianidae, notably stronger bills with sharp or serrated edges and tips, and their plumage is generally bright, in combinations of black, white, yellow, red, buff or brown. Quails of the Old World include 12 forms allocated to the genus *Coturnix*. These are smaller and less colourful than American quails, with exceptions like the tiny Indo/ Australasian blue quail (*Coturnix chinensis*), or brilliant African harlequin quail (*Coturnix delagorguei*). Worldwide attempts to stock alien quail for sporting purposes have found little success, because habitat usually proves unsuitable, but there are, for example, some resident bobwhite quail in Western Europe. Britain has small populations in Suffolk and the Isles of Scilly; however, no species of quail is permitted quarry in the British Isles.

COMMON QUAIL
Coturnix coturnix

The common quail is, as the name suggests, the most widely distributed Old World species. A migratory bird, it nests from southern Britain through Europe and Asia. It winters from the Mediterranean (which has a resident population) down into Africa, and across to Arabia, Southern India and Thailand.

At 6½ inches, it is the smallest European gamebird. It prefers cultivated land and dry meadows during the breeding season, when the staple plant diet is supplemented by insects. The male has a distinctive call note, with a different spring/ summer call designed to attract females and proclaim territorial rights.

These birds seek cover when hunted, and run rather than fly, even when confronted by a dog. Consequently, they are most often shot during migration, and over-shooting in southern Europe during their spring migration has drastically reduced the world population.

BOBWHITE QUAIL
Colinus virginianus

With an annual harvest of many millions, the bobwhite quail is one of the USA's favourite game-birds, but the hunting pressure has little impact and they remain plentiful from Canada to Guatemala.

At 10½ inches, the bobwhite is among the larger quails. The male coloration varies, but is predominantly brownish with

FLUSHED QUAIL *Quail try to evade danger by remaining hidden or by running; when flushed they fly strongly and quickly to the nearest cover, so the flight is usually brief.*

COMMON QUAIL

SCALED QUAIL

BOBWHITE QUAIL

GAMBEL'S QUAIL

MOUNTAIN QUAIL

QUAIL *With strong beaks, legs and claws, quail are well adapted for feeding by scratching up worms, grubs and roots, though some species are plant, seed or grain eaters and some also take insects.*

light underparts, white bars and darker markings, sometimes white flecked. The head is dark brown with a faint crest, a white eye stripe and a white throat. The female resembles the male, but is creamy brown where the male is white. The bobwhite's preferred habitat is cultivated land and open ground, sometimes adjoining woodland, and its diet is largely plant matter, though insects are also taken. They live in family groups.

MEARNS' QUAIL
Cyrtonyx montezumae

Known variously as black, fool, harlequin, Montezuma or Massena quail, Mearns' quail inhabit the high grass slopes of Mexico and the southwestern USA, to a height of 9000 feet. At just 8

inches long, the Mearns' is the smallest of the western quail. It has long, curved claws that assist rapid movement on steep ground, and both sexes are colourful, though females are less obvious. They have small head crests, black and white facial patterns, dark underparts and white/brown spotted flanks. The call is low and quavering. Within their mountainous habitat, Mearns' quail are frequently found among the trees (often in company with Coues deer).

CALIFORNIA QUAIL
Callipepla californica

Also known as the valley quail, the California quail is the official bird of the Golden State, although it's actually an indigenous species from Oregon

down to Baja. Of medium size (9½ to 11 inches), it has a short, curved plume on its head, and a dark throat patch with a faint white outline. The males have grey-blue scaled breast feathers, a brown underbody and bluish, white-streaked wings; females are somewhat drab by comparison.

They provide the bulk of the western quail harvest, but can be difficult to hunt in hard terrain, running and rising well out of range, if at all. When found on wooded grassland or cultivated land, however, they behave more like bobwhites, flushing en masse and then holding well in nearby cover.

SCALED QUAIL
Callipepla squamata

The scaled quail is a desert-dwelling bird of the southwestern USA and Mexico, and its local names include blue quail, blue runner and cottontop quail. It gets the name 'scaled quail' from its black-edged breast and belly feathers, which have the appearance of large fish scales. Its upper wings and back are blue-grey, while the rest of the body is grey-brown, and it has a white-tipped head crest which is raised when the bird becomes excited.

MOUNTAIN QUAIL
Oreortyx pictus

The largest native North American quail (10½ to 11½ inches), the mountain quail is found from British Columbia south to California. Along with the California quail, it has been introduced into Washington, Oregon, Idaho and Nevada. The male and female are similar in appearance, having a long, two-feathered head plume, chestnut cheeks and throat outlined in white, grey-blue upper body and breast, and chestnut flanks with broad white stripes.

As the name suggests, mountain quail inhabit mountain country, above 1500 feet and up to the timberline, and in winter they form into groups which often migrate, on foot and in single file, to lower ground to find snow-free feeding areas, covering large distances locally as they follow the snowline down the mountainside.

Their diet is predominantly of vegetable matter, including grains and seeds, fruits and berries, flowers, leaves and buds. They also eat small numbers of insects and other invertebrates.

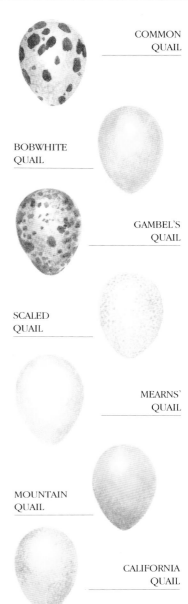

COMMON QUAIL

BOBWHITE QUAIL

GAMBEL'S QUAIL

SCALED QUAIL

MEARNS' QUAIL

MOUNTAIN QUAIL

CALIFORNIA QUAIL

EGGS *Quails' eggs, about 1¼ inches long, are laid in clutches of up to 10 or more. Their nests are lined scrapes; those of the bobwhite and Mearns' are roofed with grass.*

GAMBEL'S QUAIL
Lophortyx gambelii

Gambel's quail, the other desert species of the arid Southwest, is closely related to the California quail. About 10 inches long, the male has a black plume on its red-capped head, a dark throat patch outlined in white, and a grey breast. Its belly is yellowish with a large black patch, and the back and wings are brown with dark and white markings. The female is drabber, without the facial markings of the male.

Their habitat is desert brush, and the availability of water is the main factor determining their movements.

CALIFORNIA QUAIL

♂

♀

♀

♂

MEARNS' QUAIL

PTARMIGANS

Ptarmigans are members of the grouse family, and a number of closely-related species occur throughout the Northern Hemisphere. The most important of these are the ptarmigan, known in North America as the rock ptarmigan, the willow ptarmigan or willow grouse (of which the British red grouse is a distinct subspecies) and the white-tailed ptarmigan. They are birds of the cold subarctic tundra and the high hills, often living well above the snowline. However, although they are normally associated with the high ground, it seems that temperature rather than altitude is the critical factor determining their haunts. Their summer coloration is basically a mottled brown, but in winter their plumage is white.

PTARMIGAN
Lagopus mutus

In North America, ptarmigan (rock ptarmigan) are found across the tundra from Iceland and Greenland westwards, as far as Alaska and the shores of the Bering Straits, and in the Aleutian Islands which stretch west almost as far as the coasts of Asia. To the south, their range extends through British Columbia to the northern end of the Rockies and the Cascade Range, and from northern Montana eastwards to Maine and the higher parts of the Adirondacks.

In Europe, ptarmigan occur from northern Scandinavia and Finland eastwards across the high steppes and the taiga of Russia, Siberia and northern China. They also occur in isolated populations further south,

EGGS *Ptarmigans' eggs are about 1.7 inches long, clutches of up to 9 or more being laid in mid-May or June in nests which are scantily-lined ground scrapes or hollows.*

ROCK PTARMIGAN

WILLOW PTARMIGAN

WHITE-TAILED PTARMIGAN

notably in the high massifs of the Alps and the Pyrenees and on the high tops in the Scottish Highlands, usually above the 2000-foot contour and always well above the treeline. In the far northwest of Scotland they can be found on lower hills, only a few hundred feet above sea level.

As its Latin name suggests, the ptarmigan is the 'changeable grouse', whose plumage varies from pure white in winter to a mottled greyish-brown in summer. The variable coloration of the ptarmigan is a direct reflection of the annual changes in the appearance of its bare and inhospitable habitat, which in winter is far above the snowline. The ptarmigan's pure white winter plumage, broken only by the black markings on its tail (which never disappear) and by the cock bird's black eye stripe and prominent red wattling, gives it excellent natural concealment in otherwise bare countryside where its chief predators are the golden eagle, the peregrine falcon, foxes and, in many places, wolves.

In spring, as the snows melt, the warmer weather triggers off a change of plumage and, although the ptarmigan's underparts remain pure white, it assumes a greyish-brown plumage on its upper parts, barred with cream and buff. The female tends to have a more sandy coloration, but both sexes are well camouflaged among the sparse grasses and lichen-covered boulders.

By late autumn, the adult birds' moult will have developed further, with the males being predominantly grey while the females tend towards a greyish sandy-brown. The pure white phase of the ptarmigan's plumage is resumed from late November until late March.

Ptarmigan grow to a maximum length of about 14 inches, and a mature adult will weigh

about a pound. They have catholic tastes and will feed opportunistically on berries, such as bilberry and crowberry, on the buds of upland plants such as birch and dwarf willow, and on leaves, shoots, heather and insects.

WILLOW PTARMIGAN
Lagopus lagopus

The willow ptarmigan (or willow grouse) prefers a habitat which is more sheltered than that of the other ptarmigans. Its range is broadly similar to that of the rock ptarmigan, but it is absent from Britain and it is more likely to be found on moorland which has plenty of heather and scattered birches, willows and bushes which provide it with cover. Its feeding and breeding habits are like those of the rock ptarmigan, although in the breeding season it prefers wetter ground.

It grows to a maximum length of 14 or 15 inches, and like the rock ptarmigan its plumage changes from brown in summer to white in winter. The male's summer plumage is darker and more reddish-brown than the rock ptarmigan's; the female's usually has less of a red tint to it and the pale barring of the feathers is more conspicuous. In

WINTER PLUMAGE *In winter, the male rock ptarmigan can be distinguished from the female by his black eye stripe and more prominent wattling.*

FEET *The legs and feet of ptarmigans are heavily feathered down to the claws, which gives added protection in a cold environment.*

winter, both sexes are white with black tails.

WHITE-TAILED PTARMIGAN
Lagopus leucurus

The white-tailed ptarmigan's range extends from Alaska eastwards through the Yukon to the Mackenzie Mountains, and south through Alberta and British Columbia (including Vancouver Island) to the Cascade Mountains and along the Rockies to northern New Mexico.

These hardy birds live on high, exposed ground, sheltering among scattered rocks and dwarf willows. Both sexes have similar plumage, being all-white (including the tail) in winter, and in summer reddish-brown on the back with white tail, forewings, legs and feet, white breast and flanks marked with black bars, and the head and neck grey with delicate black, white and buff vermiculations.

The white-tailed ptarmigan is slightly smaller than other ptarmigans, reaching only 12 or 13 inches in length. It feeds mainly on buds and twigs in winter, and on leaves, flowers, berries and moss in summer. The nest, a small hollow in the ground, is lined with leaves, grass and feathers from the female's breast, and there is a single clutch of three to nine brown-speckled, parchment-coloured eggs.

TAKING OFF *Ptarmigan will usually crouch as men or dogs approach, or run ahead uncertainly, only taking wing as a last resort.*

BIRDS IN MOULT
*Ptarmigans moult in
spring and autumn,
and are white in
winter.*

MOULTING BIRDS
IN FLIGHT

ROCK PTARMIGAN
halfway through
summer moult

ROCK PTARMIGAN

WILLOW
PTARMIGAN

WHITE-TAILED PTARMIGAN

WILLOW PTARMIGAN
in summer moult

♂

WHITE-TAILED PTARMIGAN
in winter plumage

♂

ROCK PTARMIGAN *An adult
rock ptarmigan grows to a
length of about 14 inches, and
its calls include a variety of
cackles and croaks.*

WILLOW PTARMIGAN *Reaching
a length of 15 inches, the willow
ptarmigan is slightly larger than
the rock ptarmigan.*

WHITE-TAILED PTARMIGAN
in summer plumage

WHITE-TAILED PTARMIGAN
*The white-tailed ptarmigan is
easily identified by its tail: the
other two species have black
tails all year round.*

83

RED, BLACK & HAZEL GROUSE

The red, black and hazel grouse are the three most important members of the grouse family in the British Isles and continental Europe. The red grouse is one of the most famous and internationally-prized of all game birds, although its geographical distribution is limited to Great Britain and Ireland and their offshore islands, and the black grouse is a bigger, bolder-looking bird which is widely distributed in northern Europe from Britain eastwards through Scandinavia and into western and central Asia. The hazel grouse is an important and widespread grouse over much of Europe and Asia, and four subspecies have been identified. Its range extends from Scandinavia southwards into northern Spain and southeast Europe, and eastwards to Siberia, northern China and Japan.

RED GROUSE
Lagopus lagopus scoticus

The red grouse has the rounded, compact shape typical of most grouse species, and its short legs are covered with thick, light-coloured feathering which extends over the toes to the bird's claws. Adult red grouse have a dark coloration, and their plumage is not literally red but a mixture of rich, dark browns with black flecking and barring, and both sexes have black tail feathers. The hen is lighter coloured than the cock bird, and also lacks his prominent red wattles over the eyes, which become raised and swollen during the spring courtship.

The hen's eye wattles are much smaller and tend to be pinkish-orange in colour. Red grouse show considerable plumage variations from region to region, and those of northeast England and eastern and northeastern Scotland are generally much darker than their western counterparts. The red grouse of the Hebrides and Ireland are much paler, and may be slightly larger and heavier on average than their eastern counterparts, and this led to a theory that Ireland and the Hebrides had their own *hibernicus* subspecies. In fact, the paleness of the western populations is explained by their longer moulting period, a result of the mild western climate.

More than any other game bird, the red grouse is intimately associated with one type of vegetation. Ling heather, which is the dominant plant in most upland areas throughout Britain and Ireland, and also on low-lying, peaty boglands, is essential for the red grouse in various ways. Young heather shoots constitute about 90 percent of its diet, and long, older growth provides shelter for the hens and their eggs and growing chicks in spring, when they are vulnerable to predators. Long, rank heather also affords good shelter from severe upland weather in winter.

Adult cocks adopt and defend individual territories from autumn onwards, and cocks without territories are unlikely to survive the winter. Red grouse are generally monogamous, and each cock displays on his territory with leaping upward flights and steep, gliding descents, accompanied by a distinctive crowing call.

TAIL FEATHERS *The tail of the hazel grouse is slightly fan-shaped with a black border. The red grouse has a rounded tail, while that of the female black grouse is lightly forked.*

BLACK GROUSE
Lyrurus tetrix

Black grouse (or blackgame) are birds of the moorland fringes, where open hill land meets the edge of forests and woodlands, and although they look not unlike miniature versions of the capercaillie they do not share its predominantly forest life. In northern England and Scotland, which represents their principal range in Britain, black grouse are found on open heather moorland, but usually where heather is interspersed with other forms of vegetation including rushes, bracken and birch scrub. The fringes of young and middle-aged conifer plantations are also attractive to them, as are open, self-seeded birch woods on the moorland fringes.

The male (blackcock) is a substantial, chunky bird with glossy black plumage and a prominent lyre-shaped tail with vivid white undertail coverts, a conspicuous white bar on each wing and large, vivid red wattles over the eyes. The female is barely two-thirds his size, and is a greyish rufous-brown in colour, with black barring on the head, neck and tail. A mature blackcock will weigh 2½ to 3½ pounds, over twice the weight of a male red grouse, and the female (often known as the greyhen) normally weighs just

RED GROUSE *The red grouse was once thought to be a uniquely British species, but it is in fact a distinctive local subspecies of the willow ptarmigan (*Lagopus lagopus*).*

HAZEL GROUSE

RED GROUSE

BLACK GROUSE

RED GROUSE

over 2 pounds.

The breeding biology of the black grouse differs greatly from the monogamy and individual territories of red grouse, and the collective courtship ceremonies of groups of black-cock are particularly interesting and dramatic. Cock birds begin to gather at dawn and dusk at display sites, known as 'leks', from March onwards, and there will be signs of aggression between individual males.

From April onwards, lekking may involve eight or ten cocks

IN FLIGHT *The flight of the red, black and hazel grouse is strong and direct, and includes periods of gliding.*

displaying together with a series of sneezing and hissing calls, accompanied by jumping, fluttering movements and the dramatic lekking posture in which the cock bird stretches his head and neck upwards stiffly, while drooping his wings outwards and fanning his distinctive, lyre-shaped tail to reveal an arc of black feathers and a startlingly white tuft of under-

tail covert feathers. These displays help establish a hierarchy and system of territories among the males, and also advertise the whereabouts of the cock birds to receptive females.

Females wait close to the lek, and dominant males may mate briefly with a succession of females, which then leave quietly to lay and hatch their eggs and raise their young.

HAZEL GROUSE *Both sexes are alike, but the female lacks the black throat patch.*

hazel grouse

black grouse

red grouse

HAZEL GROUSE

♂

BLACK GROUSE

BLACK GROUSE *The male black grouse, with its broad, lyre-shaped tail, grows to a length of 21 inches.*

HAZEL GROUSE
Tetrastes bonasia

This rather small grouse (up to 14½ inches) is a bird of well-wooded, mountainous regions, with a distinct preference for wild, self-seeded deciduous woodlands or mixed pine forests. The severe weather of winter often forces them into the cover of dense coniferous woodlands, and they are rarely found far from the forest fringes. Despite this, their flesh rarely displays any sign of the resinous taint which can occur among other grouse species living in conifer woodlands, and the flesh of the hazel grouse is whiter than that of most other grouse species, and highly regarded from a culinary point of view.

Hazel grouse are furtive and secretive, squatting tight in dense cover when danger threatens, and they are notoriously hard to flush. Hunting traditionally involves the use of a pointer or setter, and when flushed the birds rise from cover with a rapid, noisy flight. Their fondness for dense woodland makes them difficult birds for hunters to locate and shoot.

EGGS *The red grouse lays its clutch of 5 to 12 eggs, in a simple ground scrape, in May or June. The hazel grouse's 9 to 11 eggs are laid in April, and the 7 or 8 of the black grouse in May or June.*

RED GROUSE

HAZEL GROUSE

BLACK GROUSE

BLUE, RUFFED & SPRUCE GROUSE

The blue, ruffed and spruce grouse are all birds of the North American woodlands. The blue grouse is found in the coniferous and mixed woodlands of western North America, from Alaska and the Yukon down along the Rocky Mountain chain and into northern California. The ruffed grouse is smaller than the blue grouse, but is North America's most widespread and best-known grouse, and one of its most important game birds. It occurs from Alaska through the Pacific Northwest and most of Canada, and from Minnesota through to New York and New England. The spruce grouse is widespread in Canada, but occurs only locally in the northern USA, mostly in New York and Michigan.

BLUE GROUSE
Dendragapus obscurus

Of the seven members of the grouse family found in North America, the blue grouse is the largest of the woodland species, exceeded in size only by the sage grouse and the wild turkey, which are also North American species, and by the massive capercaillie of Europe.

Like all the grouse family, the blue grouse is a stocky, rotund bird, and the average weights are 2½ to 3½ pounds, cock birds being larger and heavier than hens. Both sexes are greyish-black on the head and upper parts, with a lighter, brownish plumage on the sides, and with a greyish-blue colouring on the underparts. This predominantly greyish-black coloration makes the blue grouse rather similar in some aspects of its appearance to the black grouse of Europe, which is much the same size and weight, and it also accounts for this species' various names, which include 'dusky grouse' and 'grey grouse'. Cock birds are distinguished by their prominent red wattles and have broader tails than the females, tipped with a wide strip of pale grey.

These are birds of mature, open coniferous woodlands, especially in summer, and they eat a wide range of foods including shoots, buds, berries, wild fruits, leaves and insects. In winter, the blue grouse tends to move to thicker, more sheltered pine woods, where there is less diversity of foods, and there they eat mainly conifer needles and buds. This diet transmits a sharp, resinous taste to the bird's flesh and makes it much less palatable than in late summer.

In spring, adult blue grouse cocks adopt and defend individual territories, where they display prominently to assert

and maintain their dominance. Males are vocal at this time, calling repeatedly with a series of hooting calls, and their conspicuous, strutting courtship dances are accompanied by frequent resonant booming noises, caused by the rapid expulsion of air from air sacs alongside the throat.

The remoteness of the blue grouse's haunts have helped prevent over-exploitation by hunters. This is important for a species which is unusually confiding and tame in its behaviour, which has lead to its colloquial name of 'fool hen'.

RUFFED GROUSE
Bonasa umbellus

Rounded and compact in shape, the ruffed grouse is similar in size and weight to the red grouse of Britain and Ireland, but its plumage is a complex barred pattern of buffs and browns, with a distinctive fan-shaped tail bearing a prominent, dark, transverse stripe. There is a fringe of black feathers on the back of the bird's neck, which forms the 'ruff' that gives the

FLIGHT *Like the other members of the grouse family, the blue, ruffed and sage grouse have somewhat short and rounded wings. They fly only short distances, but their flight is strong and direct.*

BLUE GROUSE

♀

♂

BLUE GROUSE *This pair (male displaying) are the darker coastal form, the sooty grouse.*

SPRUCE GROUSE *The spruce grouse takes its name from its frequent occurrence in forests of spruce and similar conifers.*

RUFFED GROUSE *The ruffed grouse occurs in two colour phases, red and grey. These are grey phase birds, the colour being most obvious in the tail.*

bird its name.

When adult cocks take up their territories and begin displaying in spring, one of the most characteristic and unusual aspects of the ruffed grouse's behaviour is the drumming sound created by fast wing-beating, usually made as the cock stands prominently on a tree stump or fallen trunk and stretches upwards, leaning back on its tail feathers. This drumming has much in common with the spring wing-drumming sounds made by breeding cock pheasants.

Though very widespread throughout North America, the ruffed grouse is particularly fond of woodland with dense secondary growth, especially brambles, briars and other recently-regenerated growth in woodlands which have been fragmented as a result of thinning, clear-felling, wind-throw or fires. They like a variety of tree ages from seedlings to mature standards, and a range of different species, although the aspen is particularly important for them.

SPRUCE GROUSE
Dendragapus canadensis

The spruce grouse occurs over large areas of Alaska, Canada and the northern states of the USA, and at least five regional subspecies have been identified. The so-called 'Hudsonian' spruce grouse (*D. canadensis*) is probably the commonest and most typical of this group.

Slightly smaller than the ruffed grouse, the spruce grouse also lacks its distinctive ruffed neck plumage, and its general coloration is much darker, with a slightly iridescent, metallic bloom on the feathering of the upper parts. Males are marked with black and dark grey on their upper parts, and a distinctive red eye wattle is visible at spring mating time. Hens are brownish-red with black barring, and both males and females have conspicuous reddish-brown barring across their tail feathers.

Hunting often involves the use of bird dogs, but the species is notoriously reluctant to take wing and is less highly regarded than the ruffed grouse.

EGGS *The nests of blue, ruffed and spruce grouse are lined ground scrapes, and typical clutch sizes are 6-8 (blue grouse), 7-8 (spruce grouse) and 9-12 (ruffed).*

SPRUCE GROUSE

RUFFED GROUSE

BLUE GROUSE

PRAIRIE CHICKENS, SHARP-TAILED

Prairie chickens, more formally known as pinnated grouse, are birds of the open grasslands, as their name suggests, and the sharp-tailed grouse is predominantly a bird of the open prairies and natural grasslands which extend from southern Alaska through central and northern Canada and the Great Lakes region. The sage grouse is among the largest of the grouse, and is exceeded in size only by the wild turkey of North America and the capercaillie of Europe. It takes its name from its habitat, which is the sagebrush that stretches up the west central parts of North America from Arizona to southern Canada.

PRAIRIE CHICKENS
Tympanuchus cupido

The greater prairie chicken is similar in size to the red grouse of Britain. Both males and females are very similar in plumage, with the feathering of the upper parts heavily barred with brown, black and buff colouring with creamy-buff plumage on the belly, shading to near-white on the undertail covert feathers, which are lighter and more exposed than those of the sharp-tailed grouse.

Cock birds are distinguished by a prominent yellow wattle above the eyes, comparable to the vivid red wattling found in the black grouse and the capercaillie, and it also has bare patches of skin on the lower parts of the neck, where the air sacs expand during the spring courtship displays. Both cock and hen birds have conspicuous 'pinnae' – tufts of 9 or 10 pointed feathers on the sides of the neck, which can be raised and extended in display.

The lesser prairie chicken is slightly smaller, more like a rock ptarmigan in size, and there are important differences in plumage. The feathering of the back and rump are brown, rather than blackish, while the breast plumage is more distinct-ly marked with brown and cream barring, together with more heavily barred feathers on the bird's flanks. The cock bird's yellow combs are relatively larger and more conspicuous than those of the greater prairie chicken, and the naked skin of the air sacs is more reddish.

Once common across the extensive prairies and grasslands of North America, the range and distribution of prairie chickens has been severely reduced, and is now limited to a number of areas in the southern central states of the USA. Habitat changes caused by agricultural exploitation and development of the prairie lands has resulted in a serious decline in the species, more so than in any other North American grouse. Consequently, prairie chickens are accorded full protection in most areas, although limited hunting on a carefully controlled basis is permitted in certain states

BURSTING FROM COVER When flushed, the prairie chicken rises sharply and flies strongly on its broad, short and rounded wings.

where the population is deemed to be sufficiently numerous.

SHARP-TAILED GROUSE
Tympanuchus phasianellus

This grouse, which grows to a maximum length of about 17 inches, takes its name from its long, sharply-pointed tail. The feathering of the upper parts is brownish-grey marked with black and brown, with paler underparts bearing fine V-shaped markings on the breast feathers. Like many grouse,

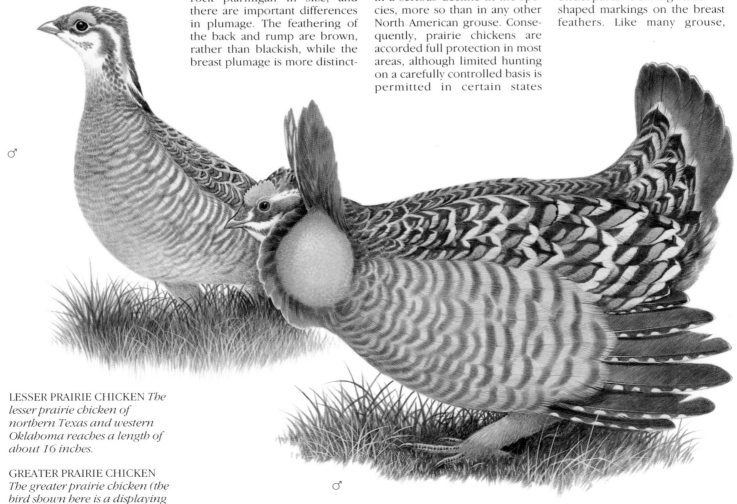

♂

LESSER PRAIRIE CHICKEN The lesser prairie chicken of northern Texas and western Oklahoma reaches a length of about 16 inches.

GREATER PRAIRIE CHICKEN The greater prairie chicken (the bird shown here is a displaying male) grows to a length of 17 inches.

♂

GREATER PRAIRIE CHICKEN

& SAGE GROUSE

SAGE GROUSE FOOT *In common with other members of the grouse family, the legs and claws of the sage grouse are feathered.*

their legs are fully feathered down to the toes. The cock bird is slightly larger than the female, and may be identified by his pale-coloured head and neck feathers and by the prominent, orange-coloured air sacs which are normally hidden by the feathers on each side of his neck until they are inflated as part of his courtship display.

The sharp-tailed grouse eats a wide range of foods, especially in the summer when there is an abundance of wild fruits, insects, vegetable matter of many kinds and the seeds of weedy

SHARP-TAILED GROUSE *The sharp-tailed grouse grows to a length of 17 inches.*

SHARP-TAILED GROUSE

vegetation and cereal crops. In winter the diet is less varied, and the birds are opportunist feeders on whatever green shoots and buds are available.

SAGE GROUSE
Centrocerus urophasianus

The sage grouse is a large, handsome upland game bird. Measuring 26 to 30 inches in length, an adult cock may weigh 7 or 8 pounds, while the smaller hen weighs 4½ to 5½ pounds. The plumage of both sexes is similar, with grey upper parts with a variegated colouring of browns and black, while the feathering of the underparts is white with dark markings on the belly and breast. The feathers of the tail are long and sharply

pointed, and the legs are feathered down to the ends of the toes. Cock birds can be distinguished from hens by their larger size and by the presence of conspicuous tufts of feathers on the sides of the neck, close to the greenish-yellow air sacs.

The leaves of the sagebrush plant are almost the sole food of this species in winter, while in summer their foods are augmented by other forms of vegetation and various insects. Their predominantly sagebrush diet is reflected in the taste of their flesh, however, which can be powerful and unpalatable in the case of old individuals.

Sage grouse have excellent natural camouflage and crouch tightly in cover, taking wing only reluctantly and rather slowly. They are normally hunted with bird dogs and provide easy targets as they rise slowly. In full flight, however, they are deceptively fast and provide the hunter with very challenging targets.

GREATER PRAIRIE CHICKEN
LESSER PRAIRIE CHICKEN
SHARP-TAILED GROUSE
SAGE GROUSE

EGGS *All four species are ground-nesters, laying their eggs in sparsely-lined scrapes. The eggs of the prairie chickens and the sharp-tailed grouse can vary greatly in colour, but those of the sage grouse are usually as shown.*

SAGE GROUSE *The sage grouse is the biggest of these three species. The male, shown here dislaying, is larger than the female.*

SAGE GROUSE

CAPERCAILLIE & WILD TURKEY

The capercaillie and the wild turkey are the largest game birds of Europe and North America respectively. The capercaillie, a member of the grouse family, inhabits the upland coniferous forests of the Scottish Highlands, the Pyrenees, Scandinavia, the USSR and the alpine regions of Europe. Its name is derived from the Scottish Gaelic *capull coille*, which means 'horse of the woods', and it is a highly aggressive bird which will even attack human intruders on its territory. The wild turkey, the largest bird of the pheasant family, has some half a dozen subspecies of which the most numerous and widespread is the eastern turkey. After a period of dramatic decline, caused mainly by loss of habitat due to deforestation, the eastern turkey was successfully introduced throughout the eastern midwest and southern states of the USA. The other subspecies include the osceola or Florida turkey, found mainly in Florida; the Merriam turkey of the Rocky Mountains; and the Gould's turkey, Mexican turkey and Rio Grande turkey of the southwest.

CAPERCAILLIE
Tetrao urogallus

The male capercaillie is a massive and spectacular bird, generally dark in colour, with dark green plumage on the breast, wings tinged with dark brown, and a dark, rounded head with a tuft of bristling chin feathers above the throat. The bill is short, stout and horn-coloured, and the legs are short and stocky and feathered down to the ankles, like others of the grouse family.

An adult male capercaillie may stand 3 feet high and weigh up to 9 or 10 pounds, while the female is barely two-thirds his size and weighs about 4 pounds. She is less dramatically coloured with a variegated reddish-brown colouring not dissimilar to that of the female black grouse, but with a tinge of red on the breast feathers, and she lacks the vivid and prominent eye wattles which make the male capercaillie appear so dramatic and distinctive.

Capercaillie, especially the males, have a wide and varied repertoire of calls. During the spring breeding season, displaying males will utter an unusual and often comic range of noises, sometimes gobbling like a turkey, and with a calling routine which may begin with a croaking rattle and culminate in a series of resounding pops, like corks popping.

Displaying male capercaillie fan out their tail feathers to exhibit an impressive black fan streaked with white, and the cock bird may be visited by a number of females which respond to his calling with a low, pheasant-like croaking. At other times of the year, both sexes are usually silent.

In many European countries, male capercaillie are traditionally stalked and shot in spring, often with rifles, as they display on the ground or while they are perched high in mature conifer trees. In Britain, however, they may only be shot between 1 October and 31 January, and enjoy full protection during the breeding season.

Capercaillie are woodland birds, and feed extensively on pine needles and the seeds, shoots, cones and buds of trees like the Scots pine. Other seasonally-available food includes fruits, berries and seeds, and insects and some other invertebrates are also eaten, especially by growing chicks which require plenty of protein.

Formerly abundant in many parts of Britain, the capercaillie eventually died out in Scotland and Ireland around 1790. It was successfully reintroduced in the late 1830s and spread widely thereafter.

WILD TURKEY
Meleagris gallopavo

The wild turkey is an even bigger bird than the capercaillie, and can weigh up to 24 pounds, although the various subspecies can vary greatly in size and weight. The little Rio Grande turkey, for example, will rarely weigh more than 10 pounds.

The wild turkey is North America's only indigenous

CAPERCAILLIE

♀

♂

CAPERCAILLIE *During the breeding season (April to June), the male capercaillie raises his tail in display to attract a number of females.*

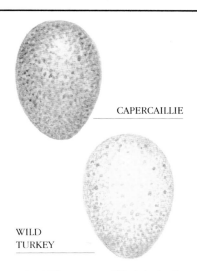

CAPERCAILLIE

WILD
TURKEY

EGGS *The capercaillie lays its 5 to 8 eggs in a shallow scrape in the ground. The 10 to 15 eggs of the wild turkey are laid in a sparsely-lined hollow during March and April.*

WILD TURKEY *The wild turkey is the largest gamebird in North America, the male (seen here displaying) reaching a length of 40 inches.*

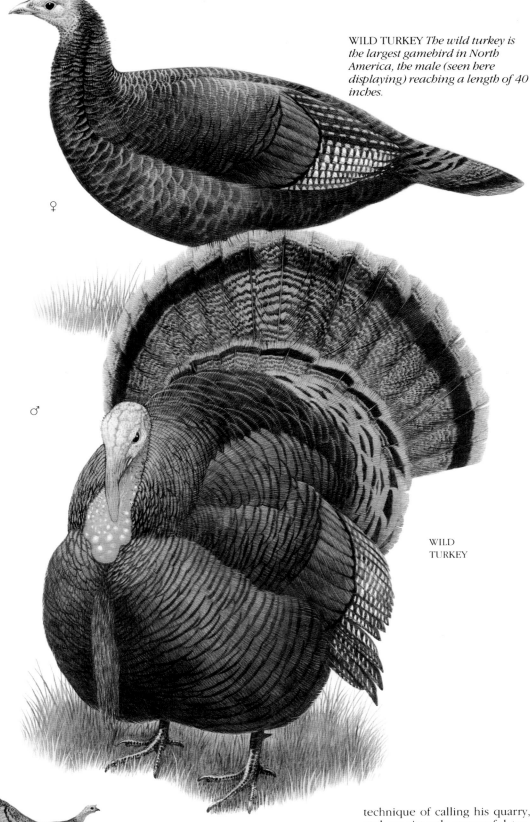

WILD
TURKEY

member of the pheasant family, but it's the biggest of them all and is a direct ancestor of the familiar domestic turkey now known worldwide. In the wild state, turkeys are woodland birds. They were formerly found throughout all the extensive forests of North America, but their range and numbers were seriously reduced by timber felling and over-hunting. The southern states of the USA remained the species' principal stronghold, but careful management and restocking programmes have restored wild turkeys to much of their former range.

Mature woodlands provide the wild turkey with its natural food of acorns, nuts of all kinds including walnuts and beechmast, and also a variety of wild fruits. With its predominantly brownish, sombre plumage it is well adapted to a woodland life. The male or tom is very much larger than the female and distinguished by his large and brightly-coloured red wattles, and by his 'beard' – a cluster of feathers on the breast.

The characteristic call of turkeys is the familiar 'gobbling'

CAPERCAILLIE   ♂

WILD
TURKEY
♂

IN FLIGHT *The flight of the capercaillie is fast, with rapid wingbeats and long spells of gliding as it skims just above the treetops. Wild turkeys are powerful flyers over short distances, but prefer to run.*

sound, and adult males in spring use this call to accompany their dramatic fan-tailed mating displays, which often involve strutting movements and vigorous attacks on other adult cocks which compete with them for females or territorial space. The turkey's distinctive call has led to the turkey hunter's traditional

technique of calling his quarry, and consistently successful turkey calling is a highly skilled sporting art.

Old males are induced to move towards the calling hunter, who may shoot his quarry either with a shotgun or a rifle. Turkeys are normally shot in this way on the ground, although a proportion will be shot from their roosting places.

PHEASANTS

Although the pheasant family (the Phasianidae) is large, comprising at least sixty different species and races which have an extensive natural distribution from the eastern Mediterranean across India and China, the pheasant as a sporting bird can be considered separately. In Britain, North America and most of western Europe, where the pheasant has particular sporting importance, it is an alien, introduced species, and one which has become thoroughly crossbred and hybridized as a consequence of the interbreeding of a number of races and subspecies through captive rearing programmes. Many species of pheasant do not lend themselves to sporting shooting, and these are of importance chiefly to ornithologists, and also to aviculturists for whom the more exotic pheasants are favourite ornamental birds. Pheasants fall into two broad groups, the northern or 'ring-necked' species and the southern or 'black-necked'.

PHEASANT
Phasianus colchicus

The first pheasant to be introduced into Europe (and later into North America and New Zealand) was the black-necked (*Phasianus colchicus*), also known as the common or Old English pheasant, which is a native of southwestern Asia. It takes its name from the region of the River Phasis in Colchis, which is now in the Soviet Republic of Georgia, and its existence there was described by chroniclers of the Greek Empire such as Aeschylus (525-456 BC).

Its western spread into Greece and Italy, and later into France and Britain, has been attributed to the pheasant's popularity as a table bird with the Greeks and Romans, who are thought to have kept captive pheasants as semidomesticated poultry throughout their empires. It is possible that the first wild-living populations of pheasants in Britain originated from escapees in Romano-British times.

Phasianus colchicus was later joined in Britain (and also in North America and New Zealand) by the ring-necked pheasant *Phasianus torquatus* of Mongolia and northern China, and in 1840 a British sporting landowner imported the Japanese or green pheasant (*Phasianus versicolor*), which is a native of the Japanese archipelago and has a predominantly dark green plumage, especially on the neck, rump and underparts. Most feral populations in Britain, augmented by reared stock from game farms, represent a thoroughly mixed combination of all these races. Although dark green and almost blackish Japanese-style birds frequently occur, as do the Old English or black-necked examples, by far the commonest pheasant in Britain, as in North America, is the ring-necked variety. Despite this, the species as a whole is generally referred to as *Phasianus colchicus*, a term which originally applied only to the black-necked pheasant.

The presence of feral populations in Britain appears to have been continuous since before the Dark Ages, and there were undoubtedly futher introductions in Norman and later times. Pheasants were attractive quarry for falconers and were also sometimes taken in nets by fowlers. This was in addition to the sport they afforded the sportsman with his fowling-piece, especially in winter when the best of the partridge shooting on the open, hand-reaped stubble fields was over. It was a regular practice to beat out the coverts for pheasants and woodcock, with several sportsmen walking-up in line accompanied by spaniels and other flushing dogs.

Today, the pheasant's introduced distribution extends from the British Isles (where it is widespread apart from in northwest Scotland) eastwards throughout Europe, except for the most northerly and the most southerly parts. Its indigenous population ranges from the Caucasus through Soviet Central Asia to the Chinese coast, and it has also been introduced into Japan and New Zealand.

In North America, it is common in Washington, Idaho and northern Oregon, and east of the Rockies from southern Canada to Kansas and from northern Missouri to New England. There is also a pheasant population in Arizona.

The dramatic and vividly-coloured males contrast strongly with the duller and more inconspicuous females, which tend to be smaller in size and are well camouflaged. A full-grown cock pheasant is a large bird, which may be 30 to 35 inches long, including its tail feathers which may account for 15 to 18 inches of that length. Cock birds may weigh as little as 1½ pounds, although individuals have been recorded weighing almost 4½ pounds. 2½ pounds is a good average, however, and hen pheasants weigh an average of 2¼ pounds.

The plumage of the cock pheasant is an iridescent combination of greens, bronze, copper and foxy-red, and there are hints of blue, with blackish barring. Individuals vary enormously in colour, from near black to pale cream, and true albino examples can also occur. Despite the wide range of colour varieties, the sporting pheasant should not be confused with the ornamental pheasant species, of which the commonest are the golden pheasant (*Chrysolophus pictus*), Reeves's pheasant (*Syrmaticus reevesi*) and Lady Amherst's pheasant (*Chrysolophus amherstiae*). These are mostly confined to collections, but there are some small feral populations.

The cock pheasant is a noisy bird whose crowing is a familiar sound in the areas in which it lives. Like many gallinaceous (fowl-like) birds, he tends to crow at dawn and dusk, and crowing may also be stimulated by loud noises, including gunshots. In addition, crowing and a resonant wing drumming sound are important features of the male's springtime display.

Pheasants have an unusual breeding system, which involves individual cock birds gathering and holding harems of several females. The hen pheasant normally takes full responsibility for the clutch and nest, and her breeding success depends on suitable habitat (often in the bottoms of hedges and woodland edges) as well as security from predation by mammals and predatory birds, and a good supply of food for the young chicks after nesting. Insects, though less important for the pheasant than for the partridge, seem to be a significant food for the chicks. Adult pheasant eat a wide range of foods, including grain, weed seeds, peas, the buds and berries of many plants, and nuts and acorns. Various types of animal food such as ants, maggots, worms and insect larvae are also eaten.

ring-necked
Japanese green

melanistic

RING-NECKED PHEASANT *The most common type of pheasant in Britain and north America is the ring-necked. A full-grown male is nearly 3 feet long.*

RING-NECKED PHEASANT

♀

♂

EGGS *The pheasant's 7 to 15 eggs are laid in April or May, the nest being an unlined or sparsely-lined hollow.*

JAPANESE GREEN PHEASANT

MELANISTIC PHEASANT

BLACK-NECKED PHEASANT

MINOR SPECIES *In addition to the ring-necked pheasant, Britain also has small numbers of black-necked, melanistic and Japanese green pheasants. In the USA, the Japanese green pheasant is now established in Virginia and Delaware.*

TAIL FEATHERS *The tail of a cock pheasant is typically 15 to 18 inches long – about half the bird's total length.*

PARTRIDGES

The grey or Hungarian partridge is the typical game bird of low-lying arable and pasture land throughout Britain and the temperate parts of Europe, and it has been introduced into North America, where it has thrived in many states and in Canada. The red-legged or French partridge, a native of southwestern Europe, has been successfully introduced into Britain, with numerous importations since the 17th century. The partridges also include the chukars, which are natives of southern and southeast Europe. These are birds of semi-arid habitats with low scrub and exposed rock, and they have been introduced successfully into similar areas in the USA.

GREY PARTRIDGE
Perdix perdix

The grey or Hungarian partridge is a small, compact game bird, 11 to 13 inches long, with the rounded body and short, rounded wings typical of most partridge species. The cock bird is slightly larger than the hen, with an average weight of 14 ounces; a typical hen weighs 12 to 13 ounces.

Despite its name, the grey partridge is predominantly brown, with grey feathering on the upper breast and neck and prominent chestnut barring on the flanks. The face and throat are an attractive cinnamon colour. The adult cock tends to have a more upright stance than the female, and this posture makes the dark brown inverted-horseshoe marking on the lower breast feathers particularly conspicuous. The hen bird is difficult to distinguish from the cock, but is in general less boldly marked.

Sometimes also known as the English partridge, it used to be a common farmland game bird throughout Britain and Ireland, and was by far the commonest sporting bird in the days before the late-Victorian upsurge in rearing and releasing pheasants on a large scale.

In Britain and Ireland, the grey partridge has tended to fare best where the landscape is broken up into a pattern of small fields containing a variety of crops, and divided by thick, well-maintained hedgerows. Recent changes in farming have entailed the loss of much hedgerow habitat, the enlargement of fields, and a tendency towards large arable monocultures.

This trend has been accompanied by increased use of agrochemical sprays, which have reduced the availability of insects on farmland in late spring and early summer. Young partridge chicks cannot survive without a high-protein diet containing much insect food. Fewer insects, combined with loss of nesting habitat, has led to a massive reduction in the numbers of wild grey partridge in Britain. The partridge crisis has been further compounded by less rigorous control of predation by gamekeepers, most of whom are now primarily involved in pheasant rearing.

Grey partridges live in family groups or coveys during autumn and winter, and these break up into breeding pairs early in the year. Birds may even pair up in December if the weather is mild.

Cock partridge, like cock grouse, are aggressive and belligerent in maintaining their territories, which are designed to ensure that the cock bird and his mate have adequate food during the harsh early months of the year, preparatory to nesting.

The hen grey partridge prefers to nest in thick vegetation, where she can cover over her eggs when it is necessary to leave them unattended when she goes off the nest to feed.

RED-LEGGED PARTRIDGE
Alectoris rufa

At close range or in the hand, the red-legged partridge looks very different from the grey partridge. It is larger (13 to 14 inches) and more vividly-coloured, with a red bill and red legs, heavily barred flank feathers, speckling on the upper breast feathers and a prominent white stripe above the eye.

On the wing, however, identification is more difficult, especially with driven birds when both grey and red-legged birds may be put to flight. This can make it impracticable to attempt to shoot selectively, avoiding one or other of the species. It is

GREY PARTRIDGE These birds are sedentary and may live all their lives in just two or three adjacent fields.
EGGS The 9 to 20 eggs of the grey partridge are laid in late April or May.

GREY PARTRIDGE

♀

♂

FLUSHED BIRDS *Partridges rise a little and fly close to the ground before settling again.*

CHUKAR AND ROCK PARTRIDGE *The chukar and the rock partridge are very similar, the most obvious difference between them being the thickness of the black band around the face and throat. The sexes are alike, and grow to about 14 inches.*

EGGS *The 6 to 14 eggs of the chukar and the rock partridge are laid from March to June, the nest being a hollow or scrape sheltered by a rock, shrub or tuft of grass. The red-legged partridge lays its 9 to 14 eggs in April or May, in a ground hollow.*

RED-LEGGED PARTRIDGE *Male and female red-legs are alike in appearance. The male shown here is resting, with his feathers fluffed out.*

ROCK PARTRIDGE   CHUKAR   RED-LEGGED PARTRIDGE

ROCK PARTRIDGE

CHUKAR

RED-LEG IN FLIGHT

RED-LEGGED PARTRIDGE

therefore possible that a hard-pressed residual population of grey partridge may be overshot if there is extensive shooting of released red-legs, since the two species may come over the guns together.

The breeding behaviour of red-legged partridges differs significantly from that of the grey partridge. Coveys break up slightly later in the spring, and red-legged partridges, uniquely among game birds in Britain, may lay two clutches in separate nests. One is incubated by the hen while the cock incubates the other, and in a successful year two broods will hatch and survive. When mature, a cock red-leg weighs approximately 18 ounces, and a hen about 15 ounces.

The eggs of the red-legs are pale with reddish-brown spotting, and laid in clutches of from 9 to 14. Unlike the grey partridge, the red-legged makes no attempt to conceal its eggs, and when left unattended many clutches are destroyed by crows, stoats, rats and other predators. Thus the higher rate of egg production is paralleled by greater losses.

As with the grey partridge, the clutch or clutches hatch simultaneously after approximately 24 days, and the chicks are active within an hour of hatching. Both cock and hen help care for the chicks, which grow rapidly and can fly short distances when about two weeks old. Insect food is less important to red-legged chicks than to those of the grey partridge, but where insect food abounds,

chick survival will almost always be better. The diet of the adult red-legs consists mainly of vegetable matter, including cereals and other grains, seeds, and the leaves and shoots of many plants growing at ground level. They often feed greedily towards sunset.

CHUKARS
Alectoris chukar and
Alectoris graeca

There are several species of chukar partridge, of which the two most impartant are the chukar (*A. chukar*) and the rock partridge (*A. graeca*). Both are similar in overall size and appearance to the closely-related red-legged partridge, but lack the black streaks below the breast band and have closer

striping on the sides.

They prefer reasonably high, stony and rocky ground, with scrub and sparse woodland, and although they can tolerate cold weather they can't cope with deep snow and so they often move to lower altitudes during winter.

Chukar and rock partridge are ground-nesting birds, laying a single clutch of 6 to 14 eggs (sometimes as many as 21), which are incubated by the female and hatch in about 25 days. Both parents rear the young, which are fully grown after about 8 weeks.

In the USA, the range of the introduced chukars extends from Nevada and Utah into Oregon, Idaho and Washington. In the east, farm-bred birds are released for shooting.

WOODCOCK & SNIPE

Woodcock and snipe are members of the large, extended group of birds known as waders. The woodcock has the long, prominent bill and weak, webless feet typical of many species of wading birds, but is technically regarded as a webless-footed woodland wader, having adapted to a mainly forest habitat. The snipe, though, with its longer legs, more slender and rakish body, its tendency to form small flocks or 'wisps', and its fondness for wet, shallow-flooded habitats, has more in common with most of the other wading birds than the woodcock does. The American and European (or Eurasian) woodcocks are closely related, and they are generally similar in their habits and appearance.

EUROPEAN WOODCOCK
Scolopax rusticola

The European woodcock is a compact, partridge-sized bird. Its plumage is a richly-variegated pattern of creams, reddish-browns, buffs and blackish-brown, with prominent dark barring on the otherwise pale underparts, and three prominent black transverse bars across the large and triangular-shaped head. Male and female woodcock cannot be told apart by their external characteristics.

Female woodcock are diligent parents and take great care of the chicks. Like many birds of the plover and wader species, they will feign injury and undertake an elaborate distraction routine to lure potential pred-

EGGS *The woodcock usually lays 4 eggs in a lined ground hollow. The snipe and the jack snipe also nest on the ground, and like the woodcock they lay 4 eggs.*

WOODCOCK

COMMON SNIPE

JACK SNIPE

ators away from the chicks. European woodcock are known to carry their chicks, which are usually held between the adult bird's thighs and carried for short distances in a heavy, laboured flight. This carrying of chicks has still to be properly studied, but there is some evidence that it may be used to transport chicks to areas of good feeding as well as to take them away from danger.

Woodcock feed primarily on earthworms, reached by probing deeply with their long bills in soft soil. They feed principally at night, particularly in winter, flighting out from their daytime roosting places in low, shrubby vegetation to feed on marshland and wet pastures during the hours of darkness, and flighting back again to roost at first light. Woodcock feed more actively by day during the spring and early summer breeding season, often within woodland.

AMERICAN WOODCOCK
Scolopax minor

The American woodcock is the North American counterpart of *Scolopax rusticola*, and its general appearance and habits are rather similar. The American 'timberdoodle' is a smaller bird, however, weighing about 5 or 6 ounces, which is little more than half the weight of the European species. It is altogether greyer in colour, with unbarred flanks and underparts which have a pleasing cinnamon-buff colouring. The head has pronounced dark transverse barring, and the bill is slightly longer in proportion to the bird's total size.

Woodcock breed widely in central, eastern and northern states, and also in Canada. As with the European woodcock, the population is largely migratory, and birds move southwards with the onset of winter weather in the northern parts of their range. Three main migra-

♂

EUROPEAN WOODCOCK
At about 14 inches, the European bird is 3 inches longer than the American.

EUROPEAN WOODCOCK

FLIGHT *When flushed, the woodcock is an agile flyer, swerving through the trees to escape danger.*

FEEDING *Like the snipe, the woodcock has a flexible bill tip which enables it to grasp food under the ground.*

tion routes have been identified: following the Atlantic seaboard; along the line of the Appalachian Mountain chain; and further west from the Great Lakes southward. The chief wintering haunts are in the

southern states of Louisiana, Mississippi and Alabama, where the creeks and bayous afford good feeding in moist soils, and there is ample daytime roosting cover in deciduous and mixed woodlands.

COMMON SNIPE

FLIGHT *The common snipe rises quickly and has a strong, zigzag flight pattern.*

FLIGHT *The jack snipe typically flies only a short distance before wheeling down.*

JACK SNIPE

♂

♂

COMMON SNIPE *The snipe is smaller than the woodcock, but it has a much longer bill and its head is striped.*

JACK SNIPE *The little jack snipe is only 7 or 8 inches long, and is a protected species in Britain.*

COMMON SNIPE
Gallinago gallinago

The common snipe of Europe, Asia and North America is related to the various species of woodcock, and there are a number of other, more closely-related species of snipe distributed worldwide. The Wilson's snipe (*Gallinago gallinago delicata*) is now regarded as being a North American race of the common snipe.

The common snipe is about 11 inches long, and almost a third of that length is taken up by the bird's long and prominent bill. An adult will weigh 3½ to 4½ ounces, and birds are at their heaviest in late autumn and winter, except when severe frost prevents them feeding, in which case they can lose weight and condition very rapidly.

Snipe are resident in Britain, Ireland and North America throughout the year, and breed extensively on high, wet moorlands and on lowland marshes. The spring display flights of the male birds are often conspicuous, consisting of a succession of deep, diving flights over the chosen breeding territory. The flights are accompanied by a distinctive 'bleating' or drumming sound, which is not a vocal sound but is produced by vibrations from the two stiff outer tail feathers which vibrate in the slipstream as the bird extends its tail outwards and dives fast at a steep angle. The distinctive, winnowing sound which this causes can be heard at almost any time of the year, but is particularly associated with the breeding season, which extends from March or April into late June.

Snipe chicks are active within hours of hatching, and are brooded and fed by both male and female during the first weeks of life. They fledge after about 3 weeks, although they do not attain full adult size and weight until late summer or early autumn.

Snipe feed by probing in saturated ground and liquid mud, especially on marshes, swamps, bogland and along the margins of rivers and lakes. The flexible tip of the snipe's bill enables it to grasp food items like earthworms and insect larvae at some depth, and swallow them without withdrawing the bill. The main winter diet of worms is augmented by many forms of invertebrate life, and in drier conditions surface insects, caterpillars and some forms of vegetable matter such as seeds are also eaten.

Snipe usually feed by night and roost by day, and the phases of the moon seem to affect their feeding activity, possibly because the lunar cycle affects the behaviour of certain species of earthworms and other invertebrate food items.

JACK SNIPE
Lymnocryptes minimus

The jack snipe is a small, rather delicately-coloured cousin of the common snipe which breeds in Finland, the Baltic States and northern Russia, and winters in the Tropics and subtropics, southern and western Europe and the British Isles.

Weighing less than 2½ ounces and with a shorter bill, it is considerably smaller than the common snipe, and it rises silently when flushed, usually in a weak, direct and short flight. Since 1981 it has been protected in Britain but is still shot in Ireland, where it can provide good sport, especially when driven in a strong wind.

97

PIGEONS & DOVES

Pigeons and doves together form the Columbidae family of birds, of which over 300 different species occur worldwide. They vary widely in size, plumage and in sporting importance, but their behaviour and nesting habits tend to be rather similar. The most important of these birds in the British Isles and Western Europe are the woodpigeon, the collared dove and the rock dove. In North America, the main species are the mourning dove, the band-tailed pigeon and the white-winged dove, and the rock dove (or domestic pigeon) which was introduced from Europe.

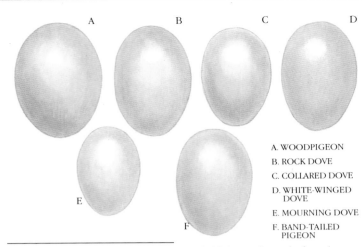

A. WOODPIGEON
B. ROCK DOVE
C. COLLARED DOVE
D. WHITE-WINGED DOVE
E. MOURNING DOVE
F. BAND-TAILED PIGEON

WOODPIGEON
Columba palumbus

The woodpigeon is by far the most important sporting species of the pigeon family in the British Isles and western Europe. It is a rounded, compact bird, and males and females have similar field characteristics and can also be very difficult to distinguish in the hand.

The plumage is predominantly grey, and in flight the bird's prominent white wingbars and white neck patches are distinctive. Young birds lack the well-developed white neck patches of the adults, and the vivid yellow-coloured eyes of adult woodpigeon develop from an almost black colour in the young. Male woodpigeon tend to be slightly larger and heavier than the females, but a good average for both sexes is about 1¼ pounds.

Woodpigeon are tree-nesting birds, building their nests in copses and woods and in high-growing shrubs in hedgerows. They also nest in single trees, especially where the foliage is thick, as when a mature tree has been overgrown with ivy. Ground-nesting is not unknown, however, in areas where few trees exist, and long heather and rough grasses may sometimes conceal woodpigeon nests.

The nest is a roughly-constructed affair, little more than a platform of twigs, built mainly by the female from fragments carried in by the male. Two or three whitish eggs are laid, and a pair of woodpigeon will usually raise at least two broods a year.

Nesting may take place in any month of the year, although late spring and summer are the peak times in Britain. This means that the growing young or 'squabs' have the benefit of ample food at harvest time, which is especially important in wheat- and barley-growing areas.

COLLARED DOVE
Streptopelia decaocto

The collared dove, a native of the eastern Mediterranean countries, is a relative newcomer to Britain and western Europe, but even though the first recorded occurrence in Britain was as recently as 1952, the current British population is probably well in excess of 100,000 pairs.

The collared dove is small – barely half the size of a woodpigeon and about a third of its weight. It is dainty and elegant in appearance, with a delicate buff-coloured plumage with a hint of a pinkish hue. There is a distinctive band of white on the tail, most visible when the bird is flying, and a prominent black collar, edged with white.

Properly cooked, the collared dove makes excellent eating and is superior to the woodpigeon.

ROCK DOVE
Columba livia

The rock dove or feral pigeon is closely related to the woodpigeon, although there are important differences in appearance and the woodpigeon has much greater significance for the sporting shooter.

Smaller and more racy and streamlined in appearance than the woodpigeon, rock doves and feral pigeons have a wide variety of plumages, from a greyish-blue to a pale cinnamon-brown, and many have prominent white rumps. They will breed on coastal cliffs and on the man-made nesting sites provided by city buildings.

MOURNING DOVE
Zenaida macroura

The mourning dove is an important sporting pigeon of Central and North America and parts of the Caribbean. It is a resident breeding bird of almost every state of the USA but also migrates, mainly in response to changing weather conditions and food availability.

It is an attractive little bird, 11 to 13 inches long, with light grey plumage on the upper parts and a pinkish-buff coloration underneath. As with many pigeon species, it can be difficult to distinguish males from females, but the female is duller and has a shorter tail.

Like most pigeons, the mourning dove flies deceptively fast and is regarded as a difficult bird to shoot because of its erratic, curling flight and its tendency to alternate fast wingbeats with rapid gliding on set wings. In some areas, shooting mourning doves is an important exercise in crop protection.

IN FLIGHT *Pigeons and doves are strong, direct and powerful in flight, and they will also glide.*

EGGS *Apart from the band-tailed pigeon, which lays a single egg, all these species lay clutches of 2 eggs. Those of the white-winged dove are buff, the rest white.*

BAND-TAILED PIGEON
Columba fasciata

The band-tailed pigeon is a migratory dove, 14 to 15½ inches long, which is highly regarded as a sporting bird throughout the western parts of North America. It used to be abundant, but overexploitation by the netting and shooting of market hunters, which was made easier by the bird's tendency to form exceptionally large flocks, led to a serious reduction in numbers. This was exacerbated by the fact that each pair of band-tailed pigeon produces only one egg per year.

With the prospect of the bird being hunted to extinction, which was the fate of its once-abundant relative the passenger pigeon (*Ectopistes migratorius*), the US government imposed controls on the shooting seasons and there has since been an upswing in numbers.

WHITE-WINGED DOVE
Zenaida asiatica

The white-winged dove is found mainly in the southwest of the USA, from Texas through to California, and southwards into Central America. At about 12 inches long it is somewhat similar to the mourning dove, having brownish-grey feathering and a distinctive pointed tail. It gets its name from its prominent white wing patch which is particularly conspicuous in flight.

White-winged doves are strong fliers and, like most pigeons, they are gregarious birds which form large flocks, especially at harvest time when they gather to feed on grain crops.

WHITE-WINGED DOVE

♂

BAND-TAILED
PIGEON

♂

♂

WOODPIGEON

MOURNING DOVE

♂

♂

ROCK DOVE

COLLARED DOVE

♂

BLACK, WHITE & BLUE GEESE

Geese may conveniently be grouped according to their predominant colours: the 'black' geese include the Canada, barnacle and brent (or brant) geese, and the 'white' geese such species as the greater and lesser snow geese and the Ross's goose. The 'blue' geese are colour variations of the lesser snow goose. The Canada goose, of which there are many subspecies, is a native of North America which has flourished in Britain and Europe since its introduction, as an ornamental species, in the 18th century. Of the other black geese, only the brent is found on both sides of the Atlantic.

CANADA GOOSE

CANADA GOOSE
Branta canadensis

The breeding grounds of the Canada goose are in the north-western USA, in most of Canada from Newfoundland to the Yukon, and through Alaska to the Aleutian Islands. Its wintering areas are localized in southern Canada and central USA, but extensive in the lower Mississippi Basin, along the Gulf Coast and the Atlantic seaboard and in California and Oregon.

The species was introduced into Britain and Europe as an ornamental species and, in Britain at least, its breeding success has been so marked that it is now considered to be an agricultural pest in many areas, and a possible competitor to the native greylag.

Canada geese are a very variable species, and as many as twelve distinct subspecies have

been identified. One of these, the cackling Canada, is one of the smallest of all geese, with a length of only 24 inches, and small females weigh about 2½ pounds. The giant Canada is the largest goose, measuring nearly twice the length of the cackling, and big ganders will weigh as much as 20 pounds. The British birds are not as big as this but, at about 13 pounds for a really big gander, they are the largest of the geese in Britain.

The main feature common to Canadas is the black head and neck with large white cheek patches that may join under the throat. The body plumage varies from greyish to dark brown, and the breast and underparts are whitish, the bill is black and the legs and feet are very dark grey. The voice of the Canada is a loud, repeated honking.

The Canada's flight is strong with steady wingbeats, and although short flights may be taken out of formation, for longer distances they adopt their distinctive V-shaped skeins. They move well on water and on land, feeding mainly on the shoots of crops and on grain. They also feed on grasses, sedges and aquatic plants, and on berries in tundra regions during the breeding season.

BARNACLE GOOSE
Branta leucopsis

Barnacle geese are clearly divided into three separate groups: birds that breed in Greenland and winter in Ireland and western Scotland, notably on the Isle of Islay in the Inner Hebrides; those that breed in Spitzbergen and winter on the Solway Firth in southwest Scot-

EGGS The white or creamy-white eggs of these geese range in size from about 2.75 inches long (Ross's goose) to nearly 3.5 inches for those of the largest subspecies of Canada goose. The nests are usually lined hollows.

land; and the third group which breeds on islands to the north of Siberia and winters in the Netherlands.

Barnacle geese have white faces and foreheads on a black head and neck, the white area being much larger than that of Canadas. Those wintering on the Solway are totally protected, and as a result their numbers, having fallen to below 1000 after World War 2, are now in excess of 10,000. Shooting is, however, allowed on the Isle of Islay. There, the great majority of the geese are concentrated at two adjacent roosts, and with the population increasing (from 2800 to 21,500 between 1959 and 1983) there was an outcry from local farmers who demanded that numbers be reduced and controlled. The shooting season was extended from two months to five months in 1977 in order to disperse the geese, and although shooting is only permitted under licence, conservation bodies are now expressing their concern that the pendulum has swung too far the other way and the barnacle population may now be under too much pressure.

ROSS'S GOOSE

SNOW GOOSE

BARNACLE GOOSE

BRENT GOOSE

CANADA GOOSE

BRENT GOOSE
Branta bernicla

The breeding range of the brent or brant goose extends further north than that of any other goose, and is circumpolar through arctic North America, northern Greenland, Spitzbergen and across arctic Siberia. European birds winter in Denmark, Germany, the Netherlands, the British Isles and France, and the wintering range of North American brent is down the Pacific coast from British Columbia to California and Mexico, and from Massachusetts to North Carolina on the Atlantic coast.

The brent's head, neck and breast are black, with a whitish, sometimes indistinct, collar around the neck. The upper parts are dark brown with grey smudging, while the undertail coverts and the sides of the rump are white and show as a distinct 'V' when the bird is in flight.

There are various subspecies of brent, and the colour of the

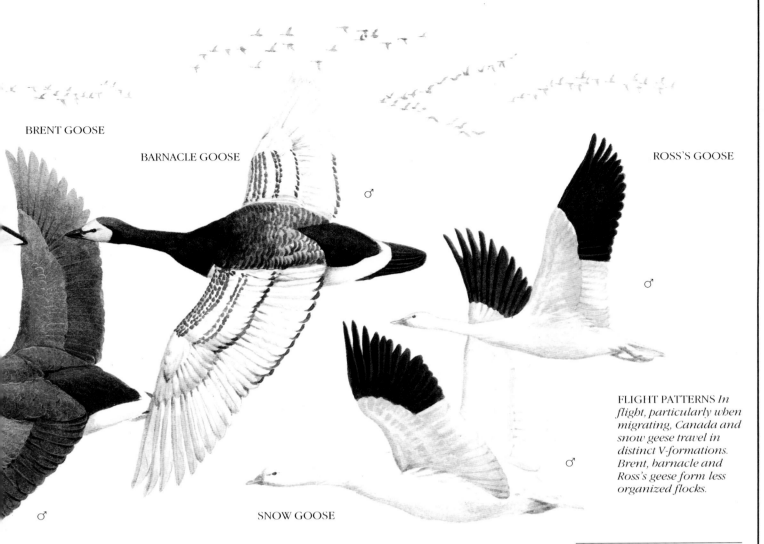

BRENT GOOSE

BARNACLE GOOSE

ROSS'S GOOSE

♂

♂

♂

♂

SNOW GOOSE

FLIGHT PATTERNS *In flight, particularly when migrating, Canada and snow geese travel in distinct V-formations. Brent, barnacle and Ross's geese form less organized flocks.*

underparts varies from one to another. For example, the underparts of the dark-bellied brent fall halfway in colour between the pale brownish-grey of the light-bellied or Atlantic brent, and the almost black of the Pacific or black brent.

The brent has been protected in Britain for many years, following its decline, and because this has brought about a reversal in its falling numbers, there are now serious conflicts with farming interests.

SNOW GOOSE
Chen caerulescens

Many authorities now consider that snow geese and blue geese are colour variations of a single

species, and that is how they are considered here. However, there has been a fair amount of disagreement on the matter and the majority of hunters still regard them as separate species in the field even if, biologically, they are the same.

The snow goose is divided into two subspecies, the greater snow goose and the lesser snow goose, the greater snow goose measuring 30 to 32 inches and the lesser averaging 27½ inches. The adult plumage of the greater snow goose is identical to that of the white-phase lesser snow goose, being all white with the exception of the black primaries and grey wing coverts, and sometimes a yellow or orange tint to the head.

There is no 'blue' phase in the greater snow goose, and all blue geese are variations of the lesser snow goose. Blue geese are, in fact, not blue at all; they have the normal white head of the snow goose, and the body is an ashy grey or light brown colour.

Lesser snow and blue geese breed largely on islands off the north coast of Canada, in particular on Baffin, Southampton, Victoria and Banks Islands, and their wintering areas are in California, Mexico, Texas and Louisiana. The Californian birds originate mainly from Banks Island, but their numbers are swelled by a Siberian population which crosses the Bering Strait in the autumn.

Greater snow geese are confined to the east of North America, and their breeding range – around Baffin Bay and in Greenland – is more northerly than that of the lesser species.

FEEDING *The barnacle, Canada, snow and Ross's geese will usually be seen feeding in fields, but the brent prefers aquatic plants where available.*

ROSS'S GOOSE
Chen rossii

Ross's goose is a little-known bird, its breeding grounds in the northwest Territories of Canada remaining unknown until 1938, and there are possibly colonies still undiscovered. Those that are known about are the original discovery in the Perry River region to the south of Queen Maud Gulf, on the McConnell River, at Eskimo Point and at Churchill (both on the western shore of Hudson Bay) and on Southampton Island. Ross's geese migrate to the south in winter, to the Central Valley of California and the Gulf areas of Texas and Louisiana.

These geese are very similar in appearance to snow geese, but they are smaller, their length being from a little over 20 inches up to about 26 inches, and there is no black 'grinning' patch at the sides of the bill. Ross's geese are gregarious and associate freely with whitefronts and the smaller varieties of Canada geese, but most especially with lesser snow geese.

GREY GEESE

The so-called 'grey' geese of the genus *Anser* – the greylag, white-fronted, bean and pink-footed geese – breed mostly in the cold, northern areas of the world. The white-fronted goose, which is the most widely distributed of all geese, is the only grey goose found in North America. Of the others, the greylag and the bean goose enjoy wide distribution in Europe and Asia, but the pink-footed goose is highly localized, breeding on a small number of remote islands and wintering in restricted areas of western Europe. The greylag, the largest of the grey geese, is very probably the source of the original breeding stock of most farmyard geese.

GREYLAG GOOSE
Anser anser

The breeding range of the greylag extends east from Iceland through Scandinavia and Finland to Russia, and into northern Scotland, Germany and Poland. The Icelandic birds winter in Britain, while the rest migrate to the Netherlands, France, Spain, the eastern Mediterranean and as far south as North Africa.

The greylag, which averages about 33 inches in length, is a brownish-grey goose with light barring on the upper and underparts and on the head and neck. In flight, the greylag displays a distinctively pale forewing. The bill, legs and feet are clear identification points in grey geese, and a good aid to distinguishing one species from another. The greylag's bill is large and orange in colour, and its legs and feet are pinkish or flesh-coloured.

However, there is an eastern race of greylag, slightly larger birds with pink bills, which breed in eastern Europe, Asia Minor and across Russia eastward from the Urals and into Manchuria. This eastern race winters in south China, Burma and northwest India.

The flight of the greylag is strong and purposeful and the birds, travelling in V-formation, never seem in any doubt as to where they are headed. They gather in a great variety of group sizes, from single family units up to flocks numbered in thousands.

Their winter habitat is on fresh and saltwater marshes and estuaries. They have a varied diet, and are regularly seen feeding on pasture land, stubble and potato fields as well as on fields of carrots and turnips.

WHITE-FRONTED GOOSE
Anser albifrons

The white-fronted goose is a slightly smaller (28 inches) and darker goose than the greylag. It is widely distributed across Europe, Asia and North America, and there are four generally-recognized subspecies, which each use different breeding grounds.

The principal subspecies

GREYLAG GOOSE

WHITE-FRONTED GOOSE

BEAN GOOSE

IDENTIFICATION *All these geese are similar in overall coloration, so the most reliable means of identification is by the colours of the bills, legs and feet. The bean goose's bill midsection may be pink, orange or yellow.*

breeds on the arctic coast of northeast Russia and Siberia, the Pacific whitefront in eastern Siberia, Alaska and northwest Canada, and the Greenland whitefront on the west coast of Greenland. The fourth subspecies is the Thule whitefront, whose breeding grounds, remarkably, are still not accurately known.

In winter, birds of the principal subspecies which have bred in northeast Russia migrate to southeast Europe, the eastern end of the Mediterranean and the Caspian and Black Seas, and to Germany, the Netherlands, Belgium and England; the Siberian birds, being more easterly, winter in India, Burma, China and Japan. Pacific whitefronts, bred on either side of the Bering Straits, winter on their respective sides of the Pacific, with North American geese going to California, Texas and central Mexico. The Greenland whitefronts winter in Ireland, notably on the Wexford Slobs (marshes), in eastern parts of England and in Scotland, particularly on Islay in the Inner Hebrides.

It should be noted that whitefronts are a protected species in Scotland; they may be shot in England and in Northern Ireland, but like all wild geese they currently enjoy total protection in the Republic of Ireland.

The head and neck feathers of a whitefront are darker than those of a greylag, but even more characteristic of the whitefront is the prominent white patch on the forehead and around the base of the bill, from which this goose gets its name. The bill itself is lightish pink and the legs and feet are orange or sometimes flesh-coloured. The Greenland race are distinguishable by their yellowish-orange bills, and their heads and necks are even darker than those of other races.

BEAN GOOSE
Anser fabalis

Bean geese breed in the northern parts of Norway, Sweden and Finland, across northern Russia and through Siberia to the Gulf of Anadyr, and into the Altai Mountains and Mongolia. Their wintering range is extensive, with eastern races of the species being found in China, Korea and Japan. Western-race bean geese winter from Asia Minor and Turkestan right across central Europe to the Mediterranean, and north to Germany, the Netherlands and parts of southern Scandinavia. Fairly small numbers winter in Britain, where they are protected.

The bean goose is much browner than the greylag and it has neither the pale forewing of the greylag nor the barred belly of the whitefront. It is the second-largest grey goose, averaging about 32 inches in length. It tends to be less vocal than other geese, but its call, when made, is not unlike that of the pinkfoot, except that it is deeper and rather more of a *honk-honk* than a *wink-wink*.

The legs of the bean goose are yellowish-orange, but the bill's shape and colour vary with the bird's geographical origin and, in addition to the more general division into eastern and western races, some authorities suggest at least six subspecies and there is certainly a clear distinction between tundra and forest subspecies. The tundra bean breeds in the northern part of the species' range, and its bill is shorter with a curved lower mandible.

PINK-FOOTED GOOSE
Anser fabalis brachyrhynchus

The distribution of pink-footed geese strongly coincides with that of the 'black' barnacle geese. They breed on islands off Spitzbergen and in Greenland and Iceland, and their wintering grounds are mainly in Scotland, England, Germany, the Netherlands and Belgium. All the birds from Greenland and Iceland winter in Britain.

Some biologists consider the pinkfoot to be a subspecies of the bean goose, but the pinkfoot

GREYLAG NEST

GREYLAG CHICK

BREEDING *All these geese lay 4 to 6 white eggs, about 3 inches long. They nest in lined scrapes, and the active, downy young hatch after about 28 days. The greylag lays in April or May, the others in June or, in the north, as late as July.*

is more coastal in its habits and it is smaller, at 24 to 30 inches long, and distinguished by its paler back and by its bill, which is smaller and black with a pink band; its main distinguishing features are its very dark head and neck, which contrast with the much paler underparts and forewing. The call note is a distinctive *wink-wink*, and on a higher pitch than that of the greylag or the bean goose.

Pink-footed geese are extremely social birds. In winter, they roost in their thousands on estuarine sandbanks, and on lakes and marshes where these remain undisturbed. At dawn they flight inland to feed on stubbles, potato fields and pastures, and on the shoots of young cereals and grasses in spring. A fairly recent addition to their diet are frost-damaged carrots left in the ground.

Although pinkfeet will roost alongside them, they will not roost on such small areas as greylags often do, and prefer more isolated sites.

PINK-FOOTED GOOSE

♂

MALLARD & PINTAIL

The mallard is far and away the most numerous and familiar species of duck and, because of its importance as a quarry species, it has been closely researched and is well understood. It is the species of duck that best lends itself to intensive rearing for release, when individuals and clubs seek to maintain duck numbers by putting some back to replace what they have taken. The pintail is a most elegant and popular duck but, in America, its fall in numbers due to environmental and hunting pressures is causing concern. American duck hunters have to stick to bag limits which state how many of which species can be shot, and when, but in the first five years of the 1980s, duck limits were more generous than they had been since the Twenties, when marshland wintering habitats were far more extensive. As a result, by the late 1980s the number of pintail in North America had fallen to less than 40 percent of what it was at the close of the Seventies. Now, many American duck hunters – being deeply concerned with the management and conservation of waterfowl species, as well as simply hunting them – are calling for an immediate reduction in the hunting season and duck limits.

TAKEOFF *The mallard, being a dabbling duck, can spring directly into flight from the surface of the water. It doesn't need a running start to take off, as diving ducks do.*

FEEDING *Mallard feed by upending and by dabbling in the shallows. They also feed on land, taking cereal grains, grazing on vegetation and dabbling in soft mud.*

MALLARD
Anas platyrhynchos

The mallard is a very well-known duck, the most widespread species of all waterfowl and common wherever climatic conditions are suitable. It will not tolerate the same degree of cold as, say, the black duck, but because it has adapted so well to changes in the environment brought about by the hand of man, it is often less affected by environmental pressures than are other species.

In Europe, Asia and North Africa it breeds almost everywhere suitable between about latitude 34°N and the Artic Circle, including Algeria, Morocco and Tunisia, and in Norway its breeding range extends as far as 70°N. In North America, its breeding range extends from the Arctic Circle south, through Alaska and the western half of Canada and around the Great Lakes, and westwards from there to the Pacific, extending south through California, Utah, Colorado, eastern Arizona and western New Mexico.

Mallard migrate south in winter, their range extending generally to about the Tropic of Cancer, but even further south in Africa, on the west coast down to Nigeria and in the east along the Nile through Egypt and into northern Sudan. In North America, the mallard's winter range covers southern British Columbia, and most of the United States south of a line running roughly from western Montana to Nebraska and east to Maryland, extending up the Atlantic coast to New England.

In Britain, tradition dictates that the name 'mallard' should really only be used in reference to the drake of the species, being derived from the Old French word *mallart*, meaning 'male'. The female is thus called the 'wild duck', and to the British is the only bird entitled to the name.

The mallard is a large bird, the drake measuring some 24 inches with a wingspan of close to 3 feet. He is clearly recognizable by his metallic green head and white collar above a purplish-brown breast and grey body. The tail is grey and white, with black central feathers that form a distinctive, tight curl, and the broad, purplish-blue speculum on the wing, set between two bars of black and white, is another distinctive feature. The drake's bill is yellowish-green tipped with a black nail, and his legs and feet are a reddish-orange.

The wild duck, which is an inch or two smaller than the drake, is drab by comparison, being mottled light brown with a pale eyebrow above a dark stripe through the eye, and her bill is olive-brown and mottled with orange at the sides. Her plumage is a much lighter brown than other ducks and that, together with her size and the purplish-blue speculum on her wing, distinguishes her from other species. It is the duck, rather than the drake, that quacks so loudly and defiantly – the instantly-recognizable call of the mallard. The drake has a much quieter *queck*, rather than a *quack*.

Mallard are found on all kinds of waters apart from the open sea. In Britain, roughly three-quarters of the total number are found on freshwater, some in close proximity to man and happily feeding from his hand; most of the rest are found on estuaries.

The mallard walks and feeds well on land, taking cereal grains, dabbling in soft mud, or grazing. In water, food is gathered by dabbling in the shallows and by upending in the classic fashion. Mallard will also dive to gather rich underwater food, for example when they are on a pond and someone throws them a handful of barley, although they can only stay under for a few seconds. This type of feeding activity is different from that of other dabbling ducks, although these can, of course, also resort to diving when wounded and pursued in water by a wildfowler's dog.

In winter, the diet consists very largely of vegetable matter, including the stems and seeds of aquatic plants, and waste cereal grains are taken from harvested fields in late autumn. They will also feed on waste tubers and root fragments in potato fields, and in wooded areas, acorns and the seeds of shrubs and marginal plants are taken avidly, in preference to any artificial feed that may be offered.

The mallard is an adaptable and opportunistic feeder, but animal matter makes up less than 10 percent of its diet. Because of this predominantly vegetable diet, there are few duck to rival the mallard as a table bird, and nothing beats a stubble-fed mallard for taste and texture.

Mallard lay a clutch of normally ten to twelve creamy-grey or buffish-green eggs in a down-lined nest, which is usually hidden in undergrowth close to water. Incubation lasts about 28 days, and the ducklings, supervised by the female, leave the nest soon after hatching and fledge in about 7 weeks.

PINTAIL
Anas acuta acuta

Also known as the northern, common, or blue-billed pintail, this duck breeds extensively throughout northern parts of the Northern Hemisphere. It breeds in western Greenland, Iceland and the British Isles, and across northern Europe and Siberia to the Kamchatcka Peninsula. In North America, its breeding range extends westwards and northwards from the

PINTAIL

MALLARD

EGGS *The eggs of both mallard and pintail vary from yellowish or greenish-cream to various shades of pale green or pale blue. The mallard's egg, a little over 2¼ inches long, is slightly longer and broader than that of the pintail.*

MALLARD

MALLARD *The male is identifiable by his green head, yellow bill and purple-brown breast, and both sexes have a bright blue, white-bordered speculum on the wing.*

PINTAIL *The male pintail is a brown-headed bird with a white breast, grey-looking flanks and back and a long, slender tail. The brownish female has a white belly.*

PINTAIL

Great Lakes, and down from the Pacific Northwest into California.

In most places it is highly migratory, and in North America it is to be found wintering in the states around the Gulf of Mexico, particularly in Florida, up the Atlantic coast as far as New Jersey, all along the Pacific coast, and into Central America and the West Indies. The birds breeding in northwestern Europe winter as far south as the Nile Valley, and other wintering grounds include western Europe, the Mediterranean coasts, tropical West Africa, the Black Sea area, Arabia, India, Burma, Sri Lanka, Borneo and some Pacific islands.

The pintail has been described as perhaps the most graceful and elegant of all ducks. The drake is about the same length as a mallard, but much slimmer in build, and he is easily distinguished by the long and thin central tail feathers that give the species its name. He has a chocolate-coloured head and neck with a white stripe on either side, reaching up from the snowy-white breast, and the back and flanks are vermiculated brown and white, which gives them a greyish appearance. The scapulars (shoulder feathers) are grey, heavily marked with black. The belly is white, the undertail coverts black, and the tail is grey

and white except for those long central tail feathers, which are black with a greenish sheen. As is suggested by the name 'blue-billed pintail', the bill is bluish-grey, and has a black central ridge and tip nail. The feet and legs are slate grey.

The duck is similar to the mallard duck, but is darker and more graceful with a longer neck and more pointed tail, and lacks the vivid speculum of the mallard. Her speculum, like that of the drake, is an obscure and rather dull purple-bronze bordered with a single white band.

Besides being described as elegant, the pintail is wild, fast, smart and shy, and tends to fly in large flocks. Drakes whistle and

ducks quack, but the pintail's quack is hoarser than that of the mallard duck. Like mallard, pintail will feed on grain fields although, in winter, they are most regularly found in coastal regions. They will also feed on potato fields after ploughing, and like mallard they make fine birds for the table.

Compared to most ducks, pintail nest with scant regard for cover, and the clutch of usually seven to nine creamy or greenish-buff eggs is laid in May or later, depending on location. Incubation takes the relatively short time of 23 days, and like mallard chicks, the ducklings are tended by the female when they leave the nest.

BLACK DUCK, GADWALL & SHOVELER

The black duck's breeding range extends from Minnesota, through the Great Lakes region to New England and southern Canada, and down the Atlantic coast as far south as North Carolina. In winter, it is found on the east coast from Nova Scotia to northern Florida, and in most areas south of the Great Lakes and east of the Mississippi. The gadwall has a wide range in the temperate parts of the Northern Hemisphere, but its distribution is irregular. Its southern limit in winter is about latitude 20°N, and in summer its northern limit is around 60°N. Even more widespread, the shoveler is perhaps the most internationally-successful duck of all, with a world range wider than that of the mallard.

BLACK DUCK
Anas rubripes

The black duck is similar in voice, shape and size to the mallard but, as its name suggests, its plumage is much darker. The drake has a blackish crown, the rest of the head being a light brown streaked with black, and at close quarters it can be seen that a dark line of plumage streaks through the eyes. The body plumage is of very dark brown feathers with pale borders, which creates a lacelike effect. The bill is greenish-yellow, and older drakes sometimes have red rather than the more normal coral-orange legs.

The duck is a drabber version of the drake, the head and neck being grey and less streaked and the markings on the body irregular, giving a striped rather than lacelike effect. The duck's bill is olive-green with black mottlings, and her legs are greenish-yellow or dull orange.

In fair light, it is easy to distinguish between a black duck and a mallard drake, which is much more brightly coloured and has a distinctive metallic-green head. However, it is easy to mistake a black duck for a female mallard, because although the black duck is a darker bird, both species show a prominent white underwing in flight.

Unlike mallard, which often feed in fields, black duck prefer to stick to water, and they are more inclined to live near the sea coasts or large lakes. However, they are able to adapt to a wide variety of habitats and show a preference for wooded areas. Animal matter, such as shrimp and marine worms, accounts for up to 20 percent of the black duck's diet, the rest being vegetable matter such as the seeds of sedges or rushes and the stems and leaves of pondweeds.

GADWALL
Anas strepera

The gadwall is smaller than the mallard, but with a maximum length of about 20 inches it is still a fairly large duck. The drake is identifiable by its black upper and undertail coverts, which contrast with its grey-brown back. The head and neck are pale buff, spotted and streaked with brown, and the crest bears bold, crescent-shaped markings. The bill is a slaty-grey or lead colour, and the legs and feet are orange-yellow.

The female is browner than the drake, with coarser markings, and although her bill is the same basic colour as the drake's, it also has a drab orange border.

The female gadwall might be mistaken for a mallard duck when seen swimming. In flight, however, the gadwall has quicker wingbeats than the mallard, and its long, pointed wings are a useful distinguishing feature. In addition, the gadwall is the only dabbling duck to show a white speculum or patch on the upperwing. This is common to both sexes and can be seen from a long distance. The drake has a harsh *kack-kack* call, and the ducks quack, but more softly than the mallard and without the same air of defiance.

Although they can be found on brackish waters, gadwall prefer freshwater lakes and ponds with thick cover and are generally more numerous at inland sites. They like thick cover to nest in, fairly close to water, and lay their eggs in May or June.

SHOVELER
Anas clypeata

The shoveler is easily recognized by its shovel-like bill, the top of which is twice as large as the base. This bill is an extreme adaptation for filter feeding, which involves straining water taken in through the tip of the bill and ejecting it through the very prominent projections, known as 'lamellae', on the upper and lower mandibles. This allows the shoveler to feed on tiny particles, including plankton in spring and summer.

For this reason, shoveler less often upend than other dabbling ducks and more commonly feed while swimming. Other

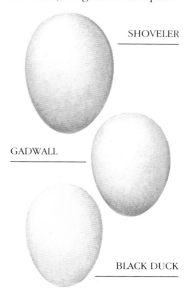

EGGS *The shoveler lays 6 to 14 eggs, the gadwall 8 to 12. The black duck's 8 to 10 pale tan eggs, often tinged with green, are laid from late April to June.*

SHOVELER

GADWALL

BLACK DUCK

GADWALL

♂

BLACK DUCK

items commonly included in their diet are seeds, weeds, insects and molluscs. In some places, such as the Ouse Washes in England, it has been found that threequarters of the shoveler's diet consists of animal material, making it the most carnivorous of the dabbling ducks.

The drake has a metallic green head, similar in colour to that of the drake mallard. The lower neck and breast are white, the flanks and belly are a chestnut-cinnamon, and the rump and tail coverts are black with a greenish sheen. The bill is black and the legs and feet are orange-red. The duck is mottled in shades of brown and buff, with a greyish-brown bill, and the length of both duck and drake is about 20 inches. Shoveler are mainly silent, but the duck sometimes utters a hoarse quack and the drake a low-pitched *tock, tock* sound. However, it is the bill that is the truly distinctive feature of the shoveler, whether at rest or in flight, when it is carried with a slight downward tilt.

In the southern extremes of their breeding range, shoveler will breed in early April, but in more northern parts they will breed as late as June. The nest, containing six to fourteen pale buff eggs, is built of dead grasses, lined with down and feathers and sited close to water.

LANDING *Being a dabbling duck, the gadwall can take off without running, and it lands on water with its wings outstretched, neck extended and feet acting as brakes.*

IN FLIGHT *The shoveler is easy to identify in flight, with its extra-large, shovel-like bill, and its wings which are set farther back on its body than those of other ducks.*

SHOVELER

TEALS & GARGANEY

The teals and the closely-related garganey are among the smallest of all wild duck. Very gregarious fliers, travelling in fast-moving flocks that constantly expand and contract, they often indulge in what can only be described as formation flying, when as many as thirty or more birds twist and turn, dive and climb, in perfect unison. Some wildfowlers would say that teal do not fly any faster than, say, the mallard, but because of their small size and rapid wingbeats, they certainly appear to be faster. Their flight is more like that of the waders than of other ducks, and they jink and swerve like a flock of sandpipers. At the first shot from a wildfowler's gun, a flock will burst like shrapnel, then the teal go into vertical thrust and head for the clouds. They are tremendously popular with wildfowlers because they test markmanship to beyond most men's limits.

EUROPEAN TEAL
Anas crecca

The European teal, also known as the common teal or European green-winged teal, is the smallest duck resident in Europe. However, besides breeding in the British Isles, central and southern Europe, Iceland, Scandinavia and the Balkans, its breeding range extends across Asia to Kamchatka, the Kuriles and Japan, and it may also be found along the Atlantic coast of North America. In winter, its range extends as far south as tropical Africa, Arabia, India and Southeast Asia.

Because of their size alone, teal present few identification problems; their length is only about 14 inches, and they usually weigh no more than 12 ounces. In the hand, the teal drake is seen to have a rich chestnut head and neck, with a broad, metallic green stripe on each side, running from in front of the eye and bordered in white; the breast is white and heavily spotted. The mantle and flanks are vermiculated pale grey and black, and these feathers are much in demand for tying the wings of the 'Teal' series of trout and sea trout fishing flies.

The speculum on the wing is metallic green and black, with white borders in front and behind. The bill is very dark grey, almost black, while the legs and feet are a dark grey with a hint of green. The female is mottled brown and buff overall, with a green and black speculum like that of the drake.

In summer, this teal is found in boggy areas of low scrub, secluded marshland, ponds and lakes, and in woodland clearings. In winter, roughly half the British teal population moves to coastal sites such as estuaries and salt marshes.

Plant seeds are the most important part of the teal's diet, representing up to threequarters of its food in many places. It also feeds on aquatic plants, plus some insects, worms and molluscs. In very shallow water, teal will feed by walking slowly, dabbling with their bills and heads submerged. In deeper water they will upend to feed, but due to the shortness of the neck and bill they are unable to feed in water more than about 10 inches deep.

In a severe winter, the numbers of teal in Britain may fall dramatically. Due to their small size, they are particularly vulnerable to hard weather, and they move south to western France and Spain.

GREEN-WINGED TEAL
Anas crecca carolinensis

The American green-winged teal is the smallest duck in North America, and the drake is very similar to the European teal. The major distinguishing features are that the European drake has a white line running along the scapulars, but the American bird has a white line running vertically down the breast instead; in addition, the clearly-defined white border of the green stripe on the sides of the head of the European drake is not nearly so clear, or absent altogether, on the American. Apart from these small differences, the American bird is basically the same in appearance and habits as its European counterpart.

It has an extensive breeding range, from California to Alaska and from northern Nebraska to Maine, and in southern Canada. Like the European teal, it is susceptible to extremes of hard weather, so while small numbers winter as far north as southern Alaska and British Columbia, it is chiefly found further south, with the greatest concentrations being around the Gulf of Mexico, throughout Central America, and in northern Venezuela and Cuba.

BLUE-WINGED TEAL
Anas discors

In the breeding season, the blue-winged teal is found on small freshwater lakes, marshes, ponds and sluggish streams from the Mississippi Basin westwards, and in southern Canada, the Yukon and Alaska.

Like the green-winged teal, it is a highly migratory bird and

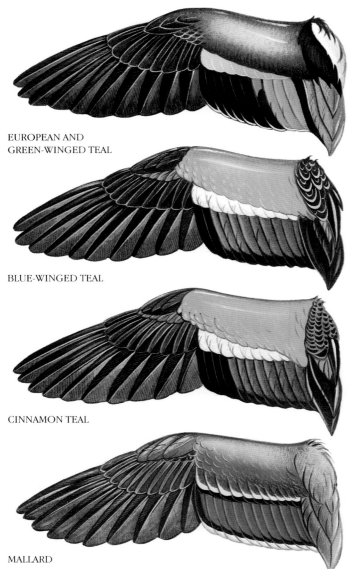

EUROPEAN AND
GREEN-WINGED TEAL

BLUE-WINGED TEAL

CINNAMON TEAL

MALLARD

WINGS *The wings of male European and green-winged teals, blue and cinnamon teals and the male mallard. In all these birds, the speculum of the female is similar to that of the male.*

TEAL

GARGANEY

EGGS *All teals' eggs vary from pale cream to olive-buff. The garganey's are creamy-buff.*

GARGANEY

♀

♂

♂

EUROPEAN TEAL

♀

will travel south over enormous distances to reach its wintering grounds which extend from the Gulf Coast of the USA to the West Indies, and through Central to South America.

The blue-winged teal drake has a very dark grey head and neck, tinged with metallic pink and violet, with a large and distinctive crescent-shaped band between the bill and the eye. The back is grey and the mantle is dark brown with buff markings. There are very vivid, light blue wing coverts, from which the teal gets its name, but the speculum is metallic green between two white bars. The bill is black and the legs and feet have a yellowish tinge. The female is basically brown overall, with blue wing coverts like those of the drake.

CINNAMON TEAL
Anas cyanoptera

Cinnamon teal are widely distributed in North and South America, and five separate races are recognized, but only the northern race (*A. c. septentrionalium*), the most cinnamon-coloured of the races, is found on the northern subcontinent. The other four are all found in South America, and these are the Argentine cinnamon teal (*A. c. cyanoptera*), the Andean (*A. c. orinomus*), Borrero's (*A. c. borreroi*) and the tropical (*A. c. tropica*).

The northern cinnamon teal drake has a deep cinnamon-red body and head, with a very dark crown. The wing is similar to that of the blue-winged teal, having the same blue wing

coverts and metallic green speculum. The bill is black and the legs are yellow-orange. It can be said that the cinnamon teal duck is more reddish than the blue-winged, but she is mottled and spotted in the same way as the blue-winged, and the shades of brown can be practically indistinguishable.

GARGANEY
Anas querquedula

Also known as the garganey teal, this duck is slightly larger than the European teal. Garganey are summer visitors to many parts of England, where they breed regularly, and occasionally to Scotland. However, they are seldom still present in Britain at the start of the duck shooting season, and so are a very rare

addition to the wildfowler's bag.

As well as the small stock breeding as summer visitors in Britain, garganey are regular breeding visitors throughout most of Europe north of the Pyrenees and Alps and across Asia to Kamchatka. The winter range is southerly, with only a few to be found in southern France and Spain, the vast majority wintering in Africa south of the Sahara. Asian breeding birds, as would be expected, winter further east in India, Burma, Malaysia, Borneo, southern China and the Philippines.

The garganey is easily recognized at a distance by the pronounced white eyebrow, which extends down the neck, and the pale grey forewing that can be seen when the bird is in flight.

WOOD DUCK & WIGEON

The breeding range of the European wigeon extends across northern Europe and Asia, and it winters as far south as North Africa. The breeding grounds of the American wigeon extend from the Great Lakes region west to Oregon and northwest to Alaska, and it winters on both coasts, in California's Central Valley and in Mexico. The wood duck, another American species, breeds in most parts of the USA east of the Mississippi, with other breeding areas in the west and the Pacific northwest. It winters in southern parts of its eastern breeding range, and in California, Oregon and Washington.

WOOD DUCK
Aix sponsa

The North American wood duck resembles the slightly smaller teal in flight, although it is not as aerobatic and seldom gathers in flocks of more than ten. Also, the prominent head crest distinguishes it from any teal.

The long crest is a particularly noticeable feature of the drake. Its head and crest are a mixture of glossy greens, purples and blues, with white lines which extend from the base of the bill over the eye, and from the back of the eye across the side of the head and down to the point of the crest.

The chin and throat are also white, as is the belly. The wings and back have metallic sheens, but the overall impression is of glossy black. The upper breast is purplish-brown with white, triangular spots, and the sides are buff speckled with black, the uppermost feathers being alternately tipped with crescent-shaped black and white feathers.

The drake's bill is as impressive as the rest of his appearance. It carries a yellow band at the base and then is red, shading through pink and yellow to white, with a black nail at the tip and a black patch between the nostrils. The legs and feet are orange-yellow, with grey webs.

The duck is a toned-down version of the dandified drake. She has various shades of grey and green on her back, with metallic sheens. Her underparts, chin and throat are white, and the crest and head down to the nape are dark grey, again with metallic purple and bronze sheens. Her bill is grey and her legs and feet are yellow with grey webs. The length of both sexes is about 18 inches.

The wood duck has a remarkable ability to fly through the tops of trees, even flying under a closed canopy of leaves in summer, and as it flies it holds its bill at a characteristic downward angle and looks from side to side.

EUROPEAN WIGEON
Anas penelope

The European wigeon holds a very special place in the affections of coastal wildfowlers. The drake's melodious *whee-oooo* whistling and the low, growling purr of the duck will quicken the heart of any hunter waiting with dog and gun on the saltings in the half-light of dusk.

The wigeon is a medium-sized duck, growing to a maximum length of about 18 inches. The drake has a number of conspicuous features, the first and foremost being the golden, custard-coloured crown to his

EGGS *The eggs of the wigeon are cream, the European bird laying 7 or 8, the American 9 to 11. The wood duck lays 8 to 10 white eggs.*

WOOD DUCK

♀

♂

WIGEON

WOOD DUCK

AMERICAN WIGEON

♀

♂

♀

♂

EUROPEAN WIGEON

chestnut head. The breast is pinkish-brown, fading into white underparts which contrast clearly with the black undertail coverts, and the flanks and back are grey and lightly barred with black. When the bird is in flight, a white patch on the front of the wing is clearly visible.

The female has no such outstanding features, being brown above and white below, but the distinctively high and rounded wigeon head, with its abruptly sloping forehead, is a useful sign as are the pointed tail and scimitar-shaped wings which are common to both sexes. The light, slaty-grey bill of the drake, tipped with black, is slightly duller in the duck, while the legs and feet of both sexes may vary from brown to grey.

Wigeon feed at night and rest by day, when some will be found on lakes and reservoirs but the majority will be at sea.

AMERICAN WIGEON
Anas americana

Also known as the baldpate, the American wigeon is the same shape and size as its European cousin. The main difference is that the American wigeon is keener on fresh water, frequenting inland marshes and lakes, and in general it resorts to the sea only on the Pacific coast.

Although it is similar to the European wigeon in most respects, there are distinct differences in plumage, particularly in the case of the drake. His

FLIGHT *Wigeon fly fast and are usually seen in quite large flocks, which fly loosely grouped or in V-formation.*

crown and forehead are white and there is a distinctive flash of metallic green from the eye to the nape, while the rest of the head is creamy-white with black spots. His upper parts and sides are a rich chestnut brown, with black vermiculations which give a lightly barred effect. The breast and abdomen are creamy-white, and the slaty-grey bill has a touch of black at the base as well as the tip.

The female differs from the European wigeon duck in that she has a white background to the head which is spotted on the crown and throat. She is greyish on the back, rather than brown.

The American wigeon stays mainly inland, usually on marshy areas close to large expanses of water, but during a winter freeze it will move to the coast or to rivers not affected by ice or frost.

POCHARD, REDHEAD & CANVASBACK

The European pochard and the redhead and canvasback of North America all belong to the genus *Aythya*, which are diving ducks. All the members of this genus, which also includes the goldeneye and the tufted duck, are expert divers, gathering the bulk of their food underwater and being able to feed at a far greater depth than the dabbling ducks, such as the mallard and the teals of the large genus *Anas*. Being diving ducks, the pochard, redhead and canvasback are shaped rather differently from the dabbling ducks, and are generally squat and rotund with heavy bodies and less pointed wings. To help them dive, their legs are set towards the rear of their bodies, whereas those of the dabblers are more central.

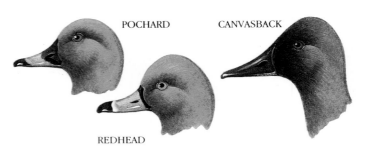

POCHARD
CANVASBACK
REDHEAD

POCHARD
Aythya ferina

The European pochard is very largely an inland species, but it is also seen on the coast and in estuaries, especially in winter. Its breeding range extends over most of central Eurasia between latitudes 45°N and 60°N, including France, Belgium, Holland, Germany, Denmark, Norway, central Sweden, Austria, Romania and Hungary, and across Russia to central Siberia. Only a few hundred pairs nest in Britain, but the British pochard population increases to many thousands when the winter migrants arrive. Apart from Britain, its wintering grounds extend from the extreme west of Africa to Japan, and include North Africa, mainland western Europe, India, Burma and China.

Identification of the drake is simple. About 18 inches long, it has a rich chestnut head, a black breast, grey back and sides lightly vermiculated with black, and a belly which varies from pale silvery grey to white flecked with brown. The bill is a light slaty-grey, dark at the base and with a black tip, the legs and feet are greyish yellow, and the iris of the eye is red. The brownish-coloured duck is rather harder to identify, but she has the same squat, rather flat appearance as the drake.

They are to be found mainly on shallow inland waters, ranging from lakes to slow-flowing rivers but, particularly in winter, they will resort to sheltered coastal sites in bays and estuaries. They often form large flocks, and in some winters more than 300,000 gather on the Danube delta.

The pochard, being a diving duck, has a mixed diet. It takes large amounts of insect larvae during the breeding season, and on the coast a substantial part of its diet is made up of crustaceans and small molluscs. In winter, however, it is largely vegetarian, which is why it shows a preference for heavily-vegetated waters then. It is a shallow diver and rarely feeds in water deeper than 10 feet.

REDHEAD
Aythya americana

The redhead is the American equivalent of the European pochard. It is a slightly larger bird, its eye has a yellow rather than a red iris, and it is a very much darker bird due to the coarser, darker vermiculations on the body. Otherwise, it is very similar in appearance and has similar behaviour, diet and habits to the pochard.

The redhead breeds from central British Columbia south to New Mexico and east to Wisconsin. Wintering grounds are from Connecticut south to the Gulf Coast and into central Mexico, with the majority wintering between Florida and Mexico.

On their winter range, redheads feed and live with canvasbacks, which are a similar and closely-related species. Indeed, the ducks are very difficult to tell apart, as would the drakes be if it were not for the canvasback drake's 'Roman' profile. The redhead duck, however, is a brown bird and her wings are grey, while the canvasback duck is more greyish with a brown tinge.

On migration flights, both species fly in formation, and redheads and canvasbacks are noted as strong fliers with a rapid, powerful wingbeat. The sound of a flock of redheads at night has been likened to that of a bunch of cats, with their alternating 'meows' and 'purrs'. That is the song of the drakes; the ducks quack, but with a higher tone than the mallard.

CANVASBACK
Aythya valisineria

The canvasback is a larger bird than the redhead, measuring about 22 inches. Its breeding range extends from Alaska and the Yukon through the Canadian prairies and into the northwestern USA. In winter, they are found in the upper Mississippi and Great Lakes area, down the east coast from New York to Florida, along the Gulf Coast, and up the west coast from Mexico to Washington. Large winter populations are found around Detroit, in the Chesa-

IDENTIFICATION *The pochard and redhead are very similar, but the pochard's bill has a larger dark patch at the base. The canvasback's head is darker and wedge-shaped.*

peake Bay and San Francisco Bay areas, and in California's Central Valley.

The colouring of the canvasback drake is very similar to that of the redhead and pochard. However, the front of the face and crown shade into a very dark brown, and the upper back and the breast are brown. The lower back is greyish brown, finely lined and speckled with grey; as with the other two species, the rump and vent are black, but the belly and sides are white. The bill of the canvasback is black, and the legs are slaty blue in both sexes; the iris of the eye is red. The canvasback duck is mottled brown on the head, neck, upper breast and back, with dark grey wings and a white belly. As a means of identification, though, it is the shape of the head that sets the canvasback apart. It is distinctly wedge-shaped with a sloping forehead and a long, tapering bill.

As with pochard and redhead, the diet is predominantly vegetarian, consisting mainly of grasses, aquatic plants and seeds, and the canvasback is particularly fond of wild celery. However, nearly a third of the canvasback's intake is molluscs and insect larvae. With vegetable matter predominating in its diet the canvasback, like the redhead and pochard, can make good eating.

During the breeding season, canvasbacks are found on flooded farmland and smallish marshes with shallow waters but, when the ducklings are fledged, the females gather on larger marshes and the drakes go off separately to favoured moulting lakes. Like the pochard, canvasbacks nest in thick vegetation either alongside or over shallow water.

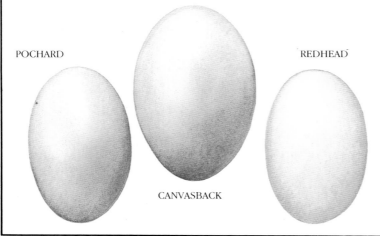

POCHARD
REDHEAD
CANVASBACK

EGGS *The pochard's 6 to 11 eggs are laid in April, May or June, as are the 10 to 15 of the redhead. The canvasback usually lays 7 to 9 eggs in May or June.*

DIVING DUCKS *Like most diving ducks, the pochard, redhead and canvasback are fast-flying birds, which means that their wingbeats are more rapid than those of the dabbling ducks. And while dabbling ducks can spring into flight from the water, diving ducks have to patter along the surface before they take off.*

♀

♂

CANVASBACK

REDHEAD

♂

♀

♀

POCHARD

♂

TUFTED DUCK & GOLDENEYE

The goldeneye and the tufted duck are widely distributed in the Northern Hemisphere; the goldeneye in North America, Europe and Asia but the tufted duck only in Europe and Asia, although it does spread down into Africa during winter. In Europe, the tufted duck and the goldeneye are two of the most popular ducks with wildfowlers, who accord them the same sort of esteem that the canvasback and the redhead enjoy in North America. The goldeneye is unusual amongst diving ducks in that it can spring into flight; other diving ducks have to run and patter along the surface before they can get fully airborne.

TUFTED DUCK
Aythya fuligula

Tufted duck are the commonest and most widespread diving ducks in Britain, where they are found almost exclusively on inland waters. They breed in Britain, Iceland and most of Europe into the far north of Sweden, Finland, Russia and Siberia as well as in the Near East and as far east as Japan. In winter, they spread to the Black Sea and Mediterranean coasts, into Arabia, India, Burma, Malaysia and the Philippines and as far south in Africa as Kenya. They regularly visit Alaska, and occasionally winter on both coasts of North America.

They nest on islands in lakes and along the banks of ponds. The nest is made of dry grass and withered rushes and reeds, filled with the duck's down. A normal clutch of the greenish-grey eggs would number somewhere between six and twelve, but much larger numbers are occasionally found when more than one duck lays in the same nest. Almost immediately after hatching, the ducklings will enter the water and begin to dive.

Tufted duck are a very distinct species, both sexes being crested and the crest or tuft being plain to see. The adult drake is a piebald bird, the crest, head, neck and back being black with a purplish gloss, and the black upper parts and tail having a greenish sheen. Wings, sides and flanks are white, and sometimes the sides are spotted. The drake's bill is slaty blue fading into white, and his legs and feet are also slaty blue.

The female is dark brown, and her crest is shorter than the drake's. The sides shade into pale brown with white on the centre of her breast and belly, and her bill and legs are duller than those of the male. The ducks and the drakes are similar in size, typically about 17 inches in length, and both exhibit a distinctive broad, white wing-bar when in flight. The duck has a harsh call, described as *curr, curr*, but the drake has a soft and repeated whistle.

Animal material accounts for more than threequarters of the tufted duck's diet, molluscs being predominant in fresh water, with some insects and plant material. In brackish water, mol-

RING-NECKED DUCK (USA)

TUFTED DUCK

RING-NECKED DUCK *On its occasional winter visits to the coasts of North America, the tufted duck might be mistaken for a ring-necked duck, but it has a crest (not always obvious) and lacks the neck ring and white at the base of the bill.*

luscs still predominate, and some crustaceans are also taken. On inland waters without large supplies of molluscs, such as Loch Leven to the north of Edinburgh, midge larvae are taken instead. Whatever the diet, although the tufted duck is certainly edible, its flesh is rather coarse.

TUFTED DUCK

GOLDENEYE

♂

♀

GOLDENEYE
Bucephala clangula clangula

The goldeneye very largely restricts its breeding range to between latitude 50°N and the Arctic Circle across mainland Eurasia and North America. In Eurasia, this includes Scandinavia, the northern parts of the USSR, Germany and Poland, but there are also breeding populations further south in Switzerland, Bulgaria and Romania. The North American subspecies (*B.*

GOLDENEYE

TUFTED
DUCK

c. americana) breeds from Newfoundland and Labrador in the east to British Columbia and Alaska in the west, but nowhere is it a common nester.

Eurasian goldeneye move south from their breeding places as autumn sets in, but cannot be expected in Britain in any numbers before the end of November. Eurasian birds winter in Britain, the southern Baltic, Black and Caspian seas, the northeast coasts of the Mediterranean, part of the Arabian Gulf, India and Burma, as well as China, Korea, Taiwan and Japan.

American birds winter in Atlantic coastal waters from the Gulf of St Lawrence to South Carolina. They are found inland on the Mississippi and Ohio rivers, and along the north shore of the Gulf of Mexico. On the Pacific seaboard, they winter from the Aleutians south to mid-California.

Goldeneye lay their eggs in enclosed sites, in burrows or crevices in rocks in treeless areas but, for preference, in cavities in dead or decaying trees. Nesting boxes are readily

EGGS *The goldeneye's 6 to 11 eggs are laid in early May or, in the north, in June. The tufted duck lays 6 to 12 eggs in April or May.*

accepted, and these are in general use throughout breeding areas. This is an ancient practice, being referred to by the 18th-century Swedish botanish Linnaeus (Carl von Linné) as a means of supplementing the diets of peasant people. In the past, Lapps not only took the eggs, but usually killed the sitting bird as well.

Until maturity, the young drakes have brown heads, mottled mantles and white wing patches, normally without the white collar visible on adults. Mature plumage is adopted in the drake's second winter. The black head and back, glossed with a metallic green sheen, contrast with the white underparts and patches on the cheek. This gives a handsome, pied appearance. The bill of the drake is almost black, and the legs and feet are orange-yellow.

The female has a dark brown head, the back being dark brown mottled with slate grey. Her bill is blackish, with a faint band of drab orange near the tip which carries a black nail, and her legs and feet are yellow. The Eurasian drake measures about 18 inches, but the duck is an inch or so smaller. The American subspecies is slightly larger, with a heavier bill.

Goldeneye occur on a wide range of habitat on fresh as well

NESTING GOLDENEYE *One of the goldeneye's preferred nesting sites is in a hole in a tree, such as a woodpecker hole, and this can be fifty feet or more above the ground.*

as salt water, but the largest numbers are normally found on the coast in tidal estuaries rather than open sea. Inland, they frequent rivers, lakes, flooded marshes and even quite small ponds. In salt water, goldeneye feed on a wide range of invertebrates: mussels, cockles and snails as well as crustaceans such as crabs, and worms and small fish. On inland waters, insect larvae are the most important food, but goldeneye will include freshwater mussels, water boatmen, tadpoles and even frogs in their diet.

SQUIRRELS, RABBITS & HARES

The squirrels are members of the Sciuridae family of rodents, which also includes chipmunks and marmots. The main feature common to all rodents is that they have sharp, constantly-growing incisor teeth, two upper and two lower, which are specially adapted for gnawing. Rabbits and hares are similar in many ways to the rodents, but they are not closely related to them: they belong to the order *Lagomorpha*, which consists of forty species of rabbits and hares and fourteen species of pikas. The Lagomorphs differ from rodents in having an additional, smaller, pair of upper incisors, and in being exclusively herbivorous.

GREY SQUIRRELS
Sciurus spp

In North America, the Eastern grey squirrel (*Sciurus carolinensis*) is widespread in the eastern half of the USA and southern Canada, and the Western grey squirrel (*S. griseus*) is common in California, western Oregon and central Washington. The Eastern grey squirrel was introduced into Britain in the 19th century, and is now so numerous that it is considered a pest species in many areas. It has found a niche in large and small woodlands, parkland and even suburban gardens, and there is evidence that the expansion of its range and the rapid increase in its numbers has been at the expense of the native red squirrel (*Sciurus vulgaris*), which has been driven from many of its former haunts over most of southern and central Britain. Today, the British red squirrel is in general decline and enjoys legal protection.

Commonly known as 'bushytails', grey squirrels are distinguished by their long and conspicuously bushy tails. Though white on the underside, these stocky and compact squirrels are generally grey in colour, although they incline to reddish tints in certain phases. Their small, slightly rounded ears lack the prominent tufts which are so distinctive of red squirrels, and body weights average about 16 ounces, with large adult specimens running up to 22 to 24 ounces.

The squirrel's nest or 'drey', made of branches and twigs, is built high in a tree, usually in a fork and close to the main trunk. They breed between December and August, during which time the female gives birth to two litters of two to five blind and naked young, which are ready to leave the nest after about 6 weeks.

Grey squirrels are common in mixed and deciduous forests, especially where there are tree species producing the nuts and acorns on which they feed. They will also eat berries and they have a fondness for the bark of certain trees, a characteristic which does not endear them to foresters, who apply major squirrel control programmes to minimize damage. In addition to these vegetable foods, grey squirrels also take insects, birds' eggs and young birds.

Another important species, widely distributed through the hardwood forests of the eastern USA, is the large Eastern fox squirrel (*Sciurus niger*). The fox squirrel's coloration varies from rusty-yellow to tawny or grey, and it weighs from 1½ to 3 pounds.

THE OLD WORLD RABBIT
Oryctolagus cuniculus

The Old World rabbit, of which there are six subspecies, is native to eastern, central and southern Europe and the Mediterranean countries. It was eradicated in Britain by the onset of the last Ice Age, and may have been reintroduced by the Romans in a semidomesticated state, as a useful source of meat, with later introductions in Norman times.

Compact and neatly formed, the rabbit is greyish-brown with a coat comprising a base of dense, short, fine hairs through which grow the longer, coarser hairs of the outer pelage and a third layer of longer, more thinly-distributed hairs. The coat tends to grow thicker and heavier with the onset of colder weather in the autumn. A mature adult rabbit may weigh

EASTERN GREY SQUIRREL

WESTERN GREY SQUIRREL

EASTERN FOX SQUIRREL

between 2 and 3 pounds, depending upon the quality of feeding available, and the males are slightly heavier than the females.

As well as its sharp front incisors, the rabbit has side teeth which are set far back and are designed to grind tough, fibrous vegetable matter. The rabbit's feeding process involves eating, digesting, excreting and then re-eating its food. This unpleasant-sounding process, known as *refection*, enables the rabbit to extract the maximum nutrition from vegetable foods by passing them through the gut several times in succession, rather than by the ruminative process of repeated regurgitation and swallowing adopted by cattle.

COTTONTAIL & SWAMP RABBITS
Sylvilagus spp

The principal species, and the most widely distributed, is the eastern or common cottontail (*Sylvilagus floridanus*), which grows to about 4 pounds in weight and a length of 15 to 17 inches, including the 2-inch, fluffy white tail which gives these rabbits their name.

The other cottontails are the New England cottontail (*S. transitionalis*) of southern New England, the mountain cottontail (*S. nuttallii*) of the Rocky Mountains, and the desert cottontail (*S. auduboni*) of the more arid regions of western North America from the Canadian border south to central Mexico. These rabbits are generally smaller than the eastern cottontail.

The swamp rabbit (*S. aquaticus*) is larger, weighing up to 6 pounds. Its habitat is the

MOUNTAIN HARE

MOUNTAIN HARE
blue coat

BROWN HARE

WHITETAILED JACKRABBIT
in winter coat

BLACKTAILED JACKRABBIT

SWAMP RABBIT

OLD WORLD RABBIT

COTTONTAIL RABBIT

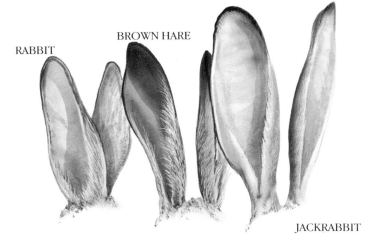

RABBIT

BROWN HARE

JACKRABBIT

EAR SIZE *One feature of most rabbits and hares is their large ears; those of the jackrabbits are particularly large.*

swamps and marshes of the southern states, and it is particularly abundant in Tennessee and the neighbouring states.

HARES & JACKRABBITS
Lepus spp

The most widespread of the genus is the russet-coloured brown hare (*Lepus capensis*). Its natural range extends from Britain eastwards throughout Europe, except for Scandinavia, through the central latitudes of Asia to China, and throughout Asia Minor and northern, eastern and southern Africa. In addition to this, it has been introduced into the Great Lakes region of North America, into Australia, New Zealand and Chile, and into northeast Ireland where it coexists with the native Irish hare.

The Irish hare (*Lepus timidus hibernicus*) is a subspecies of the mountain or blue hare (*Lepus timidus*), an upland species whose coat is a greyish-blue in late summer but turns

piebald or often pure white in winter. The mountain hare is found in the European Alps, the mountains of Scandinavia, and the high hills of North Wales, northern England and Scotland.

The greyish-brown arctic hare (*Lepus arcticus*) of the northernmost parts of Europe, Asia and North America also adopts a white pelage in winter, and in its most northerly haunts it remains white all year round.

The North American snowshoe hare (*Lepus americanus*) and tundra hare (*L. othus*) also change white in winter, their summer coloration being brownish-grey. The North American hare population also includes the blacktailed jackrabbit (*Lepus californicus*) of the west and southwest, and the whitetailed jackrabbit (*Lepus townsendi*) which is found further north and east.

WILD SHEEP & GOATS

DALL SHEEP

BIGHORN SHEEP

The various species of wild sheep and wild goats, found mainly in rugged mountainous areas and occurring throughout Asia, continental Europe and North America, are among the most demanding and sought-after trophies for the rifleman. In North America they are a more important part of the sporting scene than they are in Europe, with the bighorn sheep of the Rocky Mountains being perhaps the most coveted. The other North American species include the mountain goat, the Dall sheep and the closely-related Stone sheep. In Europe, the chief sporting species of sheep and goat are the mouflon and the chamois.

BIGHORN SHEEP
Ovis canadensis canadensis

The Rocky Mountain bighorn sheep is a massive relation of the mouflon of the Old World; a mature male may weigh more than 280 pounds and stand over 40 inches at the withers. The bighorn is primarily a creature of the high mountain pastures, grazing on sparse upland herbage and descending in the severe weather of winter to feed at lower altitudes, sometimes browsing along the treeline.

As with most mountain species, rutting takes place in late autumn and the lambs, which may be single youngsters or twins, are born in mid to late spring, when the climate is kinder and the newly-grown grasses and herbs provide a readily-available source of rich feeding.

Mature bighorn rams will compete strongly to mate with as many sexually-receptive ewes as possible, in a way reminiscent of red deer on the hill in Scotland, but their battles are more violent, involving fierce, head-on battering clashes as they strive to assert dominance.

The mountain bighorn has a relatively smooth coat of stiffish guard hairs overlaying a fleecy underfur. The overall colour is a tawny brown, with pale patches on the snout and rump and a pale belly. Both sexes have horns, but the ewe's are smaller and less curled than those of the ram, which can reach a length of 40 inches around the curl.

Closely related to the mountain bighorn, but smaller in size, is the desert bighorn, the six separate subspecies of which are found across the arid, semi-desert areas of California, Arizona, Texas and Mexico. These desert subspecies are generally lighter in colour than the mountain bighorn.

DALL SHEEP
Ovis dalli dalli

The other mountain sheep of North America are the Dall sheep and its close relative the Stone sheep (*Ovis dalli stonei*). These sheep are smaller than the desert bighorns, rarely weighing more than 150 to 180 pounds; they lack the bighorn's massive build and their horns are more slender. The Dall or white sheep has a predominantly white pelage all the year round, although its winter coat is much denser and heavier, and the Stone sheep is a dark grey.

The Dall sheep occurs mainly in Alaska and the Yukon and into the Northwest Territories, with the Stone sheep occupying a similar ecological niche further southward into British Columbia. Their habits and breeding behaviour are similar to those of the mountain bighorn, the males living in separate flocks from the females and lambs during the summer but rejoining them in autumn.

MOUNTAIN GOAT
Oreamnos americanus

The mountain goat is not a true goat, but the only North American representative of the *Oreamnos* genus of mammals, which combine something of the qualities of both antelopes and goats. Its range extends from the mountains of Alaska southward through the Rocky Mountains, although its strongholds are in British Columbia and Washington.

It has a beard, like a true goat, and its solid, humpbacked

MOUNTAIN GOAT

♂

♂

♂

CHAMOIS

MOUFLON

which the chamois graze.

The chamois rut begins in November, and a dominant male may mate with a succession of females. The females breed in their second year, but few males do so before they are three years old.

MOUFLON
Ovis mousimon

The mouflon is another long-established trophy for the upland stalker in Europe, where it occurs in central Alpine areas and also in the mountains of Sardinia and Corsica. In addition, the mountains of Cyprus are home to the only European herds of the closely-related Asiatic mouflon (*Ovis orientalis ophion*), sometimes known as the red sheep.

The mouflon is a stoutly-built, sturdy mountain sheep, and a mature male will stand about 29 inches at the shoulder and weigh about 100 pounds. Mouflon in winter have a dense coat which is a dull greyish-brown, with a blackish-coloured mane of longer hair fringing the throat. The lighter summer coat is reddish-brown, with a pale rump patch and a prominent black stripe along the line of the spine.

Only the male has horns, which are triangular-sectioned and spread outward and curl back from a thick base at the skull, and these horns develop steadily as the animal matures. The horns of a fine adult mouflon may reach a length of 30 inches around the curl.

Mouflon are herd animals, and the rut occurs in November and December, with the new season's lambs born in late April and May as the upland weather improves and fresh vegetation becomes readily available for the young animals. Mouflon subsist by grazing on the sparse but nutritious grasses and herbs of high mountain pastures, augmented by some browse foods along the tree line in winter, and their dark, tangy-tasting flesh is a delicacy for the successful hunter.

Like chamois, mouflon represent a demanding challenge to the stalker, owing to the steep and remote terrain which is their habitat, and also because of their excellent eyesight, keen scenting powers and elusive shyness. Their fondness for screes and slopes of loose, tumbled boulders makes it difficult and often dangerous to stalk them silently.

appearance is reminiscent of that of a buffalo. Standing 34 to 36 inches at the withers, it may weigh from 200 to 380 pounds, and its coat is long, thick, and shaggy and off-white in colour. Both sexes have horns, which are long and slender and bend back at the tips, and have an average length of 8 to 9 inches.

The mountain goat is exceptionally well adapted to steep terrain, and its feet and leg muscles are well-developed aids to climbing. It has a goatlike tendency to feed by browsing, and its diet also includes upland herbs and various types of lichen and moss. It feeds vigorously in summer so as to build up large reserves of fat which help it to survive the severe winter weather.

The mountain goat ruts in November, and mature males will rut with a succession of females. Although they lack the fierce aggression of species like the bighorn, males will dispute territories and access to sexually-receptive females, and the species is generally regarded as capable of coping with most threats from natural predators.

CHAMOIS
Rupicapra rupicapra

The chamois has long been an important quarry for Alpine stalkers in Europe, and its natural range includes not only the Alps but also the Pyrenees, the Jura mountains, the Carpathian and Tatra ranges of southeast Europe and the adjacent mountainous regions of southwest Asia. Chamois also occur in the mountainous parts of New Zealand's South Island, where they were introduced in the nineteenth century and have since flourished.

The chamois has goatlike and antelope qualities in its appearance and behaviour. A mature male may weigh up to 120 pounds and stand some 32 to 35 inches at the withers. The females are slightly smaller and lighter, but both sexes have distinctive horns. Unlike the antlers of deer, which are shed and regrown annually, the chamois' horns grow steadily throughout its life. The elegant

horns grow upward as a pair of slender spikes, starting high on the forehead, spreading slightly and curling backward into neatly hooked tips. As with all wild sheep and goat species, the horns of the male are heavier, longer and more widely spread than the female's. A mature male chamois may have horns measuring 9½ to 12½ inches, and anything within this range is regarded as a worthy trophy.

Chamois are well adapted to mountain life, being deep in the chest and strongly built, though with a fine-boned, elegant appearance which is reminiscent of some antelope species. Their excellent eyesight and scenting ability, very acute hearing, and their remarkable agility on even the steepest and rockiest terrain, make them elusive and difficult to stalk.

They feed mainly by browsing on twigs, buds, leaves and tree bark, which they find by foraging along the tops of the tree line, especially in winter. In summer, the high Alpine pastures provide ample grasses and other seasonal herbage on

WILD BOAR & RACCOON

The wild boar and the raccoon are two examples of successful transatlantic introduction, the boar from Europe to the USA, and the raccoon from the USA to Europe. The wild boar has long been extinct in the British Isles and Scandinavia, but its present range extends throughout the rest of Europe and across Asia to the Pacific, and round the Mediterranean into northern Africa. In the USA, it is found in many states including New Hampshire, Texas, Oklahoma, Tennessee, Georgia and Florida. The raccoon, distributed widely in North America, is a member of the Procyonidae family which also includes the ring-tailed cat, the coatis and the kinkajous. It is now well-established in many parts of northern Europe.

WILD BOAR
Sus scrofa

These animals are, strictly speaking, wild pig, but they are usually referred to as wild boar although this term should really only be applied to adult males. In the British Isles they were already declining in late medieval times and became extinct sometime before 1700. In many European countries, however, the wild boar remains common, to the extent of being classified as a pest species in certain areas, because of the damage it can do to arable crops.

Like their domestic counter-parts, the forest-dwelling wild boar are omnivorous, with large appetites. They adopt a regular routine of resting during the daylight hours in favourite parts of the forest and moving out at dusk to regular feeding grounds, where they feed greedily throughout the night, returning to cover at first light. Within the forest, boar feed on acorns, beechmast and other nuts, together with a wide variety of berries and shrubs. They also eat a good deal of miscellaneous animal matter, which may be anything from worms and grubs to young rabbits, gamebird poults, young deer fawns and assorted types of carrion.

Where forests are adjacent to arable farmland, boar feed readily by digging for root vegetables, and are especially fond of potatoes, swede, sugarbeet and turnips. They tend to feed in large family groups or 'sounders', and a sounder of boar can do enormous damage to a field of root vegetables in the course of a single night. Consequently, boar are controlled by culling in many central and northern European countries.

For much of the year, boar live in extended family groups, in which adult sows and younger males and females coexist with yearling piglets. Mature males tend to lead solitary lives outside the rutting season.

In Europe, the wild boar rut begins in late November and lasts until early January. Mature

BOAR TRACKS *Boars have four toes on each foot, but the weight is distributed equally on the two middle toes.*

males wander widely in search of sows and may move about a good deal by daylight. Rival adults and young males may provoke angry fights as the dominant male takes possession of the sounder, and after the rut the male resumes his solitary life.

After a gestation period of about three and a half months, the sow gives birth to her piglets, having first left the rest of the sounder and found a quiet place in which to farrow. Seven to eleven piglets comprise a normal litter, and these are born with attractive longitudinal striping forming a pattern of light and dark brown fur, which provides excellent camouflage

WILD BOAR *A mature adult stands 3 feet at the shoulder and weighs 200-400 pounds. The length of head and body is about 5 feet.*

WILD BOAR

RACCOON *The raccoon lives close to water, and usually finds its food along the water's edge or actually in it.*

RACCOON

within the dead leaves and shadows of the forest. This juvenile striping disappears after 7 or 8 months, and as the young pigs mature their coats darken through reddish-brown to dark brown and finally an almost blackish colouring. Adult males and females both have a harsh, bristly coat and a thick protective undercoat.

Although wild boar have few enemies or predators apart from man, they will normally retreat when disturbed and they can run at high speed for considerable distances. Their highly developed sense of smell and excellent hearing make them difficult to stalk and observe.

When pressed by hounds and when cornered, boar are extremely aggressive. In particular, the adults are equipped with two pairs of long, heavy

tusks which are so positioned that they have a continual self-sharpening effect, and the points and inner edges of wild boar tusks are sharp and formidable weapons. Tusks up to 12 inches long have been recorded, but 6 or 7 inches is an excellent average for an adult male, and anything over that length will be considered a notable trophy.

Wild boar from Europe, particularly from Russia, were introduced into the United States between 1890 and 1925, and their numbers increased considerably before excessive hunting pressure threatened to eliminate them. They were given special protection in various National Parks, and wild boar hunting is now available by arrangement with various private hunting ranches.

RACCOON
Procyon lotor

The raccoon is an important traditional sporting quarry in the southern United States, and has no direct equivalent among the native sporting species of Britain and western Europe. However, it has been introduced into Europe and is now successfully established in France, Germany, Holland, Luxembourg and the USSR.

In their native North America, raccoons are widely distributed from southern Canada southward throughout the United States and into Mexico, and over

IDENTIFICATION *The raccoon is about the same size as a cat, but is easily recognizable by its facial markings, as well as by its ringed tail.*

this range they are represented by a number of subspecies. They are rarely found far from water, and can swim strongly, taking readily to the water as a means of defence or escape.

Raccoons have a thick, brownish-grey fur, and perhaps their most distinctive physical features are a rather foxlike, distinctively-marked face and a bushy, ringed tail. An adult raccoon may weigh from 15 to 30 pounds and the species is mainly sedentary, living in hollow trees and venturing out mainly by night, when they rarely venture far from their home trees.

Like bears, raccoons are omnivorous, but have a fondness for flesh in various forms, including small mammals, grubs and items of carrion. Their diet varies with the season of the year, and may include a wide range of wild fruits, seeds, grains, nuts, small mammals, frogs, crayfish and reptiles.

Raccoons pair for mating in January and February, and gestation lasts about 2 months, with litters of young being born in late April and May. 4 to 7 young will be found in the average litter, and the family group may remain together for almost a year, only splitting up when the next season's litter of young is about to be born.

The raccoon is a resourceful animal which has few predators and a relatively high survival rate among its young, and these factors combine to enable raccoon populations to increase rapidly. These populations may reach pest proportions, especially in areas where they can do serious damage to waterfowl.

Originally hunted for their pelts, raccoons are also an important sporting species which are normally hunted with hounds, often at night when raccoons are at large away from their dens. Once they are on the scent of a raccoon, hounds will follow a trail fast and hunters encourage them to put the fleeing raccoon under pressure, which eventually forces it to take refuge in a tree. Once treed, the racoon can be shot with a rifle, shotgun or handgun, depending on the local practice.

FOX, WOLF & COYOTE

Foxes, wolves and coyotes are all members of the Canidae family, which also includes jackals and domestic dogs. The principal quarry species of this family are the red fox of Eurasia and North America, the grey fox, the grey wolf or timber wolf, and the coyote; the arctic fox (*Alopex lagopus*) is valued for its fur, but is usually trapped rather than hunted. There are three other species of wild dog in North America, the swift fox (*Vulpes velox*) and the closely-related kit fox (*Vulpes macrotis*), both now rare and endangered, and the red wolf (*Canis niger*), whose range is restricted to southeast Texas and parts of Louisiana and Arkansas.

RED FOX
Vulpes vulpes

Whatever the pressure on carnivores, the red fox – known as the common fox or simply 'fox' in most places – continues to thrive. This supremely adaptable species is the most widespread and successful animal of prey in the Northern Hemisphere, being widely distributed there and occupying every type of habitat from mountain forest to city park.

A member of the dog family, the fox is not large, its body length averaging 24 inches with a bushy tail, or brush, of 16 inches. Height at the shoulder is 14 inches and adult dog-foxes weigh 15 pounds, although much larger specimens have been recorded. The female, or vixen, is slightly smaller than the dog.

Foxes have pointed muzzles and erect ears, and the coat is thick, with coloration from sandy to red-brown. Underparts and tail tip are white, while there are black patches on the limbs, behind the ear and very occasionally on the end of the tail. They have several calls, and both sexes use a characteristic sharp bark, while the vixen often emits a wailing scream.

The fox is solitary, except when rearing cubs. Mating is preceded by play, and usually takes place in winter, though this pattern can vary. The size of the one annual litter is unpredictable, but is likely to number around four cubs, born in an earth that has probably been taken over from another burrowing animal. The dog supplies food from the moment of birth and plays with the cubs, while the vixen introduces them to hunting.

GREY FOX
Urocyon cinereoargenteus

Although called a fox, and very foxlike in appearance and behaviour, the grey fox is in fact a quite separate species of wild dog. The grey fox is native to North and Central America, and there are two main sub-species. The island grey fox (*U. littoralis*) is found on islands off the coast of Southern California, the more plentiful Eastern grey fox (*U. cinereoargenteus*) ranges from the south of Canada, through the USA and Mexico to Venezuela. The most striking characteristic of the grey fox is its prodigious climbing ability – hence the alternative name of 'tree fox'. The animal can climb a sheer tree trunk with ease, and frequently does, whether or not it's being pursued.

The grey fox has a small head with a sharp muzzle, a shaggy coat, and a prominent bushy tail that tapers to a black point and has a black stripe along its upper part. The legs, neck, the sides of the head and the underside of the tail are reddish-yellow, the back is grey and the underbody is buffish-white. In winter, the coat of animals living in the north may turn to blue-grey or all-white.

The diet is mixed: these foxes do take small animal prey like pocket gophers, mice and rabbits, and some birds and poultry, but a large proportion of their food is vegetable matter. The mating and cub-rearing habits of the grey fox are similar to those of the red fox, with an average of four young.

RED FOX

GREY FOX

DOG TRACKS

FOX TRACKS

GREY
WOLF

WOLVES *Wolves feed on small mammals, birds, carrion, deer, elk, moose and caribou.*

COYOTE *The coyote's eerie, mournful howl is an unforgettable sound.*

COYOTE

COYOTE TRACKS

WOLF TRACKS

WOLF
Canis lupus

One of the largest wild dogs, the wolf has always been abhorred and persecuted by man, but it is still surviving in Alaska, western North America, Florida, Mexico and remoter parts of Spain, France, Germany, Scandinavia and Asia. Withstanding a relentless clearance policy, the largest single population exists in the northern USSR.

A large male can be over 45 inches in length, with a 16-inch tail, a shoulder height of 32 inches and a weight of 160 pounds or more; bitches are smaller. The chest is broad, and the wolf has long, powerful legs enabling it to run for long distances, strong jaws and teeth. Fur coloration can vary from jet black to pure white, but is usually whitish grey or yellowish-grey, and the thick tail droops almost to the ground. It is easy to see that the wolf is the ancestor of the domesticated dogs, with which breeders still cross it to improve a hunting strain.

After winter mating, 5 or 6 cubs are born in spring and both parents assist with feeding and rearing. The family group remains together, hunting set territory by day and lying up below ground at night. Groups are hierarchical, and the well-known howl is used to communicate and maintain status.

RED FOX *The red fox's diet includes insects, small mammals, birds, grass, fruit and carrion.*

GREY FOX *The grey fox, seen here in its blue phase, is a shy nocturnal predator.*

TRACKS *A large dog's tracks are broad and staggered, often with splayed front toes. Those of wild canines are narrower and less staggered, with the front toes close together.*

COYOTE
Canis latrans

The coyote's alternative names of prairie wolf and brush wolf are apt, describing both the animal's preferred habitat and its appearance. However, when wolf and coyote come into contact, the wolf will always try to kill the smaller rival. But the coyote – noted for showing its mood with a variety of facial expressions – has the last laugh. Because of its small size and ability to make skilful use of cover, it has survived where the wolf cannot. Coyotes are distributed from Alaska down to Central America, except where successful eradication programmes have taken place, and are particularly common on the USA's western plains.

The jackal-like coyote is around 48 inches long, including a bushy black-tipped tail of 16 inches, and its weight reaches 40 pounds or more. The coat is thick and quite long, becoming coarse in winter, and its colour varies by season and locality but is generally greyish-yellow, with red-brown patches on neck and legs and whitish underparts.

Coyotes eat small rodents, rabbits, fruit, vegetables and carrion. Although they feed on crop pests, they are disliked by stock farmers, especially those who run sheep, as they can attack young domestic animals. They do not hunt in packs, but sometimes pursue their prey in relays. They are territorial animals which live alone or in pairs (not necessarily for breeding purposes – two barren females often share a den).

Males will fight for the attention of a female, but she may not accept the winner as her mate. Once mated, they pair-bond. Coyotes mate in January or February, with a maximum of 10 cubs born in a natural den.

WILD CATS

All cats are members of the Felidae family, which includes the big cats of the genus *Panthera* and the puma and smaller cats (including domestic cats) of the genus *Felis*. The big cats of the *Panthera* genus are now mostly rare and protected: for example, the lion (*Panthera leo*) is all but extinct in Asia; the tiger (*Panthera tigris*) is an endangered species of Asia, where the leopard (*Panthera pardus*) is also threatened; and the jaguar (*Panthera onca*) is coming under increasing pressure throughout its range, which extends from the southernmost parts of Texas, Arizona and New Mexico through Central and South America to about latitude 40°S. For the hunter, the most important wild cats are now the North American members of the genus *Felis*: the puma (or mountain lion), the lynx and the bobcat. Most other members of this genus, especially those of Europe, are rare or protected.

PUMA
Felis concolor

Known variously as the cougar, catamount, panther, mountain lion or simply 'lion', the puma is the second largest cat in the Americas, surpassed in size only by the jaguar. Once widespread throughout the Americas, the puma's range in North America has shrunk; it is now found mainly in the west, from the mountains of western Canada south to Mexico and Texas, with small numbers in Louisiana, Arkansas, Mississippi and Florida. Occasional sightings are reported from other states such as Minnesota and New York. Its preferred habitat is in remote, rugged mountain areas and in forests and swamps.

This lithe carnivore is similar to the leopard in size, with males averaging a muscular 125 pounds and females 80 pounds. They can run to over 250 pounds in the Rocky Mountains, tending to be smaller southwards into the Sierra Madre. A good-sized male is around 55 to 60 inches long, plus a long tail of 30 inches or more. The puma's upper body is usually yellowish-brown, with paler undersides, but it can also shade toward red or grey. Its ears are dark, with whitish insides, and there are white patches on the lips, which on the upper lip are divided by a pronounced dark streak. The thick tail has a dark tip, and the head is noticeably small in comparison with the body.

Like many cats, the puma is a solitary animal, with a tom occupying a territory – sometimes with its mate – which it defends against intruders. When several are found together, they will usually be a family group of female and young; the cubs remain with the mother for up to two years, until they have mastered hunting – a familiar pattern among wild cats. The cubs are born at any time of the year (but usually in June or July), three months after the puma's wild mating calls have been heard in the night. There may be as many as five or six young, but generally only two survive, and for the first 6 months they have dark spots which occasionally remain faintly evident in adult animals.

Pumas are wide-ranging, stealthy animals that prefer to hunt nocturnally. Although they willingly consume anything from vegetable matter to domestic stock if circumstances demand or allow, their main diet is deer. The cat mounts a slow stalk to bring it within striking distance, then bounds forwards to strike the prey, killing it swiftly with one bite to the jugular or the spinal cord. These shy cats very rarely attack humans, and those reared in captivity can prove extremely docile. However, pumas can occasionally become confirmed stock killers, and when they do, the result can be savage: they will kill every sheep after entering a pen, or take large numbers of immature cattle in a single night. They were, therefore, traditionally classed as vermin and ruthlessly exterminated in farming and ranching areas, and a byproduct of this process was a population explosion among the puma's natural prey such as whitetail deer and elk.

Many hunters feel that the pursuit of mountain lion embodies the twin ideals of self-reliance and freedom from restriction, but puma are now classed as a game species in some states, and hunting is becoming controlled. A puma hunt can take days, or even weeks, and it involves the use of specially-trained dogs.

LYNX
Felis lynx canadensis

The lynx's alternative name of 'Canada lynx' may suggest that this forest-dweller is restricted to Canada, but in fact this cat is found not only from Alaska eastward through Canada to Newfoundland, but also down into northern New England, Wisconsin and Minnesota, the Northwest, and Utah, Wyoming and Colorado.

The elusive lynx is valued for its fur, and those that are taken are usually trapped, rather than shot. Extreme patience, in diffi-

PUMA *The puma or mountain lion is mainly nocturnal in its habits, and because of this and its secretive nature it is seldom seen during the day.*

PUMA

BOBCAT *The bobcat or bay lynx is about 30 inches long (head and body) with a 5-inch tail, and usually weighs between 25 and 30 pounds.*

cult conditions, is needed to secure a rifle shot, and the hostile terrain inhabited by this hardy species is a deterrent to all but the most determined hunter.

The male lynx averages about 40 inches in length, including the 4-inch tail, and it weighs about 25 pounds. The heaviest are no more than 40 pounds, contradicting a widespread belief that they consistently outweigh the bobcat. This confusion is generated by the lynx's long, strong legs, which make the animal seem larger than it really is. The large feet are padded, which aids mobility in deep snow – an advantage not enjoyed by the lynx's main competitor, the fox, in the search for the snowshoe hares which are a staple food for both species. In addition to snowshoe hares, the lynx will take small rodents and birds.

The lynx has an attractive coat of mottled, yellowish-brown fur, long ears with bold black tufts, two black throat tassels, a short tail with a black tip, and large amber eyes. The kittens are born in spring, two months after mating, with the normal litter being of two to four young. They stay with the mother until she mates again the following year.

BOBCAT
Felis lynx rufus

This well-distributed species, which is also known as the bay

BOBCAT TRACKS

PUMA TRACKS

BOBCAT

♂

lynx, ranges freely throughout wooded country, swamps and rocky regions in much of North America, especially the west. Although it is generally smaller than the lynx, the bobcat becomes larger toward the south of its range, and a specimen of 70 pounds has been recorded. On average, though, the male weighs around 25 to 35 pounds, with a body length of 30 inches plus a stumpy 5-inch tail.

The bobcat's coat is a rusty yellow-brown, with large dark spots on the body and the legs, dark stripes on the face and one single dark stripe along the

TRACKS *The footprint of the bobcat is about 2 inches long, which is about half the length of the print of the puma and twice the length of that of an average-size domestic cat.*

back. The ruffed throat is white, as is the spotted underbody. Unlike the tail of the lynx, which has a completely black tip, that of the bobcat is black only on the top of the tip.

Bobcats usually hunt at dawn and at dusk, catching birds and small mammals including hares, rabbits, young deer and even domestic animals. They will also take carrion, if it is fresh, which is something the lynx will not do. They often live in family groups consisting of both parents plus two to four young, the latter being born at any time of the year (most commonly in spring).

Hunters may sometimes flush a bobcat by chance, but prefer to use dogs to find the cat in its den, which is likely to be a cave, a hollow tree or a refuge hidden beneath tangled brush or roots.

BEARS

It was formerly thought that there were many different species of brown bear, spread throughout Europe, Asia and North America, but all are now classified as *Ursus arctos* or closely-related subspecies. Browns were once common in Europe, but land clearance and hunting have severely reduced their numbers. In North America, the brown bear is represented by two subspecies, the Kodiak or Alaskan brown bear (*Ursus arctos middendorffi*) and the grizzly bear (*Ursus arctos horribilis*). In addition, North America also has a large population of black bears (*Ursus americanus*).

EURASIAN BROWN BEAR
Ursus arctos

The brown bear is scarce and protected in most of its European range, but it is still hunted in Eastern Europe and Asia. Its habitat is wild, mountainous country with deciduous or coniferous forest. The omnivorous brown bear's diet varies with the seasons, and includes roots, tubers, berries, nuts, fungi, grain, honey, grubs, birds and their eggs, fish, small mammals, carrion and occasionally large animals such as deer and moose.

The brown bear, a heavily-built animal, has a wide head with a well-developed snout and small round ears, a thick neck, broad feet with five non-retractile claws, and a vestigial tail. It reaches 7 feet in length and a weight of 500 pounds in the remoter parts of its range, but is smaller where extensive hunting has taken place in the past. The shaggy coat has soft underfur, and its colour varies from almost black through dark brown to a pale creamy fawn.

A solitary creature, it hibernates or semihibernates in a den beneath rocks or tree roots.

ALASKAN BROWN BEAR
Ursus arctos middendorffi

The Alaskan brown bear was once thought to be a distinct species, called the Kodiak bear after the rugged island off the Alaskan coast where it was abundant. The idea that it was a separate species of bear perhaps occurred because of its enormous size: it is one of the world's largest terrestrial carnivores, with a shoulder height of 4 feet and a length of 9 feet or more, and it weighs in excess of 1400 pounds. Its range extends from British Columbia to Alaska, with the largest individuals being found on Kodiak Island and the Alaska Peninsula; its colour varies from almost black to blond.

Now recognized as a subspecies of brown bear – which it closely resembles in every aspect but size – the Alaskan brown is an impressive animal, and many hunters regard it as North America's ultimate big game challenge. Unfortunately, past hunting reduced the population of really large browns, especially on Kodiak, but steps are now being taken to ease pressure and allow more trophy animals to mature.

The Alaskan browns emerge from their winter dens when the spring thaw comes, grazing heavily on sedges, roots and grasses, but the most spectacular feeding takes place when they feast on Pacific salmon during the fishes' spring and autumn runs. The bears sometimes wade to the neck into brackish water where the fish are concentrated, though this isn't a very successful method. They do better when the salmon run upstream, and they find shallow spots from which to snatch passing fish. The prey is carried to the shore and the meat removed, with the head, bones and tail being left intact.

Access to remote bear-hunting areas is usually by float plane, with the subsequent hunt taking place by backpacking or by boat. Hunters stake out favoured feeding places during the salmon run, or locate suitable animals which are then stalked.

GRIZZLY BEAR
Ursus arctos horribilis

The grizzly bear is also larger than the Eurasian brown bear, although it doesn't reach the same massive size as the Alaskan brown. Even so, a fully grown male can be over 8½ feet long and weigh 600 pounds or more.

The grizzly has a distinctively humped back and fur that can vary between yellow-brown and grey-brown. There are many silver-tipped hairs along the back, which often has contrasting darker patches, and these hairs give the bear the grizzled appearance from which it gets its name. The muzzle and snout are pointed, and the ears are small and rounded.

Grizzlies frequently live in family groups with up to four cubs. They consume large amounts of vegetable matter, particularly in the spring, and they also take fish, birds, mammals to medium size and carrion. They follow the usual ursine pattern of eating heavily to build up fat reserves, which sustain them through the winter when they spend long periods of inactivity in their dens.

Their original distribution was along North America's western mountain chain from the Arctic to Mexico, but today their range extends mainly from Alaska to Oregon. However, persistent conservation work has resulted in a slow revival in numbers towards the south of this spread, for example in Yellowstone National Park. Even so, Yellowstone's 5½ million acres hold no more than 300, and the whole state of Montana has less than 1000 grizzlies.

They are still plentiful in Alaska, though, particularly in the southeast, the rugged land of peaks, glaciers, fjords and islands along the coastal strip from Skagway to Ketchikan. Strictly controlled hunting takes place there in spring and autumn, when hunters with local guides locate individual trophy animals and mount an upwind stalk that can frequently be prolonged – grizzlies are considered dangerous quarry.

BLACK BEAR
Ursus americanus

The black bear is the smallest, most numerous and least belligerent of North America's bears. Though concentrated in the forested regions of Canada and the northern USA, this furtive creature does not require wilderness conditions to survive. It is well distributed southward, and is huntable in half the USA's states. This versatility is confirmed by the fact that Alaska is the most populous black bear state, while some of the largest specimens are found in Florida's Everglades.

Despite the name, black bears range in colour from jet black to creamy-blond; in the Rockies, where their coloration is frequently light, they are known as 'cinnamon bears'. There are also two main subspecies, the blue-grey glacier bear (*Ursus americanus emmonsii*) of Alaska and the white Kermode bear (*Ursus americanus kermodei*) of British Columbia.

The size of the black bear varies from one area to another, and although the average adult weight is 250 pounds, they can grow to 400 pounds and a boar of 800 pounds has been recorded. Their shoulder height is up to 3 feet, and their overall length to 6 feet, but their long, thick fur makes them seem larger than they are. They lack the hump of grizzlies and Alaskan browns, and have short legs and stumpy tails. They have small

UPPER TEETH

BROWN BEAR TEETH

LOWER TEETH

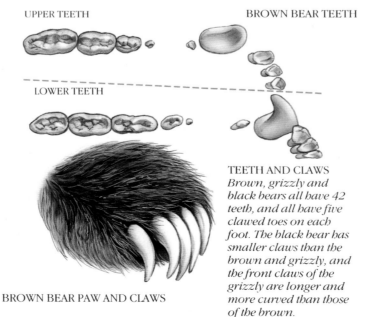

BROWN BEAR PAW AND CLAWS

TEETH AND CLAWS
Brown, grizzly and black bears all have 42 teeth, and all have five clawed toes on each foot. The black bear has smaller claws than the brown and grizzly, and the front claws of the grizzly are longer and more curved than those of the brown.

BLACK BEAR *The black bear is North America's most widely distributed and numerous bear.*

BLACK BEAR

TREE CLIMBING *The black bear is more skilled at climbing than the brown or grizzly, and is the only North American bear that regularly climbs trees.*

ALASKAN BROWN BEAR

ALASKAN BROWN BEAR *The Alaskan brown bear is larger than the grizzly and its range is much more restricted.*

eyes, well-rounded ears and narrow jaws, and the paws have five short, non-retractile claws.

Their habitat is diverse; coniferous forests are favoured, but black bears will live wherever they can find adequate cover, from swamp to high country. The diet is likewise varied, and although they are technically carnivores, they are actually omnivorous and consume anything edible they can find, including grubs, garbage, rodents, fish, nuts, berries, grass, crops, honey and fruit. Black bears are skilled climbers, and are the only North American bears that regularly climb trees as adults. They are usually nocturnal, especially when coexisting with man. They mate in June or July, but gestation is delayed until the autumn. The cubs, usually twins or triplets, are born in the winter den, and they remain with the mother for their first year or more.

BISON, MOOSE & CARIBOU

Only the most privileged hunters can expect a chance to shoot big game animals – past hunting and continuing loss of habitat have made sure of that. The bison, for example, was once among the most abundant of the large animals of Europe and North America, but was brought to the verge of extinction by excessive hunting and the spread of agriculture and other human activities. Today, the bison survives on reserves and ranches and its numbers are slowly increasing. The other large, hoofed wild mammals of North America and Europe are now largely confined to the inhospitable Arctic and sub-Arctic regions and the mountains and forests of the Far North. These include the caribou (the North American cousin of the European reindeer) and the moose (which is known in Europe as the elk), and the musk ox (*Ovibos moschatus*), now a rare and protected species whose range extends from northern Canada to western Greenland.

AMERICAN BISON
Bison bison

At its peak, the American bison's numbers probably exceeded 70 million, but wholesale slaughter in the 19th century almost led to its extinction. These peaceful ruminants once roamed the plains of central and western North America, migrating southwards from September onwards and often covering several hundred miles over well-trodden trails before returning to northern pastures the following spring. Now, they are confined to reserves such as the National Bison Range in Montana and Wood Buffalo Park in Alberta. A limited number of old bulls are culled annually, but bison are no longer hunted as regular quarry.

The bison (also and more popularly known as the buffalo) is a powerful animal with a massive, bearded head, humped shoulders and short, curved horns. The coat is thick on the head, neck, shoulders and forelegs, but thinner on the flanks. The coloration is dark brown,

darker on the head and throat. They reach a height of 5 or 6 feet and a weight of from 800 to 2000 pounds, and can live for up to 30 years; calves are born singly, after a gestation period of about 9 months.

The total population of wild bison is now about 30,000 but there is growing interest in farming bison for their meat, which is lean and can be excellent and surprisingly tender. There are now some 1200 bison ranches in the USA, with a total stock of about 100,000 head.

There is some dispute as to whether the European bison (*Bison bonasus*), also known as the wisent, is actually a different species or is the same as the American bison, but there can be no doubt that it has fared even worse than its American cousin. It is a forest rather than a grassland dweller, and it became extinct in the wild (in Lithuania and the Caucasus, its last remaining homes) in 1925. However, a new herd (which has thrived) was formed from zoo and park animals in Poland's Bialowieski Forest.

The European bison eats leaves, browsing on heathers and evergreen shrubs in winter, and rarely feeds on grass, unlike the American bison whose diet is predominantly grass. It is physically similar to the American bison, but the shaggy coat is shorter and the hump less pronounced. The sole remaining herd numbers only about 400, and it is strictly protected.

MOOSE (EUROPEAN ELK)
Alces alces

The North American moose and the European elk are essentially the same species, although the moose has four recognized subspecies. These imposing animals, which are the world's largest deer, are an altogether

BISON

♀

BISON *The bison is a relative of our domestic cattle, with which it can interbreed. Both sexes have horns, which are unbranched and are never shed, unlike the horns of deer.*

HAIR *The head of the bison appears more massive than it is,*

because of its thick, curly hair and long, shaggy beard.

more challenging quarry than the caribou: despite their huge bulk and clumsy antlers, they inhabit broken country, seek thick cover, flee at the first signs of danger, and swim and dive strongly.

The coat is grey-brown to near black, with lighter snout and legs. The muzzle is broad, long and downturned at the end, and ears are large and the neck is short. There is a pendulous flap of hairy skin at the throat, and a slight mane. The bulls have massive, flat antlers which are palmated and have many small tines.

In summer, the main foods of these herbivorous animals are aquatic plants and young shoots, and they spend much of their time browsing in shallow water and on marshy ground. In winter, they move to higher, forested areas where they feed on twigs, bark and saplings.

The range of the European elk extends from Scandinavia and Finland through northern Poland and across the northern Soviet Union. Their numbers are satisfactory, and their range is being extended in northern Russia.

In North America, the four subspecies of moose together amount to over 800,000 animals, with a legal annual harvest of 90,000. Eastern moose (*Alces alces americana*) are found from the northeast coast of the USA westwards to the Great Lakes region and northwards to the northern treeline of Canada. Northwestern moose (*A. a. andersoni*) are found through the upper Midwest, across Canada to the Pacific Coast and down into Washington, and Shiras moose (*A. a. shirasi*) inhabit the northern Rockies from Alberta to Wyoming. The Alaska-Yukon moose (*A. a. gigas*) is the largest subspecies, with specimens of nearly 2000 pounds on record.

CARIBOU
Rangifer tarandus caribou

The North American caribou and the European reindeer are slightly differing forms of the same species, sharing similar habitat, physical characteristics and behaviour patterns. The reindeer (*Rangifer tarandus tarandus*) is the deer of the European North and once roamed the summer tundra in countless numbers, with great herds migrating southwards to the Scandinavian and Siberian woodlands in winter. Today, wild reindeer are scarce; they still thrive, but only as the domesticated or semidomesticated servants of nomadic Lapps, giving food, clothing, warmth and transport.

Both the reindeer and the caribou are unusual among deer in that both males and females are antlered to assist survival in unfriendly conditions. The antlers rise from the upper skull, and in bulls the brow tines are well developed and descend over the face. The ends of the antlers are broad, and the animals use them like shovels to dig down through the snow to reach food beneath it. In addition, their broad, spreading hooves help them to move freely across snow or boggy summer ground.

There are three main races of caribou: the barren ground caribou, which is found on the tundra between Hudson Bay and Alaska; the larger and darker woodland or forest caribou which lives in the forests to the south of the tundra from Alaska to Newfoundland; and the mountain caribou of the northern Rockies, which can run to 700 pounds, notably in British Columbia. The numbers of all three have declined through loss of habitat or human interference with their traditional migration routes, to the point where only the barren ground variety remains plentiful.

Male caribou stand up to 48 inches tall at the shoulder and reach a length of about 70 inches, with the woodland caribou male weighing from 250 to 600 pounds and the barren ground bull from 250 to 400 pounds. The females are smaller, weighing from 150 to 350 pounds (woodland) or 150 to 250 pounds (barren ground). The coat of the woodland caribou is a dark chocolate-brown, with a lighter underbody and white on the neck, rump and tail. The barren ground caribou is paler, and at the northern extremes of its range it may be almost white in colour.

Grasses, leaves, mosses and lichens form the bulk of the diet, and barren ground caribou migrate in search of food. They spend the short summer on the tundra, but when the first snowstorms break they migrate southwards, sometimes for hundreds of miles, before overwintering in the forest fringes.

MOOSE *A bull moose can stand 6 feet at the shoulder, and weigh over 1000 pounds. Females weigh 600 to 800 pounds.*
CARIBOU *The male caribou, shown here in scale with the moose, can weigh from 250 to 700 pounds.*

MOOSE

CARIBOU

RED DEER & WAPITI

The red deer and the wapiti, along with the much smaller sika, are all closely-related species, as might be inferred from the similarities in their general appearance and the configuration of their antlers. The wapiti or North American elk is the giant of the trio, and is a coveted sporting species for American and Canadian deer hunters. The wapiti is usually hunted with rifles, as is the red deer, although there is an ancient European tradition – dating from before the Middle Ages – of hunting red deer stags with hounds. This tradition persists in France and Belgium, and also in the English counties of Devon and Somerset, but it has otherwise died out and been replaced by shooting with medium-calibre rifles, usually according to a predetermined culling plan.

RED DEER
Cervus elephas

The red deer is the largest wild land mammal in Britain and Ireland, where it reaches the most westerly limits of its wide range which extends from western China across most of temperate Asia and Europe and parts of North Africa.

The size and weight of adults varies with habitat and available food, but a mature woodland stag may be as much as 55 inches at the shoulder, while a hind on the hill in Scotland may be as little as 40 inches. Body weights are similarly variable, and the live weight of males and females may be as low as 175 pounds and 125 pounds for hill deer, and up to 440 pounds and 270 pounds respectively for woodland stags and hinds.

In summer, the red deer's coat is a darkish red-brown with a cream-coloured rump, and the coat normally has no spotting. Both sexes have a short tail, about 6 inches long. Mature stags develop a shaggy, mane-like growth around the neck and withers prior to the rut, which takes place in late September and in October. Both sexes have a rough and thick dark greyish-brown coat in winter. The young or calf of the red deer is born with a light brown coat heavily spotted with creamy-white markings, which fade as it matures.

A red deer stag's antlers are rounded in section, with multiple points and a generally branching configuration. Antlers are shed annually in spring, with the mature stags shedding first. Growth in velvet takes place during the summer and antlers will be hard and clean by September. The size, length, weight and number of points on the antlers are not necessarily a reliable indictaion of age, and have more to do with the local availability of suitably calcium-rich foods.

Like fallow, red deer are herd animals, living in separate stag and hind herds through most of the year. The hinds are usually accompanied by their calves and also the yearlings, and woodland red deer normally form smaller herds than do those which live on the open hills and moorland.

Though normally silent, hinds

WAPITI *The wapiti is found both in woodland and on open ground, feeding on bark, twigs, herbs and grasses and also raiding vegetable and grain crops.*

call to their calves with a bovine lowing, and there is also a distinctive bellowing when hinds are calving. When alarmed, red deer may give an intermittent coughing bark, but their most familiar call is the roaring of the stags in the rut, which is a long, cattle-like bellowing.

Red deer feed by browsing on the twigs, shoots and leaves of a wide variety of trees and shrubs, and will also graze on grasses, and on heather in Scottish mountain habitats. Deer living close to arable land will frequently raid the growing crops, especially root crops such as turnips and potatoes.

In western, central and southern Europe, the red deer occupies an ecological niche similar to that of the wapiti in North America. Typically a woodland species, the red deer never attains the great body weights and size of the wapiti but it is nevertheless a massive animal. Some of the heaviest stags and the finest antlers have come from the unusually large strains of woodland red deer found in Hungary, Poland, Yugoslavia, the Carpathian Mountains of Czechoslovakia and Romania, and parts of Spain.

WAPITI (AMERICAN ELK)
Cervus elephas canadensis

The wapiti is a large North American relative of the European red deer, with which it can interbreed. Confusingly, it is often referred to in North America as an elk, although this name should properly be reserved for

RED DEER *The red deer is one of Europe's most prized game species.*

RED DEER

♀

♂

first year

third year

ANTLER DEVELOPMENT
In its first year, the antlers of a stag develop from the pedicles into simple spikes. These are shed and regrown in the second year, but when they regrow in the third year, they are branched.

the European moose (*Alces alces*). It is the second largest deer in the world, inferior in size only to the moose, and a mature male or bull may stand 5 feet or more at the shoulder and

weigh over 1000 pounds live weight. The females are smaller, typically weighing 600 to 700 pounds.

The wapiti's North American range was formerly very extensive, from the Pacific seaboard eastwards to the Atlantic states, and from Georgia and Mexico up to northern Canada. Overexploitation has greatly reduced this, but recent conservation and reintroduction measures now mean that wapiti are present in over twenty states of the USA, as well as in some parts of Canada.

There are four known subspecies of wapiti, and their habits and life cycle are similar to those of red deer. Stags, distinguished by their large, branching and multitined antlers, tend to live in separate bachelor herds, while females with calves and yearlings form their own herds.

Wapiti are polygamous, like red deer, and rutting begins in September and peaks in early October. A hind will normally

give birth to one calf a year, usually in June. Winter mortality may be high if the weather is severe, and wapiti are annually forced to leave their high summer pastures for lower wintering grounds.

The calls of wapiti are similar to those of red deer, with a long, drawn-out bugling note which hunters imitate, vocally and with a variety of artificial calls, to attract wapiti during the autumn hunting season.

Wapiti have been introduced to New Zealand and to some deer parks in Britain and Ireland, where they have interbred freely with red deer and produced fertile offspring. These offspring usually display evidence of their wapiti blood by their large size and, in the case of the males, by the weight and wapiti-like configuration of the top tines of their antlers. These traces of wapiti may persist through many subsequent generations of breeding back with pure red deer.

WHITETAIL DEER

Every year, America's millions of deer hunters eagerly await the open season and dream optimistically of that ever-elusive big buck. However, despite their abundance in most parts of the USA, deer are no easy quarry, and many disappointed hunters return empty-handed from the woods. Perhaps that is predictable, because for most the quarry will have been the whitetail deer which, although it is North America's most common cloven-hoofed animal, is one of the most difficult to hunt. Not only does it possess a keen sense of smell and exceptional hearing, but recent research has conclusively dispelled the myth that this animal suffers from poor vision. Indeed, it has now been estimated that a whitetail can register the flicker of a human eyelid at a distance of 20 yards, and that they have night vision up to five times better than a human's, seeing as well by moonlight as we do on a dull day. On top of all that, they may not, after all, be colour-blind, which is bad news for hunters who are into self-preservation through wearing red or blaze orange.

WHITETAIL DEER
Odocoileus virginianus

As a result of firm management and the general decline of natural predators, there are more whitetails today than at any time during the last 300 years. The numbers are impressive: for example, the annual harvest in Pennsylvania alone runs to 150,000 bucks, with the same quantity again of antlerless deer taken, while New York State regularly produces more than 175,000 animals. Texas has a population in excess of 4 million whitetails, living 100 to the square mile in some parts of the state; many of these are small, but there are some exceptional animals on well-managed hunting ranches where quality is more important than quantity.

The whitetail deer is widely distributed in the lower half of North America, from southern Canada down through the USA, with related forms in Central and South America. Whitetails are generally bigger towards the north of this range, where there are large subspecies such as the Dakota whitetail (*Odocoileus virginianus dacotensis*) and the northern woodland whitetail (*O. v. borealis*) which regularly feature in the record books, while the smallest members of the clan are the little key deer (*O. v. clavium*) of the Florida Keys, which weigh only 50 pounds or less. In all, there are no less than 39 subspecies of whitetail.

The whitetail is classed as a medium-sized deer, and a large buck will stand up to 45 inches at the shoulder, have a length of around 80 inches plus a 12-inch tail, and weigh up to 400 pounds. The whitetail's coat changes in colour from a reddish-brown in summer to a grey-brown in winter, and the rump and the underside of the tail are white.

Only the bucks have antlers, and these are relatively short: 5 or 6 equally-spaced points are usual, although 10- or 12-pointers are not uncommon in areas where bucks are allowed to mature fully, and the antler spread can exceed 30 inches. It takes about 4½ years for a male to reach full maturity, but few survive as long as this where hunting pressure is heavy. Most are taken in their second or third years. In any event, life expectancy is usually no longer than 8 to 10 years, although some venerable beasts are known to have reached 20 years of age. Young males with simple, unbranched 'spike' antlers are common, but this usually reflects poor nutrition rather than their tender age: animals that mature to trophy class will invariably manifest small points on their first-year antlers.

In summer and autumn, whitetail deer are solitary or live in small groups (doe plus fawns), but they will often come together into gatherings of 25 or more when facing severe winter weather conditions. Whitetails are skilled at concealment, and can seem to vanish without trace into the lightest of cover. As a result, they can exist happily in close proximity to man, as well as occupying more natural forest or wilderness habitats. When frightened, a whitetail will usually – but not always – erect its distinctive large tail as it flees, showing the white underside of its tail and its white rump. This sight resembles nothing so much as a rapidly-waving white flag.

While it may make a loud, whistling snort when disturbed by the sight, sound or smell of possible danger, and occasionally emit a shrill whistling sound at night, the whitetail is normally a silent creature. As exceptions to this rule, bucks will grunt during the rut and does may call to their young with a soft munching noise, the young replying with a quiet bleating. Badly wounded animals will bleat piteously.

A wandering browser, the whitetail feeds steadily on twigs, buds, fruit, fungi and fresh grasses and herbs. It looks up frequently while it feeds, and is always on the alert. It prefers to feed at night and in the half-light of dawn, and to lie up during the day, although it will sometimes emerge to feed or simply to move from one place to another.

The breeding season is from November to February, sometimes sooner in areas with mild climates, and the rut frequently produces dramatic and prolonged battles between rival bucks, which sometimes end in the death of the loser. Small individual territories are rigidly defined and fiercely guarded, with mature males marking their boundaries with glandular secretions on trees. They also soak chosen patches of earth with urine, a practice which serves the dual purpose of warning off competing bucks and attracting does.

Gestation takes from 196 to 202 days, and a doe may give birth to up to four young, although two or three is more common. The fawns are reddish-brown and spotted with white for the first four months of life, by which time they will have been weaned and become self-sufficient feeders. The fawns may run with their mother for up to a year.

Whitetail deer have been successfully introduced into New Zealand and Finland and into

WHITETAIL DEER *When it's alarmed, the whitetail raises its tail as a warning signal, and it can run at up to 40 mph.*

COUES DEER *The little Coues deer (O.v.couesi) is a subspecies of whitetail which occurs in the deserts and mountains of the Southwest.*

COUES DEER

Czechoslovakia, where there is a herd of some 200 animals which are descended from two males and four females brought from the USA in 1852. These stocking ventures underline the whitetail's popularity as a game species, despite its innate caution.

One well-used hunting technique involves the building of a high seat – or just getting comfortable – in a tree overlooking a likely crossing point or feeding area, the hunter remaining in this vantage point until a whitetail strays within range. Another method is to drive the deer through cover, sometimes (in the Southeast) using hounds, toward waiting hunters.

During the rut, some hunters (especially in Texas and the Southwest) lure bucks toward them by rattling a pair of antlers together, mimicking the sound of two bucks fighting over territory or does. Any curious buck which comes to investigate the noise can be picked off.

Stalking is also frequently attempted, after a suitable animal has been sighted from a distance with binoculars or a sighting scope, but stalking whitetails is very difficult because of their great alertness. Perhaps the most popular method of all is still hunting, which involves moving through the woods – very slowly, with infinite patience and stealth – before standing motionless in a chosen stand for up to ten minutes. By this means, the hunter hopes to see a whitetail and get a shot off before spooking the animal; here, the one rule is that, man or deer, the first to move will be spotted.

WHITETAIL DEER

ROE DEER & FALLOW DEER

Roe deer and fallow deer, both primarily woodland deer, are found in most countries from Britain to western and southwestern Asia. Fallow have also been introduced into New Zealand and into the USA, where they are kept on many private hunting grounds and wild herds have become established in Kentucky and other southeastern states. The roe's sporting status declined in the 14th century and the species' range and distribution in Britain shrank seriously. It became extinct in England and Wales, surviving only in Scotland until introductions from France and Germany re-established it in southern England from where it has since spread rapidly.

ROE DEER
Capreolus capreolus

In appearance and behaviour, the roe deer is the original 'Bambi'. A small deer, which stands only 26 to 28 inches high and weighs abut the same as a labrador dog, the roe deer is widespread throughout Britain and other temperate parts of Europe and Asia, although it is absent from Ireland. Its appearance is fine-boned and delicate, standing upright on slender legs and having a compact body, a slim neck which thickens with age, and a delicate head with upright ears.

Young roe deer, known as kids, are born in May and twins are normal. Roe have a long gestation period, with the rut taking place in late July and early August but the growing foetus not developing much before January or February, owing to delayed implantation. In the first few months of its life, the roe kid is dappled with irregular white spots against a brownish coat, which gives it excellent camouflage as it lies motionless in the variegated light and shade of summer woodlands. By September, this spotting will have faded.

The adult males (bucks) shed their antlers in late autumn and regrow them during the winter months, which distinguishes them from other British and European deer. A mature roebuck in late spring and summer will usually display a symmetrical head of six points, three on each antler, although individuals with up to ten points have been recorded. Antler coloration becomes richer and darker as the buck burnishes its antlers to strip off the velvet, and rubbing the antlers on coniferous saplings gives them a much darker colour than does rubbing them on deciduous species.

In continental Europe, and increasingly in Britain, the roe is a highly-prized sporting species. Roe antlers make attractive and conveniently small trophies, and a six-pointer adult buck which has enjoyed good feeding during the winter months may have antlers measuring up to 11 or 12 inches in legth, with long points and thick beams roughened by the 'pearling' characteristic of this species.

In summer, the roe has a bright foxy-red coat with a pale creamy underside, and the colouring is uniform and unbroken by spotting. There is a lighter, creamy-yellow patch on the rump, while the nose is black and glistening. In winter, roe grow a much thicker, dark brown pelage, which is sometimes greyish in colour. The hairs on the rump, which can be flared out if the animal is excited or frightened, become pure white in winter, and there may also be one or two white patches on the throat. Although the roe deer has no visible tail, females in winter pelage have a distinct tuft or 'tush' of hair on the rump, which helps to distinguish them from antlerless males.

Although roe are essentially a woodland deer, preferring a forest habitat broken up with open patches, they are also found on arable farmland or open ground close to woods, where they live in thick hedgerows and small copses.

Roe feed by browsing on the leaves, shoots and twigs of a wide range of trees and shrubs. They will also graze on grass, cereals and other ground herbage, and on farmland will occasionally join with cattle feeding on silage or hay. They seem to have a strong aversion to sheep, however, and will keep well away from them.

ROE DEER

♂

♀

ROE DEER *Roe deer live alone or in small family groups, and unlike fallow deer or red deer they are not a herding species.*

FALLOW DEER

♂

♀

FALLOW DEER *The male fallow is unique among the British deer in having palmated antlers. These are shed and regrown each spring.*

April. Fallow rut in October and the young, known as fawns, are born the following June. Does rarely produce more than one fawn each year.

Although not as vocal as roe deer, fallow also call to each other. The does and fawns utter high calls, and does may give deep grunts when alarmed, while adult rutting bucks give a characteristic series of belching or groaning calls. The fallow buck's palmated antlers should help to avoid misidentification with red deer or sika, and the latter also has prominent pale-coloured hock glands and a distinctly white tail, while the fallow's tail is usually dark brown or black.

Fallow are a familiar ornamental, parkland deer, but their natural habitat is mixed or deciduous woodland broken up by open pasture land or arable farmland. Bucks and does tend to live in separate herds, only coming together in the autumn rutting season. They are much less territorial than roe, and adult bucks in particular may wander widely during the year.

Both fallow and roe deer will cause considerable damage to trees and arable crops if thoughtful land management is not allied to intelligent culling. The role of the informed woodland stalker, professional or amateur, has become increasingly important in reconciling the needs of agriculture and silviculture with the maintenance of healthy, well-balanced populations of wild deer.

FALLOW DEER
Cervus dama

Fallow deer probably originated in Asia Minor, and today they are widespread from there westwards across northern Africa and western Europe. Many of the European populations, including those in Britain and Ireland, can be traced back to deliberate introductions in Roman and medieval times.

Fallow are much bigger than roe deer, and a mature buck will stand about 36 inches at the shoulder, which is some 2 or three inches taller than a doe; a big fallow buck can weigh up to 200 pounds.

Fallow come in a wide range of colours, ranging from a creamy white to almost black, but the commonest is a chestnut brown flecked with white spots in summer, which darkens to a uniform brown in winter. Other fallow, known as menil, have particularly distinct spots in summer and retain some of these during the winter, while the melanistic variety is a very dark brown all year round. The white fallow, which is not an albino strain, is usually a pale creamy white, but pure white individuals also occur.

Uniquely among deer in the British Isles, mature fallow bucks have palmated antlers, the main beam rising above prominent brow points and spreading out in a broad, flat formation in the upper part. The antlers are grown during the spring and summer months and will be in velvet until August, after which the bucks are in hard antler throughout the winter months before shedding them again in

COLOUR VARIATIONS *Fallow deer colour variations include the dark (rear), white (centre) and menil (front) forms.*

CHINESE WATER DEER, MUNTJAC &

Originating in Asia, the muntjac, sika and Chinese water deer have established thriving feral populations after being introduced into Britain and continental Europe. The Indian muntjac or 'jungle sheep' (*Muntiacus muntjac*) was introduced to Woburn Abbey in Bedfordshire late last century, but that population was shot out after a few years and replaced by the smaller Reeves' muntjac (*Muntiacus reevesii*). This deer is now widespread throughout central and southern England, with isolated populations in other places, and may be England's most numerous deer. The sika deer which were introduced into the British Isles and western Europe in Victorian times were brought from Japan, Formosa (Taiwan) and Manchuria (northeast China). Introduction was widespread in southern England, Scotland and Ireland, and feral populations are now found in all these areas, but populations of the third feral species of Asian deer, the Chinese water deer, are much more localized. Chinese water deer, which are natives of southern China, Korea and Southeast Asia, were brought to Britain and introduced into private collections and zoos around the turn of the century. Escapes inevitably occurred, and feral populations became established in many parts of eastern England.

CHINESE WATER DEER
Hydropotes inermis

The little Chinese water deer rarely exceeds 20 inches in height at the shoulder; a buck may weigh 30 to 40 pounds, and a good average weight for a doe is 35 pounds.

These deer are attractively coloured with a uniform reddish-brown coat in summer, which darkens in winter to a duller greyish-brown, and the hair appears coarser than that of the roe or the muntjac. The pelage of young fawns is dark brown, with rows of cream-coloured spots which fade quickly as the youngster develops. Close examination of dead or captive specimens will reveal the presence of a very short tail, which is not usually visible under normal field conditions.

Uniquely among the six species of deer present in the wild in Britain, Chinese water deer males do not have antlers, but the mature bucks have long, slightly curved tusks in the upper jaw, which protrude below the lips and may be almost 3 inches long. The females also have tusks, but these are smaller, shorter and less obvious.

Because of their small size, Chinese water deer are unlikely to be confused with other species of deer, with the possible exception of the muntjac. However, they have a more leggy and less piglike posture than the muntjac, and their long hind legs give them a rather forward-sloping appearance when seen from the side. In addition, they lack the prominent tail and white tail patch of the muntjac.

In their native parts of Asia, Chinese water deer inhabit wet grasslands and the reedy margins of rivers and other swampy areas. In Great Britain, they have adapted readily to a similar sort of habitat, especially in unreclaimed areas of the eastern Fenlands, but they are also present in dry mixed woodlands and copses adjoining arable farmland.

Chinese water deer feed primarily by grazing on many species of herbage, including grasses, growing cereal crops and other shoots. They will also eat root vegetables, including swede, sugarbeet and potatoes, and they often browse, especially in the winter months when other food may be limited.

These deer tend to be solitary, with adult males and females occupying fixed home ranges and the males showing particular territorial behaviour at rutting time, in December. Bucks proclaim their territories by some barking, and also by scent marking with urine and with secretions from glands below the eyes.

Gestation lasts about six months, and fawns are born in June and July. Each doe gives birth to two or three fawns at one time, and births of five or six have been recorded, but the survival prospects for these larger multiple births are much reduced. The fawns grow rapidly, and are mature at seven or eight months.

MUNTJAC
Muntiacus reevesii

Muntjac are piglike in appearance, with a humpbacked and rather hunched posture which is accentuated by the shortness of their legs. An adult, buck or doe, will stand 18 inches at the shoulder and may weigh up to 35 pounds.

The spotting on the coats of young fawns disappears quickly as they grow, and the muntjac's summer coat is a bright, unspotted foxy-red. Because of this colouring and its short stature, it is easy in summer to mistake a muntjac for a fox. In winter, though, this confusion is less

CHINESE WATER DEER *The male Chinese water deer is antlerless, but has a pair of tusklike teeth protruding from its upper jaw.*

♂

likely because then the muntjac's coat becomes a rich grey-brown.

The muntjac has prominent ears and a relatively long tail, which it carries upright when alarmed, rather as a goat does. Both bucks and does have a prominent V-shaped pattern of ridging on the face, which in the case of bucks is extended into long pedicles with short antlers, which are rarely more than two simple spikes only 6 inches long or less.

The time of shedding antlers varies from one individual to another, as does the breeding season. Unlike the indigenous deer of temperate regions, muntjac have no regular breeding cycle, and females will produce a single fawn approximately every seven months, with mating taking place again within a week or two of giving birth. Consequently, it is difficult to define a desirable closed season

MUNTJAC ANTLERS *The short antlers of the muntjac buck are usually shed in May or June, but the time of shedding can vary greatly from one individual to another. The doe lacks the antlers and prominent, fanglike teeth of the buck, and has a dark, triangular patch on her forehead.*

MUNTJAC

SIKA

CHINESE WATER DEER

SIKA

SIKA A small relative of the Eurasian red deer and the American elk, the sika stands about 3 feet tall at the shoulder.

MUNTJAC The little, piglike muntjac stands some 18 inches high at the shoulder and weighs up to 35 pounds.

♂

♂

MUNTJAC

for muntjac does, and there is no official closed season for them in Britain.

Muntjac are territorial and live in small family groups, rather like roe deer. They bark readily and for long periods when disturbed, or when other deer intrude upon their territories, and because of this they are also known as barking deer. They make territorial marks with their antlers and with their prominent, fanglike teeth, and bucks and does both have large scent glands below the eyes (suborbital glands) which also play a part in territorial marking.

Muntjac are unlikely to be mistaken for any other species of deer, except perhaps the Chinese water deer, but even then their roach-backed, piglike stance and posture, short legs and tusklike teeth give them a quite different appearance.

In its natural Asian range, the

muntjac lives in tropical forests and its twenty subspecies are distributed throughout India and east to China and Taiwan.

SIKA
Cervus nippon

Sika are closely related to red deer, with which they can interbreed to produce fertile hybrids. The various subspecies of sika which occur in eastern Asia represent an Asian form of red deer, while wapiti (American elk) constitute an extremely large form of the same family of deer at the extreme western edge of its range, in North America.

Sika are smaller than red deer, and an adult may stand 32 to 36 inches at the shoulder, which is similar to the size of a fallow deer. Live weights of adults vary according to local conditions of feeding and habitat, but a mature stag may weigh

up to 175 pounds, with a hind weighing 80 to 95 pounds.

In summer, sika are a bright brownish-red with slightly indistinct creamy spots. Both sexes have a bright white rump area, somewhat heart-shaped, which can be flared out when the individual is alarmed. There is a short tail, and the rump and tail area have a dark brownish-black border. In winter, sika lose their summer spotting and assume a dark greyish-brown pelage, the stags inclining to blackness with a thick, mufflike mane.

The antlers are similar to those of the red deer, but rarely exceed eight points in a mature stag. They are shed in spring and grow throughout the summer, being clean by September prior to the rutting season in October.

During the rut, sika stags give a loud and distinctive whistling call, quite unlike that of any

other British or European deer. It is rare for sika hinds to produce more than one calf, and this is usually born in June.

Sika are found in deciduous and mixed woodlands, and are widespread in the damp coniferous forests typical of many parts of northern Europe, and in southern, northern and western Britain and in Ireland. They will occasionally live on open moorland, like hill red deer, and they feed principally by grazing, with some browsing on twigs, leaves and shoots. Sika tend to form separate groups of stags, and hinds with calves and yearlings.

They can be distinguished from fallow deer by the stags' round antlers, and from both fallow and red by the distinctive V-shaped ridging of the facial bones, which gives them a somewhat disgruntled appearance. They are much larger than the roe, the muntjac or the Chinese water deer.

MULE DEER, BLACKTAIL DEER & PRONGHORN

For reasons of economy, convenience or lack of time, most deer hunters in the USA concentrate their activity in hunting areas which may be reached with relative ease. This means that the ubiquitous whitetail deer inevitably makes up a high percentage of North America's annual deer harvest. However, although the whitetail is by no means an easy animal to hunt, those hunters seeking a challenge greater than that offered by lowland deer can find it in the mule deer and the pronghorn, animals that occupy more demanding terrain than that favoured by the whitetail.

MULE DEER
Odocoileus hemionus

The mule deer, although closely related to the whitetail, lives on more broken ground and at higher altitudes, or in arid desert regions. The species is abundant, being widely distributed from Mexico up through the western USA to the north of British Columbia, and thriving as natural predators such as the puma have declined. In some areas they even reach a density of one animal per ten acres, a stock level far too high to permit survival for all in harsh winters when food becomes scarce.

Despite their abundance, however, hunting top-quality mule deer can still be a considerable undertaking. The best mule deer country is often diffi-cult to reach, by horse or on foot, and it may be necessary for the hunter to remain there for some time if a trophy-class animal is the target. Finding and stalking a good buck on open ground isn't always easy, and after a successful hunt, rack and meat may have to be back-packed out over a long distance. The prize can be very worth-while, though – the sturdy antlers of mule deer bucks usual-ly have ten points on the main beam, with fork-shaped branching, and double-forking can produce spectacular multipointed antlers with up to fifty points.

A big buck can reach 400 pounds in weight, standing 42 inches at the shoulder, though the average is nearer 200 pounds. The length of the head and body is about 60 inches, and the 8-inch white tail has a dis-tinctive black tip; the does are about two-thirds the size of the bucks. The mule deer's coat is generally tawny, being a reddish or yellowish-brown in summer, with a whitish rump, head, inner ears and underbody. In winter, the coat grows longer and takes on a blue-grey tinge.

Mule deer often move from high ground at the end of sum-mer, congregating in large groups and using regular migra-tion routes down the mountain-side – to the obvious advantage of hunters who have studied their habits. Bucks gather small harems for the rut, which occurs from October to December, and the one to three (usually two) spotted young are born after a gestation period of 180 to 210 days. After wintering in the woodland or brush of sheltered valleys where there is a plentiful supply of food – grass and other herbage, twigs and evergreen foliage – the mule deer return to higher ground when spring breaks.

They are at their most active in the early morning and the late evening, and will also feed

MULE DEER

♂

♂

MULE DEER *The mule deer is widely distributed through the west of North America, but the largest individuals are to be found in the Rockies.*

BLACKTAIL DEER *The blacktail of the Pacific coast is a subspecies of mule deer, although it was once thought to be a separate species.*

BLACKTAIL DEER

on moonlit nights. They can be incautious in their habits, but in areas where hunting pressure is high they have become wary, skilfully seeking the cover of thick brush, trees, hidden draws or gullies. The bucks are particularly cunning, often not showing themselves at all until after the season has closed.

BLACKTAIL DEER
Odocoileus hemionus columbianus

The blacktail deer is today classified as a subspecies of mule deer, but it was formerly considered to be a separate species (*Odocoileus columbianus*). Its range is restricted to the ocean side of the mountains in the wetter regions of the Pacific coast, from Alaska down through British Columbia to California. Some authorities divide the blacktail into two races, the Columbian blacktail (*Odocoileus hemionus columbianus*), occurring from California north to Vancouver Island, and the sitka blacktail (*O. h. sitkensis*) which occurs from British Columbia to Alaska.

The blacktail deer – a graceful animal which shares with the mule deer its characteristic habit of 'stotting', bounding through the air for considerable distances before landing stiff-legged on all four feet – is

HORNS *The pronghorn has true horns, not antlers. The horns (present on both sexes) have bone cores, covered by sheaths of compressed hair which are shed annually.*

PRONGHORN BUCK

similar to the mule deer in appearance, behaviour and diet, but is slightly smaller. The coat is reddish-yellow in summer, becoming brownish-grey mottled with black in winter. The chin, the upper throat and the underside of the tail are white; the tail itself is rather bushy, like that of a whitetail but smaller, and its black upper part is what gives the deer its name.

The antlers resemble those of the mule deer, with an upper fork, although this fork is occasionally absent on some individuals. Blacktails are not nearly as plentiful as mule deer, and tend to occupy territory that is even more remote, so consequently they do not figure large in the yearly harvest returns.

PRONGHORN
Antilocapra americana

The pronghorn, North America's oldest hoofed game animal, is the only member of the Antilocapridae family. It is found only in North America, and after decades of arguing over whether it is a deer, an antelope or a goat, zoologists finally decided that the pronghorn isn't closely related to any of them and put it in a family of its own.

Once present in countless millions on the prairies between the Rocky Mountains and the Missouri, the pronghorn had been hunted to the verge of extinction by the end of the 19th century. Happily, numbers have recovered to the point where strictly-controlled hunting can be allowed, and its present range extends roughly from

PRONGHORN *The pronghorn is a species unique to North America and the only member of the Antilocapridae family. It usually lives in small groups, on the prairies and sagebrush plains of the West.*

PRONGHORN

southern Saskatchewan to western Texas, southern California and northern Mexico.

The pronghorn stands some 36 inches tall at the shoulder and can weigh up to 130 pounds. The length of the head and body is about 55 inches, but the tail is only three or four inches long. The overall colour is light tan, with a darker face and a slightly maned neck, prominent white patches on the throat and cheeks, and white underparts, flanks and rump. The horns, which are present in does as well as bucks, curve outward from the head, recurving in at the tips. The single branch, snag or eponymous prong projects forward about halfway up the stem, and the outer sheaths of the horns are shed annually.

During the rut, which occurs from August to October, the bucks maintain modest harems of three or four does. The young, usually twins, are born in April or May in the south, but often not until June in the north. The mother leaves her young alone during the first weeks of their lives, returning only to clean or suckle them.

Like the mule deer, the pronghorn is at its most active in the morning and in the evening. Its favourite food is sagebrush, but it browses on a variety of plants including weeds and grass.

The pronghorn has an acute sense of smell, and can pick up the scent of predators (including hunters) over great distances if the wind is in its favour. When it does so, it spreads its white posterior hairs into a stiff fan and gives off a strong odour which alerts any other pronghorns in the area.

TECHNIQUES

As the Game Species section of this book shows, the modern sporting shooter has a wide and varied range of gamebirds, waterfowl and other birds to choose from, in addition to mammals varying in size from rabbits and hares to heavy mountain sheep and massive deer. So it is hardly surprising to learn that the sporting pursuit of these creatures involves a variety of different techniques.

Just to add some additional variety, and to increase the challenging range of skills which the all-round sportsman has to try and master, many sporting species can be hunted in more than one way. If we think of just two groups of sporting animals – deer and waterfowl – there are, in general terms, at least two proven, effective and exciting ways of going about your hunting. The deer hunter's high seat and the wildfowler's hide or blind mean that, if these places of concealment have been properly sited, the shooter can lie in wait to intercept deer moving about within their accustomed area, or to shoot waterfowl flying on known flight-lines or coming in to strategically positioned decoys. But a more active pursuit, and under some circumstances a more effective one, is for the shooter to be on the move. For the deer hunter this entails stalking across open ground or moving stealthily through woodlands in a technique known as still-hunting, while many a good bag of waterfowl has been made by jump-shooting, where the birds are walked up from flooded drains, flashes of water and other places in marshland and similar habitat. All the widely used modern shooting techniques can provide excellent sport, and many are not easy to master fully. None is in any sense better or more sporting than the others; each has its role to play, depending upon the circumstances. Sporting shooting is a pragmatic affair in which the individual sportsman, or perhaps a team of sportsmen working in unison, must adopt the tactics and techniques best suited to the expected quarry, the habitat, the physical capabilities and the standard of marksmanship of the individual or the group, and also individual preferences. We must never forget this last point, for sport is meant to be enjoyable! At its best, sporting shooting will always be exciting and productive, whatever technique or approach is used, but experience is the sportsman's best guide in helping him make his choice.

It is often said, with some justification, that a good rifle shot is seldom an outstanding performer with a shotgun, and that accuracy with a handgun calls for a third and very different type of skill and approach. In fact, experience, practice and a degree of natural aptitude can make one individual quite proficient at all three types of shooting. Nevertheless, there are important fundamental differences in using three such different types of sporting firearm. The modern single-barrelled rifle has been developed to a high pitch of technical perfection, enabling the firer to place a bullet with extraordinary accuracy at ranges of many hundreds of yards. This requires great care, deliberation and steadiness in taking aim, firing and 'following through' after the shot. Such careful steadiness has no place in sporting shotgun shooting, where the essence of good marksmanship is to be found in the confident, deft and fluent movement of the gun as it comes to the shoulder and is swung onto and through the line of a moving target. The handgun, when used as a sporting firearm, is brought into play under conditions which are very different from the controlled, stable environment of the practice range, and a capable performer has to learn to place his shot accurately under field conditions, always mindful of the handgun's strict limitations of accurate range.

Like everything in life which is challenging and worthwhile, mastering the techniques of sporting shooting and applying them under practical conditions cannot be achieved overnight. Practice makes perfect, in shooting as in most other skilled activities. Regular practice, on the rifle range, on the handgun range and with clay pigeons, should be a regular part of every sporting shooter's activities. The beginner should acquire all his basic training on the range or the sporting clays layout before tackling live quarry, while even the most experienced sportsman can benefit from an hour or two's practice or tuition, especially before a new season begins and when our guns may have lain unused for several months. The range and the clay shooting ground are also important aids to maintaining the standard of your shooting, and helping to diagnose and cure problems with individual firearms or ammunition. In the middle of a busy sporting season you may suddenly find you are having unaccountable misses with your deer rifle, and an hour's firing on the range often serves to show where the problem lies, perhaps indicating that the action or barrel should be re-bedded, or that the gun requires nothing more serious than a simple re-zeroing of a scope sight which has received a knock. The shotgun shooter can have his problems too, and you may suddenly find you are missing straightforward shots which have hitherto presented you with no problems at all. A round of sporting clays, with a competent shooting coach watching you, should quickly reveal what has gone wrong.

Good marksmanship, whatever the gun you use, is a useful skill and a satisfying activity. When it is combined with the skill, sportsmanship and fieldcraft which the pursuit of wild and elusive quarry demands, the combinations of skills involved come together in a uniquely pleasing and gratifying way. Practice, and the advice and tuition of experienced fellow sportsmen, are among the most important aids to achieving successful shooting and shooting techniques. In the pages which follow, however, you should find reliable guidelines for all the forms, styles and varieties of techniques which the modern sporting shooter is likely to require.

CHOICE OF TECHNIQUE

Proverbially, 'there is more than one way to skin a cat'. The same principle applies to sporting shooting and the ways we go about it. If we consider the various types of sporting quarry, group by group and even species by species, we will see that we have to resort to quite a variety of different techniques and tactics depending upon the quarry we are after, the lie of the land, the form the day's sport is to take and the capabilities and limitations of ourselves and the equipment we use.

Small, fast-moving birds and mammals, whether a bursting covey of quail, a rocketing pheasant or a bolting rabbit, give no opportunity for deliberation in shooting, and the shotgun handled quickly and swung with easy speed is the natural choice. Likewise large game, especially when we measure the shooting distance in hundreds rather than tens of yards, calls for the very different skills of the rifleman, taking a deliberate aim and delivering a single high-velocity projectile to a lethal point on a static target, often at long range. A fast-flying pheasant or duck could conceivably be shot with a rifle bullet, and it has been done, but it cannot be done consistently. Similarly, a charge of birdshot from a shotgun can kill large mammals when fired at very short range, but it is inappropriate, inhumane and ineffective for tackling larger species such as deer, boar and other sizeable sporting mammals under normal conditions.

Your individual choice of shooting technique will be determined not only by your personal preferences, the requirements of your chosen quarry species, your physical limitations and the ballistic capabilities of your chosen firearm, but also by certain legal restrictions. Every sportsman should make certain that the tactics, methods, weapons and equipment he uses conform to the laws which apply in the area concerned, and also to the unwritten but important code of sporting behaviour and ethics to which every sportsman should adhere.

Where shooting is organized and formal, much of your mastery of sporting technique boils down to your own ability to shoot safely and skilfully. By contrast, rough shooting, decoying and stalking are often less formal and offer greater scope to the individual sportsman. Success or failure often hinge upon the individual sportsman's personal resourcefulness and fieldcraft.

ROUGH SHOOTING FOR PHEASANT

WILDFOWLING

CLAY TARGET SHOOTING

TECHNIQUES AND GUNS
SHOTGUNS (for live quarry)
Walking-up, Rough shooting,
Jump shooting, Pass shooting,
Decoying, Shooting from
blinds/butts
Covert shooting
Driven game shooting
Shooting over dogs
SHOTGUNS (for clay
pigeon shooting)
All types and specialized
disciplines of clay pigeon
shooting, invariably 12-
bores and principally
over-and-under and semi-
automatic types.
AIR RIFLES
Small game at short ranges

SMALL-BORE RIFLES (.22
rimfire)
Small mammals at up to
100 yards
CENTREFIRE RIFLES (.222
cal. and upwards)
Woodland stalking
Open ground stalking
Shooting from high seats
Still-hunting
HANDGUNS
As for rimfire and centrefire
rifles, but effective
ranges much shorter;
quarry usually smaller.

BEATERS DRIVING PARTRIDGE

WOODLAND DEER STALKING

SAFETY & MAINTENANCE

Guns kill, and must therefore be treated with the greatest respect. A statement of the obvious? Perhaps – yet while the basic rules of gun safety *are* obvious, when looked at logically, it remains a sad fact that hundreds of sportsmen around the world are injured, maimed or killed every year because simple rules are ignored. Some shooting accidents are the result of thoughtless action in the excitement of the moment, but most are caused by sheer carelessness.

Experienced shooters should know all about gun safety, and make a conscious effort to practise the rules at all times. It is also essential that young people coming into the sport should be made aware of safety procedures, by instruction, example and constant reminder if seen to transgress. Equally, though sometimes this is more difficult, any mature individual who transgresses should also be confronted.

In 1909, the British sportsman Mark Beaufoy wrote a poem for his son Henry, who had reached the age of 13 and was about to start game shooting. This famous poem is not only a reminder of the importance of educating young shooters, but also contains much sound safety information. Called *A Father's Advice*, it goes like this:

If a sportsman true you'd be
Listen carefully to me.
Never, never let your gun
Pointed be at anyone;
That it may unloaded be
Matters not the least to me.
When a hedge or fence you cross
Though of time it cause a loss,
From your gun the cartridge take
For the greater safety sake.
If 'twixt you and neighbouring gun
Bird may fly or beast may run,
Let this maxim e'er be thine;
'Follow not across the line.'
Stops and beaters, oft unseen,
Lurk behind some leafy screen;
Calm and steady always be;
'Never shoot where you can't see.'
Keep your place and silent be;
Game can hear, and game can see;
Don't be greedy, better spared
Is a pheasant, than one shared.
You may kill, or you may miss,
But at all times think of this –
'All the pheasants ever bred
Won't repay for one man dead.'

So just what are the rules? The following apply specifically to sporting shotguns, but the principles are valid for other disciplines. Always assume that a weapon is loaded, even if you have removed the cartridges yourself, and never pick up a gun without checking to see if it is loaded. In no circumstances point a gun at or near another person, as a shotgun can discharge even with the safety catch on because sears and tumblers are never immobilized, only the triggers.

Safe gun handling, to paraphrase an old maxim, must not only *be* done, but also be *seen* to be done. In the field, a gun must be unloaded when not required for immediate use, and left opened to *show* everyone it's safe. A loaded gun should not be laid down, or taken into a vehicle or building. Carry a weapon in one of two rest positions: in the crook of

the arm, with the barrels pointing to the ground; or over the shoulder, triggers up and barrels to the sky.

When in a state of readiness, the gun should be pointed forward and slightly to one side, with barrels well up. If you're walking, make sure that the gun does not swivel towards the next in line as the natural 'across the chest' position is unconsciously adopted. A gun should be opened and cartridges removed when crossing obstacles, and not handed to a companion unless he can see that it's unloaded.

In the immediate excitement of the moment, when faced with quarry, it is easy to get carried away and make dangerous mistakes. The rule here is that a shot must *never* be taken unless the shooter has a clear field of vision and is *certain* that nobody can be hit, whether they are visible or potentially

One of the safest ways to carry a loaded double-barrel shotgun is to open it and rest it in the crook of the arm.

concealed in cover. To repeat Henry Beaufoy's instruction: 'Never shoot where you can't see.' When rifle shooting, this aspect is even more important, as the killing range of a rifle is so much greater than that of a shotgun.

A shotgun is unlikely to injure the user unless it is fired when the barrels are obstructed, which may cause a burst. This is a risk when stalking or wildfowling, when mud can enter a barrel without being noticed as the shooter manoeuvres for position; snow is also a hazard. Check regularly while you're out with your gun, to make sure that your barrels are clear.

A weapon with worn mechanism may discharge accidentally, but this should cause no injury if

BREAKING DOWN A PUMP-ACTION SHOTGUN

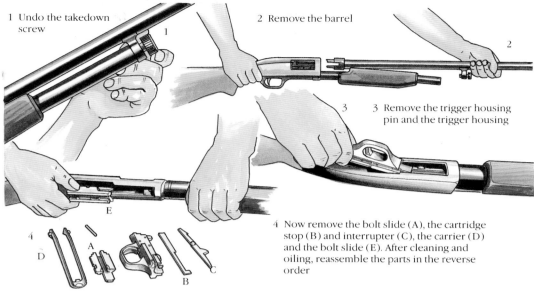

1 Undo the takedown screw

2 Remove the barrel

3 Remove the trigger housing pin and the trigger housing

4 Now remove the bolt slide (A), the cartridge stop (B) and interrupter (C), the carrier (D) and the bolt slide (E). After cleaning and oiling, reassemble the parts in the reverse order

SHOTGUN MAINTENANCE *After every outing, a shotgun should be broken down and carefully cleaned and oiled. This also allows you to check it for wear or damage.*

SHOTGUN MAINTENANCE

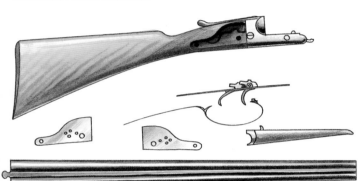

A sidelock-action double-barrel shotgun is easily dismantled for routine cleaning, oiling and maintenance.

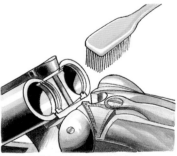

A toothbrush is useful for cleaning the bolt faces.

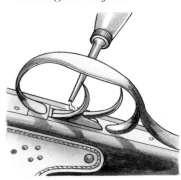

the routines described above are followed. But it's worth remembering that a gun pointing 'safely' at the ground can still be trained on a gun dog.

However, there should be no problem if a weapon is kept in good working order. Routine maintenance must be undertaken after every outing – the gun broken down, dirt and grit carefully removed, barrels cleaned inside and out and action wiped with an oily rag. A drop of oil in the trigger slot will inhibit internal rusting.

Major repairs and maintenance are best left to a gunsmith. Any gun can become unsafe in adverse climatic conditions, or through neglect. Swelling of the wood can stop sears from engaging fully, and

this will allow any sharp jolt to discharge the weapon. Worn sears can result in the gun firing on 'Safe', and trigger pulls can become so light that the gun will fire at the slightest touch. If a gun receives a professional overhaul once a year, such faults will be identified and rectified before they become dangerous.

If you keep your guns well maintained, and always observe the basic safety rules, then you will never become that most unpopular of characters – the dangerous shooter. Neither will you have the injury or death of another human being on your conscience. The etiquette and good companionship central to the pleasure of shooting is based on observance of rules formulated for mutual security.

A brush-tipped cleaning rod pushed through the barrels will remove any residues.

A little drop of oil in the trigger slot will help to inhibit internal rusting.

BASIC SHOTGUN TECHNIQUES

The shotgun has evolved and developed as the sporting firearm best suited to shooting gamebirds on the wing and small to medium-sized mammals running. This is made possible by the fact that it does not deliver a single projectile but instead fires a charge of shot pellets that form a roughly circular pattern which spreads out as the distance from the gun muzzles increases.

Whereas the sporting rifleman takes careful and deliberate aim before discharging his single bullet at a specific lethal point on the body of a static animal, the shotgunner must *point* his gun rather than aim it. The essence of good shotgun shooting is quick, deliberate and fluent movement of the gun, very different from the steady immobility of a well-aimed rifle.

Before the sporting shotgunner fires a shot he must make a number of vital decisions very quickly. Is that bird or animal a legally shootable species? Is it within range? Is the direction and angle of the shot safe? Will the firer 'poach' a bird from one of the other guns? Practice and experience mean these questions can mentally be answered in milliseconds, and if the answers are satisfactory it is legitimate to attempt a shot. But good, consistently-accurate shotgun shooting in the field is a considerable skill, and one which is best developed in the more controlled environment of a shooting school and under the watchful and helpful eye of an experienced shotgun shooting coach.

Clay pigeon layouts can present the shooter with artificial targets which simulate most of the types of shot the sportsman will encounter in the field, and repeated practice enables the novice and the experienced shotgunner to acquire and maintain competence in dealing with them.

Whatever your choice of shotgun as regards bore and style, you should first make certain that the gun is a good fit. A competent gunmaker or shooting coach should ensure that the length and angle of the stock have been adjusted to fit the individual firer before he begins to use his gun.

An ill-fitting gun, on which the stock is too long or too short, with too much 'drop', or too little, and with the wrong 'cast off' for the right-shouldered shooter or 'cast on' for the left-hander will cause unnecessary problems from the outset, especially by upsetting the quick, comfortable and snug gun-mounting which is the essence of all consistently accurate shotgun shooting.

'Gun-mounting' simply means raising the gun from the 'ready' position into the shoulder, to bring the barrels to bear upon the target. Correctly done, it should consist of one continuous, fluid movement as the muzzles are raised by the forward hand while the rear hand brings the stock into the shoulder with the barrels correctly aligned with the shooter's eyes. The movement of the gun should then flow on in an unbroken movement as the shotgunner picks up his target and swings onto it.

Good gun-mounting is essential in the field and can be developed on the clay pigeon shooting range, but many sportsmen practise regularly at home. There is no need to fire live cartridges to practise mounting the gun smoothly and swinging it with an even, free style. A picture-rail or the line of the ceiling makes a convenient 'flightpath' along which to choose an imaginary spot for your 'bird', mounting the gun onto it and swinging along the line smoothly. (Never snap the locks on a shotgun with chambers unloaded – be sure to use 'snap caps' with spring-loaded plungers to avoid damaging the

MOUNTING AND FIRING

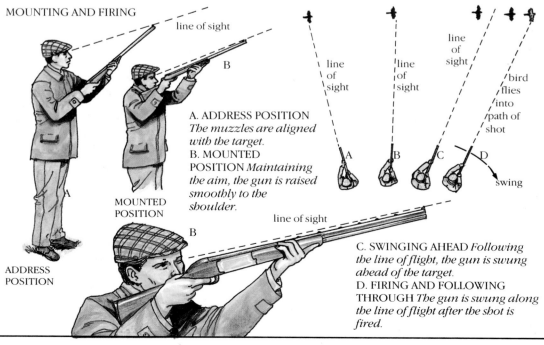

line of sight

B

A. ADDRESS POSITION *The muzzles are aligned with the target.*
B. MOUNTED POSITION *Maintaining the aim, the gun is raised smoothly to the shoulder.*

ADDRESS POSITION

MOUNTED POSITION

line of sight

B

line of sight

line of sight

line of sight

A   B   C   D

bird flies into path of shot

swing

C. SWINGING AHEAD *Following the line of flight, the gun is swung ahead of the target.*
D. FIRING AND FOLLOWING THROUGH *The gun is swung along the line of flight after the shot is fired.*

cated light guns with short (25-inch) barrels and a fast, instinctive shooting style in which the gun was raised, swung and discharged all in one quick, continuous movement. According to Churchill's theory, if you have good hand and eye coordination then it is unnecessary to think consciously about giving a moving target a chosen amount of lead, and some of the most outstanding game-shots have proved the success of this method. It is generally acknowledged, however, that it is not suitable for everyone.

Third, and perhaps most popular and widely successful, is the 'tracking method' which lies between the extreme deliberation of the sustained lead method and the fast, instinctive Churchill style. It involves smooth, deft gun-mounting which brings the shotgun barrels to bear on the track of a bird, beginning behind it. The barrels are swung through to blot out the target, and kept swinging as the trigger is pulled and as part of a smooth follow-through after the shot has been discharged. This is the style of shooting discussed here.

A well-fitting, well-balanced shotgun should rapidly become an extension of the shooter's body which he can move and direct in harmonious co-ordination with his hands and his eyes. Shotgunner-and-gun co-ordination goes even further, and the shooter's stance, the position of his feet and the distribution of his weight are all important, as also are the ways in which he can flex and twist his ankles, knees, waist and shoulders to accommodate a variety of shots at many different heights, angles and speeds.

A right-handed shooter preparing to take a shot at a high bird, coming directly forwards or crossing high in front, should stand in a comfortable, upright posture, holding his gun at the 'high port' position with muzzles raised and with the left hand supporting them at just below eye level. The heel of the shotgun stock will be approximately level with the bottom of the firer's ribs, and the shooter will look forward steadily over the top of his muzzles. His feet will be comfortably placed, with the left foot slightly forward and the right foot angled outwards.

As the target appears, the shooter should gently move his

A proper stance and a smooth swing are essential for accurate shotgun shooting.

firing mechanism.)

Different sportsmen and shooting coaches advocate different styles of shotgun shooting, which fall into three general catagories. The 'sustained lead' method is the oldest, and probably dates from the muzzle-loading days of black powder and flintlock-actioned guns. It involves swinging the barrels through the line of a flying bird and bringing them to bear on a given point ahead of it, and continuing to swing the gun to maintain that lead during and after the firing of a shot.

The 'Churchill method' is named after Robert Churchill, the famous London gunmaker and shooting writer. He advo-

SHOOTING FORWARD

When shooting forward, stand with your leading foot about 12 inches ahead of your rear foot and slightly across the front of your body. Swivel smoothly from the hip to swing the gun, with your rear heel just clear of the ground.

12 ins

SHOOTING LOW AND FORWARD

To shoot low-flying or running game, put most of your weight onto your leading foot and use your rear foot for balance. Lean forward to maintain the correct angle between the stock and your shoulder.

SHOOTING DRIVEN GAME

Shoot the nearest bird when it's about 35 yards away, then go for the next with your second shot.

35 yards

weight forward onto the front foot, leaning slightly into the shot and keeping his eyes glued on the target as he begins to mount the gun. The barrels should swing smoothly up and onto the line of the target's flight, directed by the forward (left) hand while the right hand smoothly raises the gun into the shoulder, where the comb of the stock should lie against the cheek and below the ridge of the cheek-bone.

All the shooter's actions and movements so far will have combined to place him to fire an accurate shot at an oncoming or crossing target. Whatever the direction of the target, the muzzles should pick up the line of its flight and track that line as the muzzles are pulled or pushed onwards past the target, to swing smoothly through and

ahead as the trigger is pressed – and the barrels must continue to swing with uninterrupted ease during and after the shot. Failure to follow through usually means abruptly stopping the gun's swing, which will result in a miss behind the target.

When shooting clay pigeons, either as a sport in its own right or as practice for live-quarry shooting, the conventional rules dictate that guns must be carried unloaded and open at all times, except when the firer is preparing to fire. Field conditions for the live-quarry shooter mean the gun is usually carried loaded, with the action closed and the safety firmly at 'on'. This calls for great care in handling, and it requires coolness, good judgement and experience to decide what shots can safely be fired.

SKEET SHOOTING

The origins of skeet shooting lie in game shooting. It was designed as a form of practice for the types of shot that are likely to be encountered afield: crossing and quartering 'birds' fly at a variety of angles and have to be killed at ranges out to 25 yards. However, the similarity with game shooting has been buried by the technicalities of this particular discipline. For instance, excessive choke is a handicap to the skeet shooter, making it maddeningly hard for him or her to break close-range targets, so skeet guns have wide chokes to open up the pattern and to throw a long shot string, and Beretta has patented a 'retro choke' system which has the opposite effect to that of a normal choke and has proved itself on the international competition circuit.

Skeet is a complex sport, made more complicated by the fact that three different versions are shot around the world. In Britain – but nowhere else in the world – English skeet is the most common. American skeet is shot widely in America and sometimes in Britain, Japan and other countries where the American armed forces have bases. In the rest of the world, including Europe, the USSR and South America, the rules fol-

lowed are those of the International Shooting Union (ISU).

A skeet layout consists of two trap houses facing each other and seven shooting stations arranged in a half-circle between them. In American and ISU skeet, but not in English skeet, there is an eighth station situated midway between the two trap houses.

The distance the targets are required to travel is another distinguishing feature. In English, this is 55 yards, in American it is 60 yards, making the game faster, and in ISU skeet the distance is 72 yards. These distances are measured from the inside edge of each trap house.

The two trap houses stand opposite each other, the high house on the left, the low house on the right. The former launches targets from 10 feet above the ground, while the latter shows targets starting at 3½ feet. The traps of both are fixed, to show clays in a consistent arc.

The clays' crossing point is half a radius of the circle beyond the eighth station, so obviously this depends on which version of the game is being shot. At this crossover point, the clays should pass through a hoop on a long pole when this is held up by the referee if a mutinous squad complains that the traps have been set up wrong and are not throwing at the right angle.

This is all very well in calm weather conditions, but when a fierce wind is blowing, the skeet layout becomes a very different creature. Shooters take a shot, then duck to avoid gale-blown debris, and it can be very frustrating for people who have come to expect regular target

flight patterns.

A round of skeet is shot by a squad of five shooters in American and English skeet, but six in ISU. They start at the first stand, alongside the high house, and progress from stand to stand. The birds are a mixture of singles and doubles, the precise order of which varies between the three disciplines, but in all of them the high bird is taken first on singles, and on doubles the bird from the nearer house is taken first.

In English skeet, singles and doubles are shot on stands one, two, four, six and seven, and singles are shot on stands three and five. The 25th bird is an optional high or low on the seventh stand if the shooter has not missed any during the round. If this is not the case, the first bird lost has to be taken again.

In American skeet, singles and doubles are thrown on stations one, two, six and seven, and singles are shown at stations three, four, five and eight. The 25th bird is an optional high or low bird on stand eight – most shooters go for the low bird. As with English skeet, the first miss is shot a second time.

In ISU skeet, on stand one a single high bird is shown, followed by a double. On stands two, three, five and six, a high bird, then a low bird, then a double are shown. A double release is at stand seven, and two singles at stands four and eight. This totals 25, which leaves no room for an optional target.

When calling birds, the shooter says 'pull' for the nearer house, 'mark' for the further one. Doubles are released

A skeet shooter at the first shooting station, in front of the high trap house which is on the left of the layout.

simultaneously, and 'pull' is the word here. When calling the birds, the release has to be instantaneous in English and American skeet, but when shooting ISU there can be a delay of up to three seconds.

There are other differences in the rules, with one of the grey areas being shot sizes. In England, sizes six and seven are to be seen often enough, even though all skeet disciplines are supposed to be shot with 1⅛ ounces of number nines. It has to be said that large shot sizes create less dense patterns, so perhaps these people are doing themselves no favours at all. This rule is strictly adhered to in other parts of the world: number nines are adequate for this close-range game, and run out of steam within 100 yards, making shooting safer.

Some rules are a little quaint. In ISU skeet, for example, if a shooter kills both birds of a double with one shot, it counts for nothing and the pair must be repeated, and if this happens three times in a row, a loss is recorded. If the shooter misses the first bird of a double and his shot accidentally smashes the second, the fact is scored as a miss – but the pair has to be taken again.

The trick is not to miss, of course. Top shooters on the international circuit score 600 straight when they need to. However, a lot of practice is needed to reach this sort of standard – it just takes several truckloads of shells to get there.

SKEET SHOOTING LAYOUT *The basic layout for English, American and ISU skeet consists of 7 shooting stations on an arc of 21 yards radius, measured from the target crossing point. American and ISU skeet layouts have an eighth shooting station, 15 yards in front of station 4 and midway between the two trap houses.*

SKEET LAYOUT

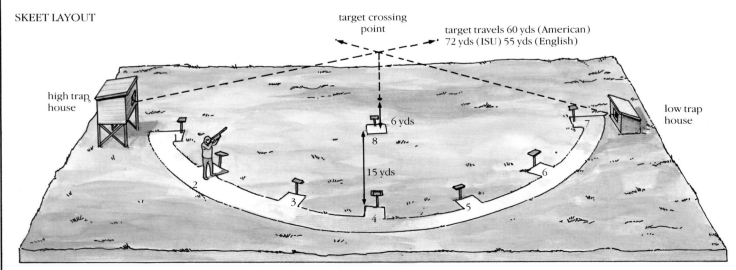

target crossing point

target travels 60 yds (American) 72 yds (ISU) 55 yds (English)

high trap house

low trap house

6 yds

8

15 yds

1

2

3

4

5

6

7

TRAPSHOOTING

In clay target shooting, the repeated exposure to shotgun noise makes the use of ear protectors a wise precaution.

The various trapshooting disciplines have sprung directly from the sport of shooting live pigeons released from traps, and much of the terminology of clay shooting stems from this sport. Live pigeons are still shot in Italy, France, Spain, Portugal and Latin America, although the sport is outlawed in Britain and most of the USA.

The birds are either trapped in cities or specially bred, and kept in aviaries near the shooting ground. There, an underground chamber has access to the bottom of a small cage – the trap. When the shooter calls 'pull', the trap is opened and the bird flies off. It has to be killed before it goes outside a circle marked on the court.

Live pigeons having more independence of thought than clays, the birds sometimes hop out of the trap and walk a few yards before flying off. Others walk all the way to the edge of the circle, and freedom. To prevent this, some types of trap catapult the birds into the air, and in the *columbare* shoots of the Gulf States and Mexico a thrower (human) stands inside the ring and hurls the bird into the air. Needless to say, the losers end up in pies. Among the spectators, losers can end up spectacularly broke: a lot of money is bet at these events.

Some of these Continental club houses and grounds, set amid sun-baked hills under deep blue skies, have an elegance and tradition that makes people hesitate before labelling their sport as barbaric. Nevertheless, clay pigeons require considerably less searching of the conscience.

Nowadays there are several different branches of trap shooting. These are Down-the-Line (DTL), which is called Trap Shooting in America; the more complicated Olympic Trench (OT), which is the discipline shot in European, World and Olympic championships; and Universal Trench (UT) and Automatic Ball Trap which are both simplified versions of Olympic Trench. In all of these disciplines, the birds fly away from the shooter.

The standard DTL layout consists of a traphouse with five shooting positions 16 yards behind it. The squad of five shooters takes up position on the stands, and the first man calls for his clay. He is permitted to have the gun at his shoulder, sighted just above the traphouse roof.

When a shooter calls 'pull', the referee releases the clay electronically. In America, only one shot may be taken, but in Britain, the shooter scores three points for a first shot kill and two points if he uses his second barrel.

The clay is thrown in an arc of 45 degrees either side of an imaginary line running through the centre of the traphouse. The precise angle is unpredictable, but the clay is about ten feet up at ten yards from the trap and travels about 50 yards. Each shooter has one bird, with the sequence moving from left to right down the line. After each shooter has taken five birds from one position, everybody moves one stand to the right and takes another five birds.

In America, a handicap system is frequently operated. The shooting positions extend backwards by 18 inch increments to

Trapshooting is a popular sport which attracts a good deal of commercial sponsorship.

27 yards. (In Britain, this variation is infrequently shot, but there the increments increase by one yard at a time.) The distance from which a competitor shoots depends on his previous scores: the better he is, the farther back he must stand.

Another variation on this theme is the 'double-rise', where two birds are thrown simultaneously from a DTL trap, usually at fixed angles. Most shooters take the left hand bird first from shooting positions four and five, and the right hand bird first from stands one, two and three. From these angles, the bird is travelling straight away from the shooter. It can be quickly powdered, allowing more time to take the angled bird before it starts dropping and presents a tougher mark.

Olympic Trench is a 24 yard long trench, containing 15 traps, split into five groups of three, each group sited 16½ yards in front of each of the five shooting stands. Each trap fires only one height and angle. The 15 traps cover a total arc of 90 degrees, with the clays varying in height between 3½ feet and 13 feet at eleven yards from the trap. Birds travel nearly twice as fast as DTL targets, at around 90 mph, and travel nearly twice as far – about 85 yards.

While the line of shooting positions is slightly curved in DTL, in OT it is straight. Squads consist of six shooters, with the sixth waiting behind the first stand. OT shooters move position after each shot, so the sixth man prevents the shooter on position five from having consecutive shots when he moves up to the first stand.

Targets are released electronically when the shooter shouts 'pull' into a microphone situated at his feet. Each group of three traps releases birds either left, right, or straight; a computer decides which trap is to fire, but by the end of each round competitors will have been presented with a fair balance of angles. Two shots can be fired, with no points system as in DTL: only kills count. However, many shooters fire the second barrel even after killing with the first. They kill again a chip of clay, thereby keeping in practice for when they miss with the first barrel and have to rely on a second shot.

Similar rules prevail for Universal Trench shooting, the main difference being that five fixed-angle traps are used, one in front of each shooting stand, instead of the five groups of three. Any trap may throw a bird, so the shooter on stand one who has a bird released from trap five, for instance, will be presented with a tricky, sharply-angled mark.

In Automatic Ball Trap, the shooting positions are curved, as in DTL, and there is only one trap. This, however, is computer controlled so that it varies at random the heights and angles at which clays are thrown, and it is possible to simulate the angles and arcs of an OT layout. ABT is, however, very much cheaper to install and operate than an OT layout.

Starshot is a recent innovation which started as a gimmick to boost the televisual appeal of clay shooting. A grid, shaped like the top half of a dartboard, is set in the ground in front of two pairs of shooting positions. It can be shot by day or night.

Four traps fire clays vertically in front of the four segments of the grid, and each segment is divided into sections. Each of these is marked with the number of points available in that section. The white clays that are used are brightly lit by the television lights and stand out sharply against the night sky. When burst, the 'smoke' shows up clearly inside a scoring section.

In the TV version of this game, two shooters from the international circuit team up with two celebrities, hence the 'star' part of Starshot.

AMERICAN TRAP/DOWN THE LINE (DTL) LAYOUT

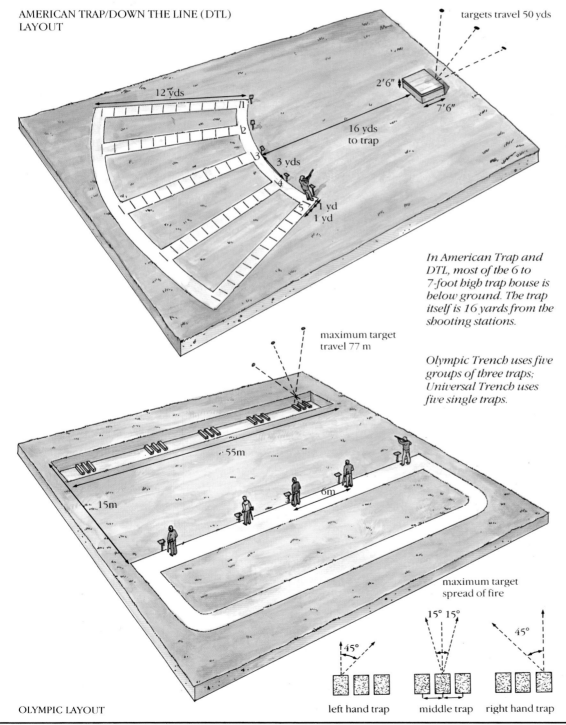

In American Trap and DTL, most of the 6 to 7-foot high trap house is below ground. The trap itself is 16 yards from the shooting stations.

Olympic Trench uses five groups of three traps; Universal Trench uses five single traps.

OLYMPIC LAYOUT

left hand trap   middle trap   right hand trap

SPORTING CLAY SHOOTING

The 'Sporting' discipline of clay pigeon shooting started out as a simple means of practising to shoot game. It has since become the toughest of the various competitive disciplines, and the sport's leading performers are consistently brilliant at smashing fast, awkward targets.

The sport has moved far from its roots. Not only are the guns and ammunition widely different from those used afield, but no bird yet hatched has the agility and speed to take off like a modern competitive clay target. At the most basic level, sporting clays are to be found at many small country fairs around England during the summer. Alternatively, a bunch of shooters take a couple of traps out to the fields and endeavour to hit the simple targets thrown by these machines. Again at the basic level, shooting schools have straightforward sporting layouts. These are used not just to tutor novices, but also to provide more seasoned shooters with practice before the game season commences.

It is ironic that several of the top international shooters in this discipline no longer have any interest in game, finding the shots too simple and unrewarding. They prefer to break clay pigeons because they jump at tricky angles or fly high and fast. This ambivalence also applies to the guns that people use. Those who regard sporting clays as a warm-up for the main event shoot with a standard side-by-side game gun. Those who consider this discipline to be sufficient sport in itself generally use an over-and-under trapgun.

One major difference is to be found in the degree of choke used. Targets are often fast and rangy at the best competitions, so barrels are choked around a quarter and threequarters. Compared with normal game loads of $1\frac{1}{16}$ ounces, sporting loads are $1\frac{1}{8}$ ounces of size 7 shot under English rules, while European rules permit a gun chambered for $2\frac{3}{4}$-inch cartridges firing a $1\frac{1}{4}$-ounce load. In Europe, official competitions may not be shot with hand loads, although these are widely

Sporting clay shooting, where fast-moving targets appear from awkward angles, is the toughest clay-shooting discipline.

used in America.

Other differences in regulations by the sport's governing bodies separate European from English sporting. In England, the gun should be clear of the shoulder, while European shooters are expected to adopt the gun-down position before calling the birds. In this latter position, the gun's butt must be readily visible below the right elbow, and touching the hip, where it stays until the target appears.

When the shooter is ready, he or she tells the referee, who

verse countryside to permit varied, safe shooting. At its best, a sporting layout is as exciting for spectators as it is for competitors: birds suddenly appear through gaps in the trees and vanish just as quickly. There are basic ways of showing the birds, but the world's top shooters in this discipline experience little difficulty in breaking the clays. They appreciate clever variations that add interest to the layout.

There are several accepted types of sporting layout, but a basic system is a long avenue with thirty traps located in the surrounding bushes. Some throw singles, others doubles, and by the end, some fifty birds

will have been shown at a variety of quirky angles and speeds. With its roots firmly in the shooting field, many stands emulate game-shooting situations. Driven partridges come across a hedge some 35 yards out; springing or rising teal appear dramatically, ascending vertically like rockets headed for the stratosphere; and for driven grouse, the shooter stands in a butt, taking the first bird in front, turning to take the second bird behind.

Pigeons come spinning over the treetops. At the sound of the shot, a second bird is released in a different direction. Another interesting combination is the rabbit and snipe. The first clay

half spins, half bounces over the ground, then a snipe zips back low on a different tangent.

Driven pheasant come from a tower that is at least 75 feet high and could easily be over 120 feet tall. At that height, the clays look like aspirins and take some hitting. Many shooters pysch themselves into missing these high screamers. Others have no problem at all in smashing them. That, however, is the charm of sporting clays: they aren't easy to hit. Very few people ever manage to shoot a complete round without dropping at least a couple of clays. Such is the nature of this game – the better the layout, the tougher the birds.

EXAMPLES OF SPORTING LAYOUTS
In the 'springing teal', the targets rise vertically within a spread of 10° to 20°. 'Driven partridge' appear suddenly over a hedge, while 'high pheasant' are launched from a tall tower.

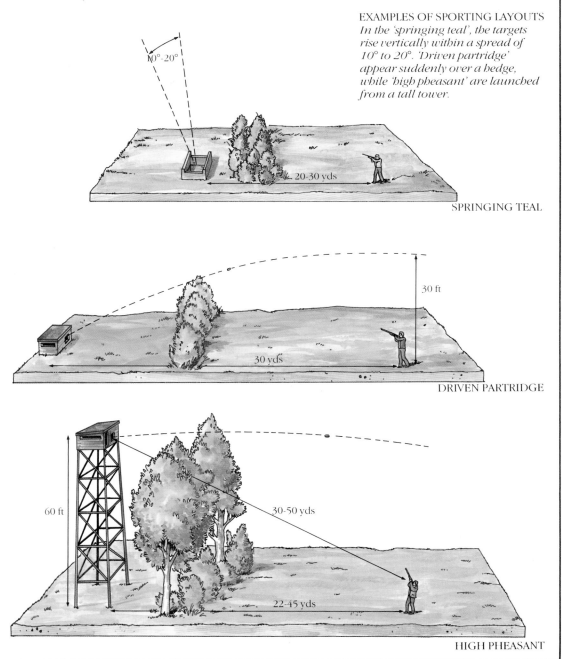

buzzes the trapper to release the birds. This 'silent rise' method is more appropriate to the unexpected way in which game appears. In England, double targets are shot one with each barrel, while in Europe the second barrel may be fired at the same bird after missing with the first.

For safety purposes, the stands are sited in a long line over open ground. The firing positions are largely enclosed to protect spectators, and only the angles of the traps add variety to this uniform scene. However, sporting layouts vary widely in quality, and a major competition requires large quantities of traps and equipment, together with sufficient acreage of di-

BASIC RIFLE TECHNIQUES

It is interesting to compare and contrast sporting shooting with a rifle and with a shotgun: there are important similarities, but many fundamental differences. Common to both is the vital importance of the sportsman's careful handling and safe use of all firearms at all times, and of his intimate familiarity with the characteristics and workings of the individual firearms he uses. As regards technique, whereas the successful use of a sporting shotgun for running or flying game depends upon quick, deft gun-mounting, a fluent swing and the ability to point and move the shotgun in an appropriate way for a moving target, the rifleman has to discharge a single, small projectile, *aimed*, not pointed, with care and deliberation, at a lethal spot on the body of a static animal, and often at very much longer ranges than a shotgunner.

Successful sporting rifle shooting involves all the basic abilities of the competitive target-shooting rifleman, plus a host of additional skills to enable him to make best use of his rifle under practical field conditions. The target rifleman shoots under much more controlled conditions than his sporting counterpart, even in the outdoor sport of high-power target shooting on open ranges.

The relative positions of the target rifleman and his inanimate target are more precisely defined, the distance between the rifle and target is known exactly, and range firing involves precise procedures, rules and facilities which make the firing of an unwise or dangerous shot very unlikely. The target rifleman fires from a steady prone, sitting or standing position on firm ground, in the knowledge that his target has a solid backstop and an adequate safety area of empty ground beyond and around; and the taking of life and the possibility of causing a painful, non-fatal wound by a bad shot simply do not arise in properly-organized target shooting.

The sporting rifleman, by contrast, is contending with living creatures which it is his duty to shoot selectively and humanely. (In the case of dangerous game his responsibility may extend further, to saving his own life and that of his companions and others by never leaving wounded, danger-

ous game at large.) Deer stalking, in woodland and on the hill, may involve having to fire shots at various distances and in a variety of conditions of light and weather, often adverse, and in many physical postures.

Conditions of light, especially at dawn and dusk and in misty hill weather, make accurate judging of distance even more difficult. The heat of summer or the numbing cold of winter, the presence of insects, soaking clothing, physical tiredness and the disorientation which often accompanies a disruption of normal patterns of eating and sleeping, mean that the stalker has to discipline himself to fire accurate shots when a variety of stresses may be making life very disagreeable for him. And all the time he must handle and use his rifle thoughtfully, constantly aware of the tragic consequences which might ensue if there is not an adequate backstop for his bullet, which has a long lethal range. The wise, capable rifleman knows when *not* to attempt a shot.

Safe, successful sporting rifle shooting should begin long before the sportsman makes his first outing after live quarry. Ideally, it should begin in childhood, with encouragement and instruction in the use of an air rifle under the watchful eye of a parent or other experienced adult. The earlier in life that habits of safe rifle handling and correct shooting technique are inculcated the better.

The guiding principle must be to ensure that the muzzle is at all times pointed in a safe direction, and the safety catch applied as an additional measure of caution, until the shot is about to be taken, and then only at a clearly discerned and identified target with a safe backstop behind it.

The sporting rifleman's early career often begins with an air rifle, but even the most experienced riflemen also find that regular practice with air rifles and .22 rimfire rifles helps them maintain their rifle shooting skills. These cheaper, simpler rifles are not costly in ammunition and can be used in places where the use of large-calibre rifles would be dangerous, and antisocial on account of the noise.

Whatever the calibre, and provided it has been zeroed carefully and the sights remain

correctly set, the firing of an accurate rifle shot depends upon the degree of control the rifleman can apply in holding and aiming his weapon and in squeezing off a steady, careful shot. This calls for co-ordination of eyes, limbs and muscles, and experienced riflemen develop a remarkable ability to control their breathing, physical position and muscle tension to promote consistent accuracy. This ability to fire consistently accurate shots is common to both the target shooter and the sporting rifleman, and should be practised and mastered on the range before a stalk after live quarry is attempted.

The sporting rifleman in Britain and Europe, and also in many parts of North America, will usually find that one .22 rimfire rifle and one larger bore centrefire rifle of a suitable calibre and style will suffice for all his sport. For most riflemen the latter involves buying one of the many varieties of bolt-action magazine rifles which are available in a bewilderingly large range of calibres.

The vast majority of riflemen whose quarry is deer and other medium-sized game will opt for calibres within the 6mm to 8mm range, which includes such widely-favoured types as the .243 Winchester, 6.5mm, 7×57mm Mauser, .270 Win, .308 Win, .30-'06 and the 8×57mm Mauser. Smaller .22 centrefire calibres like the .222 Remington and the .22-250 may be appropriate for the smallest deer, and larger bores like the

9.3mm and the .375 H&H magnum for wild boar and large elk and moose.

In sporting rifles of normal weight (say 7½ to 9½ pounds complete with scope sight) all these calibres deliver some degree of perceptible recoil or 'kick', which may cause a novice to develop undesirable tendencies to flinch unless correct methods of holding and firing the rifle have been learned from the outset. Properly handled, none of these calibres need cause recoil problems, even for lightly-built women and teenage children. Just as successful shotgunning depends on good gun-mounting, good rifle shooting calls for a firm, snug hold on the rifle.

'Dry firing' – snapping the trigger and firing pin on an empty chamber – does not harm a bolt-action rifle, and regular dry-firing practice is an important training aid for every rifleman, helping to develop and maintain steady holding and the gentle squeezing-off of a steady shot. You can practise it at home, sighting on a mock target across a room, and by firing from various postures – standing, kneeling, sitting, lying prone and so on. But *always* ensure that full safety procedures are followed and that all your ammunition is securely locked away.

The squeezing-off of a shot, in practice or at a quarry animal, must have a steady 'follow-through', as you hold your aim and let the rifle settle back out of recoil into a firm position

BASIC FIRING POSITIONS

USING TREES *To use a tree for support, rest your non-shooting hand, not the gun, against the trunk.*

The use of a stalking staff is a common continental European technique which is increasingly being adopted in Britain and Ireland and elsewhere.

after the shot has been fired. Through your scope sight or over your iron or open sights you must also watch carefully for the animal's reaction to the shot. A clean miss may puzzle you unless you have watched closely and, for instance, seen that puff of spray as your bullet passed over the animal's belly and kicked up a momentary shower of raindrops off the wet grass.

A gut-shot animal tends to hunch up and move away slowly. A bullet may merely clip the spinal column or the antlers or horns, but the beast is likely to drop on the spot, apparently stone dead but possibly only stunned. A heart-shot beast often makes a headlong lunge forward, running off at full tilt for up to 100 yards or more before collapsing dead. You may think you have missed completely unless you saw that tell-tale puff of hair fly off his coat. Best of all is if you can develop the ability to *hear* the dull plop of your bullet as it strikes flesh. With concentration and practice it can be done.

Train yourself aways to reload *instantly* after firing. This becomes a subconscious reflex with experience, and with modern rifle actions it can be done very fast, giving you a second shot in immediate readiness if it is needed.

When setting off out with a rifle, ensure that it is clean and free of grit, sand or excess oil in the barrel. Take the appropriate ammunition (it is surprisingly easy to take the wrong package) and load the magazine with care. Smooth reloading and the avoidance of damage to bullet tips can depend upon this. Carry you rifle slung from your right shoulder (for a right-handed shooter); the muzzle-up position is best for a long trek, or on the open hills or in mountainous terrain, while the European-style muzzle-down position is best if you are hunting in woodlands.

Take great care to avoid getting mud, sand, snow or water into the barrel: a wild shot or a bulged or burst barrel can result. Place a strip of thin clear sticky-tape over the muzzle to keep the bore clear – the bullet can pass through with no loss of accuracy.

UNSUPPORTED *In this stance, the non-shooting arm is kept against the body for stability.*

USING A STAFF *Many European riflemen carry a long stick or 'stalking staff' to use as a support.*

SITTING AND KNEELING *When shooting from these positions, use your knees as support.*

LYING PRONE *When shooting from a prone position, support yourself on your elbows.*

BASIC HANDGUN TECHNIQUES

Normally, the handgun hunter is using his or her weapon for one main reason – the challenge that this difficult form of hunting presents. Anyone who is a reasonable shot with a rifle or a shotgun can, with enough perseverance, eventually make a kill. A handgun hunter, on the other hand, requires marksmanship, fieldcraft and equipment of the highest standard.

Hunting with handguns is a long-established sport in North America, where it is currently enjoying a rapid growth in popularity. In Britain and Europe, however, because of tradition, a smaller range of possible quarry species and restrictive hunting and firearms legislation, handgun hunting is virtually non-existent.

Many American gunmakers produce pistols – revolvers, single-shot handguns and automatics – intended specifically for hunting, but most hunters prefer to use revolvers or single-shot handguns rather than automatics because they can handle more powerful cartridges.

For small game and varmint species, such as squirrels, rabbits, hares and woodchucks, .22 calibre handguns are by far the most popular, especially rimfire revolvers. Hunting medium-sized quarry, from foxes up to whitetail and mule deer, obviously calls for heavier and more powerful arms, with .38/ .357 revolvers being the most useful and versatile for animals in this category. For big game,

including bears, elk and lion, the most suitable calibres are those from .41 magnum up. However, when you're using a pistol, only an accurate brain or spine shot will reliably stop an angry bear or lion, so if you intend to take dangerous species such as these with a handgun, you should hunt with a companion armed with a rifle who can act as a backup if you get into trouble.

Once you have decided on the type of game you are after, and have equipped yourself with a suitable handgun and ammunition with which to take it, your next job is to find out your limitations.

Knowing the extent of your own abilities, and the limits to the accuracy and range of your

Whatever stance you adopt – sitting, kneeling, lying prone or standing – always use a double-handed grip.

gun and ammunition, is essential, so you should find these out before you go hunting. If the maximum range at which you can achieve a 4-inch group in a target is, say, 30 yards, then there will be no point in building yourself a blind about 50 yards from the favourite drinking hole of your intended quarry. Equally, your equipment must suit the terrain you are going to hunt on: scoping a handgun is great for the longer range shots and for gathering a little extra light in the early morning or late evening, but a scope is a definite disadvantage in close cover.

In handgun hunting, the most important single factor is bullet placement, so you should use any and every aid to achieve a good shot. This should include, wherever possible, getting yourself into a position from which you can shoot supported, using a prone position or, when the ground is unsuitable, making use of a tree or a rock as a hand rest. If you have to shoot unsupported, then the best stance to adopt is probably the Weaver, as used in Practical Pistol shooting. This stance gives good stability, a reasonable sight picture and excellent recoil recovery, enabling a rapid, *aimed* second shot should one be needed.

After marksmanship (and assuming that you have already matched your ammunition to your intended target), good fieldcraft is paramount, even more so than in rifle hunting because of the handgun's shorter range.

First of all, you need a good knowledge of your quarry. You need to know where you're likely to find it, and at what times of the day it is likely to be feeding, resting or on the move. Then you have to locate it, perhaps with the aid of binoculars or a spotting scope, and to be able to get close enough to shoot it.

Most animals are naturally very wary, using their highly-developed senses of smell, hearing and sight to warn them of any approaching danger. The basis of a successful approach is to keep downwind and to move silently and slowly from cover to cover. Don't do it like Rambo, crawling through thick bushes, because the noise you will make will greatly outweigh any advantage you gain from being in better cover.

Your chances of making a silent approach will be much improved if you wear suitable clothing and footwear. Light-soled boots will help you to tread quietly, and if your clothes are made of natural materials such as wool then they won't rustle as you move. It's also a good precaution, before you set out, to make sure you're not carrying anything that will rattle, such as coins or keys.

When you're using a single-action pistol, or manually cocking a double-action gun, use your thumb to cock it.

Once you spot your target, freeze, even if you are out in the open – although most game animals have excellent vision, they will usually ignore a stationary man because they associate danger with movement. Wait until it looks away and begins to feed before moving slowly to cover to begin your stalk, but freeze again instantly if it looks up again.

If you can learn how to sneak to within 25 yards of an alert rabbit, then you should be able to get to within 40 or 50 yards of a deer. With practice, it is even possible to get to within 20 yards of a wary whitetail by simply freezing whenever it looks up from feeding.

Always remember that when you take up handgun hunting you are pitting yourself against your chosen game at a definite disadvantage, but when you do succeed in taking that trophy animal then the feeling of achievement will make it all worthwhile.

BASIC HANDGUN GRIP

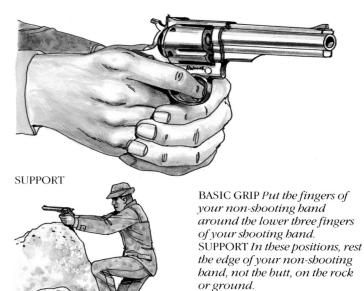

SUPPORT

BASIC GRIP *Put the fingers of your non-shooting hand around the lower three fingers of your shooting hand.*
SUPPORT *In these positions, rest the edge of your non-shooting hand, not the butt, on the rock or ground.*

BASIC AIRGUN TECHNIQUES

Air rifles, even the most powerful ones, are only effective over short ranges. Forty yards is a fair limit for most standard weapons, while seventy yards is the outer practical distance for even the most powerful rifle. Pellets travel considerably farther, of course, but do not retain sufficient energy to kill quarry cleanly. This gives air rifle hunters an edge over those who shoot cartridge rifles: there is no worry about stray shots doing damage a mile or more away. Another advantage is that of noise; at twenty yards, a silenced air rifle makes as much noise as a bicycle pump.

The comparatively puny nature of air weapons demands a high standard of woodcraft for consistent results in the field. When shooting at such intimate ranges, it is important to keep concealed from wary eyes, ears and snouts. Air weapons are best suited to the smaller species from the quarry list – rabbits, squirrels, pigeons, doves and the like. Even so, a high degree of accuracy is necessary to place pellets where they will produce their most lethal effect.

Fortunately, ammunition is so inexpensive that abundant practice is possible. Any target will do – pine cones, wild fruits, tin cans, stones, and so on, but the knock-down field target is ideal for this purpose. As with all forms of rifle shooting, it is important to recognize how gravity and the breeze affect the pellet's flight path. Naturally enough, these aspects are particularly noticeable on air weapons.

The majority of air rifle hunters get close to their quarry either through stalking or by waiting in a blind. Whichever method is preferred, concealment at close range is essential, and this generally requires the use of full camouflage. However, even a full suit of camouflage clothing is not enough if you are light-skinned. For close-range work, it is important to hide as much of this as possible through the use of a hat, face paint, fingerless gloves or whatever. There is the risk of looking like a terrorist, but the advantages outweigh this.

Shooting from a hide is most effective when the hide has been built in territory that is popular with the selected quarry species. The site should be chosen after considerable

Full camouflage makes you less conspicuous and helps you to get within shooting range.

An alternative to stalking your quarry is to wait quietly for it to come within range.

observation through binoculars, and places to note are those where quarry feeds, drinks, rests or roosts. These change with the seasons, but familiarity with these habits enables the hunter to predict the best opportunities for success.

A camouflage net forms the basis of most blinds, unless the natural cover is conveniently situated within range of the action. It is important to remember that most quarry species are familiar with their back yard and have no difficulty in spotting obvious changes. A blind, therefore, should be small and unobtrusive, the netting carefully concealed with whatever vegetation occurs naturally on site – and which won't wilt and change colour when the sun shines on it. The cover needs to

be thick at the back of the hide lest suspicious eyes catch sight of a dark object moving against chinks of light shining from behind.

In practice, it is easy to construct an unnoticeable coccoon anywhere, and not just in the more obvious locations. Inconspicuous firing points can be made along the bottom of a fence – even in the middle of an open field. It is important to be comfortable, otherwise stiffness, cold, damp or the fidgets cause interest to dwindle at the precise moment when the expected quarry turns up.

When the right moment does arrive, the quarry should be sufficiently relaxed to allow the shooter time to wait until it is presented best for an effective

shot. The pigeon resting on a branch will ultimately waddle clear of the screen of twigs, and the rabbit may hop closer.

At other times, stalking produces more interesting shooting. Clothing for this purpose should be rustle-free and silent, and footwear supple. Woodcraft has to be of the highest standard because of the need to creep so close before taking a shot. Unless a specific creature has been marked for a stalk, the best ploy for creeping through woodland is to walk slowly between patches of cover about a gunshot apart, and then pause for a few minutes. It takes time to absorb the scene, to spot the blob of feathers that is a dove, the bright eyes of a squirrel watching from a high branch, or the ears of a

rabbit concealed by grass.

Even after taking a shot, it is wise to keep still for a few moments in case the slight disturbance makes something else show itself. This particularly applies to rabbits, which show stalking with air weapons in its best context. One of the most effective ways of harvesting rabbits is at night with an air rifle (this may be illegal in some parts of the USA). During the autumn months it is easy to stalk close, dazzling them in the beam of a forehead-mounted spotlight, which picks out their gleaming eyes.

Another lamp, mounted above the scope via a single scope mount. fixed upside down, pinpoints the rabbit. The method is deadly where the

rabbits have long grass or stubble to lie out in. When they crouch at the shooter's approach, they show little to shoot at. Precision shooting is required under these conditions, especially since optimum weather conditions are those of damp and breeze to cover all sound of approach.

Modern air rifles are highly accurate weapons, and the best hunting grades come fitted with beautiful stocks. In skilled hands, they are deadly – and the inexperienced can have abundant practice without sounding like the start of World War III.

If you are fair-skinned, you may need face paint and a hat as well as a full suit of camouflage clothing.

STALKING ON OPEN GROUND

Locating, stalking to within range and bringing off a successful shot at deer, wild goats or mountain sheep on open ground requires different skills and a very different approach from that of the woodland deerstalker. Deer and other ungulates behave differently on open ground, and the nature of the terrain, the long vistas and the comparative absence of cover for concealment mean the stalker must adopt special tactics if he is to be successful

Probably the most highly-developed and organized present-day form of open ground stalking with a rifle is practised in the Scottish Highlands, in pursuit of the red deer which have taken up a wild existence there on the open, heather-covered hills since the great Caledonian pine forest was destroyed some two centuries ago. (In Scotland the term 'deer forest' is still used, even though the area concerned may be bare of anything taller than a small shrub.)

The rifleman is normally accompanied on a Scottish deer forest by a professional stalker, who guides his 'rifle' throughout the day, making all the critical decisions. His task is to manoeuvre himself and his 'rifle' into position to shoot a selected animal and to extract the carcase and (in the case of a stag) the trophy, the former going to the game larder while the sportsman will probably want to retain the latter.

In Britain, the red deer shooter's rifle must, by law, be .240-inch calibre or larger, and calibres like the .270, 7×57mm and the .308 are particular favourites. The rifle should have been carefully zeroed to provide accurate shooting at distances of up to 200 to 250 yards, although it is rare for a stalker to permit even the most skilled 'rifle' to fire at longer ranges than 150 to 175 yards. The advantages of the modern, flat-trajectory calibres like those just mentioned are particularly evident in this sort of stalking, where the shots tend to be taken at much greater distances than in woodland.

Transport from the estate shooting lodge, the hotel or the stalker's cottage will nowadays often be by some form of all-terrain vehicle like the popular Argocat, which has largely replaced the traditional hill pony

on which the gentleman 'rifle' of earlier years used to set off for a day's hill stalking. However, ponies are still used on the roughest ground.

Many Highland forests have more than one possible starting point, and your stalker's choice of which one to use will be based on his knowledge of where deer are likely to be, and will take into account the prevailing weather, and especially the wind direction. For hill stalking, the stalker and rifleman must be constantly aware of the wind direction, both as regards the prevailing wind and also the differing directions of local swirls and eddies which occur among hill ridges, valleys and corries. The slightest whiff of scent will betray the presence of a stalking party to deer half a mile or more downwind, clear-

ing that ground of deer for at least the rest of that day, and making the animals jumpy, extra alert and almost unapproachable.

'Spying for deer' is a deliberate, careful procedure, and most professional stalkers use a 30× or 40× magnification, three-draw telescope, although binoculars of 7× or 8× power may also be carried for making a general scanning sweep of a large area of hillside. But a high-powered telescope remains essential if distant herds of deer and individual beasts are to be scrutinized carefully, which is important for successful stalking and selective shooting.

Typically, the stalker will spot and select a party of deer which may be a mile or more distant, and the approach may involve

In Scottish hill stalking, the visiting rifleman is usually accompanied and guided by a professional stalker.

traversing two or three times that distance by a circuitous route, to ensure that at all times the stalker and the rifleman remain out of sight, hearing and scent of the deer. In addition to quite exceptionally highly-developed scenting powers, red deer on the open hill have good eyesight, are especially quick to spot movement, and are usually more suspicious of static figures and any alien objects than their woodland counterparts are.

The early stages of the approach rarely mean heading straight towards the deer, and are more likely to involve striking off at right angles or even doubling back on your tracks to

begin a long, roundabout route. At first, the pace may be a steady, plodding walk, but the stalker will be constantly careful to keep out of sight of the deer and to avoid any unnecessary sound such as the rattling of loose stones or the scraping of nailed boots on bare rock. He will also beware of accidentally disturbing other parties of deer which may take flight and frighten off the deer being stalked. Every advantage is taken of the lie of the land, and most stalkers prefer to keep to high ground, well above the deer being stalked and often using the dead ground behind the crest of a ridge to keep them out of sight. Deer seldom anticipate danger from above, and a high ground approach is often best, provided the wind direction remains suitable.

The later stages of the approach usually involve making use of the clefts and gulleys created by hill streams to provide concealment, and broken, hummocky ground or patches of broken peat hags can also be an advantage, but at this point you will often move forward by stooping or crawling to keep a low profile. Whatever the terrain of the deer forest, the final movement of the stalker and his 'rifle' into a suitable firing position will be made with a low crawl on hands or knees, or a belly-flat wriggle.

If all has gone well, the deer will be within reasonable shootable range and grazing or resting quite oblivious of the stalking party's presence. A hasty or snap shot is not normal, and the stalker usually has a little time to make sure that his 'rifle' has settled into a comfortable, steady firing position.

As in all deer stalking, the rifleman should aim to place his bullet within the animal's chest cavity which contains the vital heart and lungs and the large thoracic arteries and blood vessels. The neck shot, while it may mean minimal meat damage, should not be attempted at any range, whatever the conditions. It is unwise to fire at any beast on the hill unless it is standing up and presents a broadside shot.

A carefully squeezed-off shot should be followed by instant reloading, while watching carefully how the chosen beast reacts to the shot. A professional stalker ought to know instantly what has happened, and the experienced sporting rifleman learns to spot the telltale signs of a clean miss or a hit which, though it may be fatal, does not drop the beast on the spot.

A successful shot is followed immediately by the 'gralloch' or evisceration, and scavenging creatures like the hill fox and the hooded crow will be quick to take advantage of this. Carcase extraction and a return to the lodge by all-terrain vehicle or pony marks the end of a successful Scottish Highland stalk.

The same broad principles apply to stalking the other hill species, such as chamois in the Alps or wild sheep in the mountains of Asia and North America. Here, however, truly mountainous conditions of sheer slopes and bare rock are the norm, and the rifleman may not have the benefit of an expert stalker to guide him, although the chances of success are always much better if an experienced guide with local knowledge can be obtained. Because of the need to cover long distances over rough country, often in adverse weather and with great care, all mountain stalking calls for physical fitness and stamina combined with a constant awareness of the need for concealment and taking wind direction into account.

Some high-mountain rifle shooting may require more long-range shooting than in Scotland, and rifle calibres like the .20-06, the 7mm Rem. magnum and the .300 are particularly well-suited to accuracy at these longer distances. But great care is needed to judge distances accurately when shooting across a valley, where range can be very deceptive. Similarly, when shooting steeply up or down a slope the angle must be taken into account and the point of aim for an uphill shot will be lower than for a level shot, and slightly higher for a steep downhill shot, to ensure that the bullet strikes the intended vital organs.

Finally, stalking in hills and mountains can be hazardous, and a bad fall, a sudden change in the weather or a rock slide may cause a tragedy unless the party is experienced, well equipped and behaves coolly and promptly in an emergency. The pleasures of stalking in wild and remote hill country have to be paid for by careful preparation, planning and procedures.

KILLING ZONES

When shooting deer, the aim should be to place the bullet in the animal's chest cavity. Because of the great accuracy needed, the neck shot should be avoided.

WOODLAND STALKING

If it is to be productive and effective, stalking must be a well-planned, systematic activity rather than a random stroll in a forest in the hope of encountering a deer by chance and having an opportunity of taking a shot at it.

Reconnaissance of the area to be stalked is vital, and in an unfamiliar area the help of a local stalker or guide should be secured. In Britain most woodland stalking is carried out by individual 'rifles' conducted by foresters, professional stalkers or other experts, except where the individual stalker owns or rents stalking rights to a particular area of ground. In much of Canada and the USA, however, deer and the various species of mountain sheep and goats are often hunted by unaccompanied stalkers. For them, and anyone who hunts on new ground, preliminary reconnaissance and careful study of the stalking grounds will greatly improve the chances of success.

Successful stalking of any wild creature means taking account of its habits and movements, the natural rhythms of its routines of feeding, resting and moving about. These can vary according to the time of the year and the weather on the day, and deer are always most active at the very times when human activity is at a minimum – around dawn and dusk, and during the hours of darkness. The successful stalker must therefore be out and about when he would normally be sleeping, eating or resting. However, it is this break from the humdrum routine of life which helps give stalking its unique appeal and satisfaction.

Woodland stalking involves the use of all the senses, considerable fieldcraft and a high level of concentration and self-awareness if the stalker is successfully to outwit wild creatures which are vigilant, shy, nervous and uniquely well-endowed with acute hearing and a wonderful sense of smell. Stalking in wild woodlands, perhaps from a rough camp far from highways, is physically very demanding, but the mental strain of woodland stalking should also not be underestimated. Often distances of barely a mile may be covered at a snail's pace, with the stalker's every sense alert, over a period of several hours and the stalker may feel exhausted afterwards.

Stalking has as its aim the methodical control and management of deer populations, to regulate numbers, maintain health and vigour among the deer, and strike a balance between old and young, male and female.

There are legally defined open seasons for the various species, and within each species for males and females, and these must be scrupulously observed, except when it is necessary to shoot an animal to prevent suffering or, in exceptional cases, to prevent intolerable damage to trees and crops. Thus the stalker goes out with a fairly well-defined idea of what species of deer he wishes to shoot,

and within that species he will select males or females according to the statutory seasons, and try to shoot selectively to cull a high proportion of young animals and the very old.

In woodlands with which the stalker (or his guide) are familiar, the species and numbers of deer should be known fairly accurately and a shooting plan, however rudimentary, will have been decided upon. Previous outings and regular observation will have familiarized the stalker with the whereabouts of various family groups and larger herds of deer, their resting and feeding areas and the routes taken when moving between them.

If deer are known to feed at

regular times and in established places, the stalk will begin with a slow, silent approach which avoids disturbing not only the feeding deer but also any other creatures which may be encountered during the stalk. The stalker should be constantly aware of the risk of disturbing other stray deer as he moves, and many species of birds may betray his presence by their alarm calls and movements.

Deer and other big game are quick to spot sudden move-

Woodland stalking means setting out around dawn, or at dusk, to find the deer while they are feeding. During the day, they lie up in thick cover.

ments, but their eyes have little resolving power for static objects. The stalker's movements must therefore be slow and cautious, and clothing should be coloured and patterned to blend with his surroundings. Loden-type stalking jackets, capes and trousers in sage green, dark green and brown are excellent, and in the mixed deciduous and coniferous woodlands typical of temperate lands the 'distruptive pattern material' (DPM) developed for

Deer are wary creatures, alert to signs of possible danger even when they are feeding. A slow, silent and cautious approach is essential.

British military use is ideal, breaking up the outline of the human figure and helping it to merge with surrounding cover.

To reduce further the likelihood of being given away by sound, the stalker should adopt another military idea, which is to jump up and down vigorously before he moves off. This helps identify any equipment or fittings which may clink or rattle, such as coins, knives and other metal objects. Any metallic sound is alien to wild creatures and may cause them to take alarm immediately. Hands should be masked by camouflage cream or covered by fingerless mittens, and some stalkers also use veils, masks or

camouflage cream to conceal the conspicuous pallor of the face.

Every woodland stalker makes incessant use of his binoculars, which should be of the finest optical quality and the maximum light-gathering power consistent with a manageable size and weight. A leather or plastic flap will protect the eyepieces from raindrops, and the neck-sling should be broad to spread the weight.

Most important, however, is the line of the stalker's approach relative to the prevailing wind, which may carry his scent to the deer and alarm them. While wind direction in open country is often fairly easy

to determine, woodlands cause the breeze to swirl and eddy in many unpredictable ways as the pattern of trees, clearings and woodland rides deflects the wind and changes its direction. A woodland stalker must always move upward or at least across the wind, and in his slow progress he will constantly reassess wind direction by watching the movement of grasses and leaves, by feeling the fanning of the breeze on his face and by pausing regularly to test the wind. This can be done with the flame of a cigarette lighter (but *not* a match – a discarded match, not properly extinguished, can cause a disastrous fire), by blowing a puff of talcum powder from a small rubber puffer, or by shaking fine wood ash from a small bag or sachet of cheesecloth or muslin.

A soundless approach means moving at a slow, measured pace, carefully avoiding dead leaves and twigs which may rustle and crackle, and not splashing through puddles. Footwear must therefore be light enough to let the stalker feel his way step by step, detecting twigs and branches by touch before he steps on them. Light-soled shoes and boots are best, except in very cold weather, but the heavy, insulated footwear of winter is often offset by the muffling effect of a covering of snow on the ground.

Deer may also be alarmed by noises caused as twigs and vegetation scrape over unsuitable clothing. Synthetic materials are particularly prone to rustling as the wearer walks, and scrape noisily against vegetation and undergrowth. Clothing made from natural fibres like wool and cotton is silent, comfortable to wear, and the number of layers worn can be increased or reduced as the temperature varies, from season to season and even from hour to hour during a stalk. The traditional European woodland stalker's clothing of loden cloth and the New Zealand-made 'Swandri' material are uniquely water-resistant, and will keep a stalker dry and warm while still enabling him to move very silently.

During winter, the lack of foliage makes it easier to spot the deer, but it also means that there is less cover for the stalker during his approach.

STILL-HUNTING

Still-hunting is a specialized techique for the stalker hunting deer on foot. More than any other style of woodland or farmland deer stalking, still-hunting depends for its success upon the most extreme concentration and alertness on the part of the hunter, and calls for great qualities of patience and self-control. The correct physical and psychological approach, when allied to skill in woodcraft and marksmanship under field conditions, makes still-hunting a challenging and exciting field-sport, and an effective form of deer management.

The modern form of the ancient technique of still-hunting was first described in detail by the North American hunter and author Theodore Van Dyke, whose book *The Still-*

hunter (1904) is an important and influential study of this hunting craft. Among the many skills called for in still-hunting, Van Dyke placed particular emphasis on careful observation: success comes from knowing what to look for and how to look for it during the course of the stalk. The still-hunter trains himself to use his eyes as precision instruments, looking slowly and in depth – searching for signs far more subtle than the obvious images to which modern man's eyes are normally attuned. The still-hunter must learn to find critical evidence in the most minute traces over which the eye might otherwise pass unawares.

Faced with an area of forest or woodland, perhaps interspersed with clearings, open valleys and

cultivated land, the still-hunter's first task is to ascertain where the deer are likely to be found, and to take the trouble to study the movements, habits and behaviour of the deer within that area.

In Britain and western Europe, the still-hunter's principal quarry is usually the roe deer. Except in the most remote and undisturbed forests, roe will be largely nocturnal and crepuscular in their movements, lying up by day and moving as the light begins to fade at dusk. Movement and feeding during the hours of darkness will continue in the early mornings, before the deer slip back into cover. The deer have developed this pattern of behaviour in response to the disturbance caused by many human activi-

Moving slowly through the woodland, the still-hunter watches for signs of deer such as hoofprints or droppings.

ties during the normal working day. The stalker using still-hunting techniques takes careful account of this general pattern of behaviour, often modified by particular local conditions, to make his stalking most productive.

In some areas, for example, deer regularly re-emerge from cover around mid-morning, to feed briefly and enjoy a final period in the sunshine before returning to cover. This is often the case in areas which have been regularly stalked and disturbed at dawn, and where experience has taught the deer that the disturbance is over and the danger is past by mid-morning. Deer which are jumpy and difficult to approach at first light may be more approachable three hours later.

The still-hunter's progress in woodland or along the woodland edges should be painfully slow, and a novice stalker invariably proceeds much too fast. Even a careful upwind approach means the stalker's alarming scent is drifting across an extensive downwind area, and his progress through a wood will eventually succeed in alerting almost every deer in it. A slow advance minimizes the rate of disturbance and gives maximum opportunity for spotting the droppings and hoof marks of deer, the flattened areas where they have bedded, the tracks and gaps they use and the scrapes and fraying places they visit. Even without seeing a deer, all these traces help to build up a picture of how the deer live and behave within that particular area.

But the still-hunter's ultimate aim is to locate, select and shoot his deer, so the preliminary reconnaissance and process of familiarization with the area should culminate in a quest for the deer themselves. Once he knows where and when deer are to be found, the still-hunter can move to a likely area and may then spend several hours

Deer, such as this whitetail buck, are adept at concealing themselves. The still-hunter should be constantly alert to any signs of their presence.

within just a few acres and moving no more than a few hundred yards, and possibly much less.

Deer in the open, on arable fields, downland or in clear-felled areas are conspicuous, but the still-hunter is moving and watching for deer in or close to cover. This calls for meticulously careful observation to pick up signs of the presence of deer. Vegetation breaks up obvious outlines, and while the stalker may see a deer in full view on occasions, he is more likely to locate it by the sharp-eyed identification of a patch of hair on flank or rump, the twitch of an ear or the flick of a tail.

Binoculars are a vital aid, even in the thickest cover. An indistinct silhouette or outline, or a hint of deer-like colouring among the undergrowth only a few yards ahead, may need to be scrutinized minutely through binoculars, and this close-quarters approach means binoculars must be raised with infinite care. A still-hunter may raise and lower his binoculars many scores of times during a two- or three-hour outing, and absolute familiarity and skill in their use is essential. The rapid, all-round sweep with binoculars may be appropriate for open ground or hill stalking, but the woodland still-hunter does everything in slow motion, avoiding abrupt movements and paying minute attention to outlines, shadings of colour and the complex pattern of forest shapes. Constant glassing like this benefits greatly from the

availability of top-quality stalking binoculars with the finest optics.

The careful, steady and cautious use of binoculars, and later of the rifle, is made much easier if the still-hunter carries a proper stalking stick or staff, a common practice in Europe but virtually unknown in the US. Long, motionless standing and glassing, and accurate shooting while standing, are much easier for the stalker with a strong, straight stick of hazel or ash, tipped with a rubber ferrule for grip and silence. Once familiar with its use as a monopod for steadying binoculars and rifle, and as an aid to crossing country stealthily and quietly, no stalker will hunt without his stick.

The still-hunter's repertoire of skills is wide, and his approach needs to be intelligent and almost infinitely flexible if local conditions are to be turned to his advantage, but one technique should be mentioned in conclusion. Deer feeding warily in glades, along woodland edges and in more open situations, can sometimes be approached to within satisfactory shooting range by a 'grandmother's footsteps' advance. This relies for its success on the relative inability of deer to see and resolve static human figures. Thus a stalker advances carefully and steadily while the beast is in a head-down feeding position, freezing when it raises its head. An advance is made in this stop-start way, and the still-hunter may be rewarded by an opportunity for a shot.

SIGN RECOGNITION

TREES *The damaged bark of a tree shows that a deer has been rubbing its antlers on it.*

FALLOW DEER

MUNTJAC

ROE DEER

WHITETAIL DEER

DROPPINGS *A good sign that deer are in the area is the presence of their droppings; the size and shape vary from one species to another.*

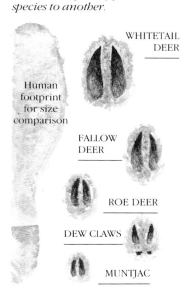

WHITETAIL DEER

Human footprint for size comparison

FALLOW DEER

ROE DEER

DEW CLAWS

MUNTJAC

TRACKS *The hoofprints of whitetail, fallow, roe and muntjac; the whitetail's print is about 3 inches long. The dew claws often leave prints when a deer jumps into soft mud.*

USING HIGH SEATS & BLINDS

'High seats' and 'blinds' are only two of many terms which sportsmen use to describe fixed positions from which quarry can be observed and shot. Others include the hurdle screen of the driven partridge shooter, the stone or turf-built butt of the driven grouse shooter, and the slit trench or sunken barrel favoured by some wildfowlers. These and other concealed or semi-concealed shooting stands are discussed elsewhere, in connection with the specific type of shooting to which they primarily relate.

'High seat' is simply a direct translation of the German hunters' term *Hochsitz*, and it denotes a raised seat or platform from which deer, wild boar and, very occasionally, mouflon can be observed and shot. (A similar type of shooting stand, called a *machan*, was used in Indian big-game hunting, especially where leopards or tigers were lured to a tethered bait or a carcase below the stand.) The principle of the high seat is a simple but important one, aimed chiefly at overcoming the extraordinary scenting powers of deer and other wild ungulates.

It allows the hunter or observer to watch and shoot selectively, from a secure position where his scent is carried away on the breeze above the sensitive noses of his quarry. Scent carried on the breeze is generally dispersed downwind and at the same height or slightly higher than its source, except when atmospheric conditions cause temperature inversion. Once established quietly in position in his high seat, the hunter's scent should be undetectable to his quarry, although he must ensure that no abrupt movement or alien sound puts them on the alert or frightens them off. The essential stalking skills of silence and slow movement still remain important when shooting or watching from high seats.

The high seat confers other benefits, too. A shot fired from a high seat placed some 12 to 15 feet above ground level means that the bullet's flight will be downward, and a shot which

misses or a bullet which passes through a beast's body should bury itself harmlessly in the ground. This is especially important when shooting in densely-populated areas or close to roads, tracks and rights of way, and also where the general terrain is flat and does not provide a close, solid backstop for the bullet. In many parts of Britain and Europe, the flatness of the land or the proximity of other human activity has led State forestry bodies and private proprietors alike to insist that all sporting shooting of deer must be carried out from high seats, for safety reasons.

The style and construction of a high seat can take many forms and it can be permanent, semiportable or fully-portable, depending on local conditions and the individual stalker's requirements and preferences.

Permanent high seats are built to stand firmly and remain useful for long periods, perhaps up to 20 or 30 years. They are often free-standing structures, built from selected timber which has been impregnated or treated against rot, and are often fitted out quite elaborately. Looking like military watchtowers, they often consist in essence of a large box on stilts, with seating to accommodate up to two or three stalkers and their guides, together with all their equipment and perhaps

also a small dachshund-like deer-tracking dog. There may be shelves and ledges for placing equipment, and some incorporate simple heating and cooking facilities, especially useful in cold winter conditions.

The semiportable or temporary high seat is a simpler, lighter structure intended either for a brief working life or for occasional movement to new locations. It may be either free standing or lean-to, and the latter type is propped ladder-wise against a suitable supporting upright such as the bole of a mature conifer or straight, upright hardwood tree. The usual construction is of sawn or peeled timber, protected against rot and designed for simplicity and lightness combined with the security which every high seat should have if it is to be used with confidence and safety.

Finally, the fully-portable high seat uses a ladder-type construction of tubular aluminium, and a number of ingenious and practical designs are readily available and widely used. Used in free-standing or lean-to modes, the portable aluminium structure enables a stalker to move his high seat with mininum trouble, and the light construction means that it can be carried easily by one person even into the most awkward and remote places. Painted

in dark greens and browns, it can merge well with its surroundings, and the Slingsby-Peill and Crosby-Holme designs are especially good.

The essential qualities of every high seat, whether permanent or portable, single-seater or multi-seater, are that it should be secure and comfortable to use. A shaky ladder or rotten wooden supports may mean a crippling fall, perhaps when the stalker is alone and miles from help. A rickety, unstable seat which sways with every puff of wind is unlikely to promote untroubled watching or straight shooting.

However well designed and comfortable the seat, its positioning is critical to its effective use. The effort and expense of constructing a high seat makes it imperative to study the movements of deer carefully beforehand, to ensure that a major, permanent structure will provide a clear view of deer moving and feeding over many years, during which time the trees will grow substantially and deer movements may be affected by other forest activities like clear-felling and new planting, or changing land use on adjacent farms.

A semipermanent or portable structure may be preferable in areas where open, recently-planted areas, with wide roads and rides, are likely to grow up

For duck shooting, the blind can be a simple screen of wire and rushes, high enough to provide cover but low enough to give a clear arc of fire.

This woodland high seat is a simple wooden ladder and platform built among the lower branches of an oak tree.

take up a concealed position close to his pattern of decoy birds placed on a likely feeding area.

The farmland pigeon shooter may place decoys on fields of oilseed rape, clover or cereal stubbles after harvest, and his ideal hide position is often along a hedgerow just upwind or across wind from the decoys. Pigeon shooting hides can be constructed using ex-military camouflage nets, augmented with assorted greenery and branches cut from the hedgerow. A shooting stick or an improvised seat made from a padded, upturned wooden box, and a convenient position for the cartridge bag, vacuum flask and so on, complete the hide's internal arrangements.

The hide's effectiveness is greatly increased if the shooter takes pains to dress appropriately, and military-style disruptive pattern material (DPM) with mittens for the backs of the hands, a hat with a good brim or peak and a face veil are all useful aids. Clothing and hide construction should also not impede the shooter when he wants to rise quickly and easily from a sitting position when a shot is to be taken.

The hide or blind requirements of the inland duck shooter or coastal wildfowler can vary considerably. Inland, where flight ponds are fed regularly to attract waterfowl, simple screens of wattle or rushes may give sufficient concealment while providing the clear overhead arc of fire which the shooter needs. Coastal wildfowling calls for careful and constantly-updated reconnaissance to establish the birds' flightlines and to allow blinds to be placed accordingly. Natural features including gulleys and creeks may give the fowler adequate cover, but coastal marshes and the tideline may call for structures improvised from rocks, available vegetation and driftwood, to which light netting may be added.

As for high seats, effective shooting from hides and blinds means the hunter must get into position in good time and without disturbing his surroundings or intended quarry.

and close in within a few years, severely limiting the fields of view and arcs of fire available from the seat. For a few years it may give excellent service, after which it can be removed and repositioned to take account of changed forest conditions. The portable aluminium seat is enormously versatile but placing still remains critical. Facing at the wrong angle or placed just a few yards wide of the mark, it can mean endless frustration as one shootable beast after another appears in an unshootable position.

Once in his high seat, whatever its design, the rifleman should have an exceptionally comfortable and steady position from which to watch and shoot. Sitting in a comfortable, relaxed fashion, he suffers from none of the physical tensions and breathlessness which can afflict the stalker on foot, although concentration and watchfulness impose the same nervous strain. Binoculars can be used methodically and steadily to scan an area and study individual beasts as they appear, and a thoughtfully-placed ledge or bar should give his forearm a secure rest when a shot is taken. Whether padded or not, the woodwork or metal of the rifle itself should on no account be allowed to touch the bar, which is intended only to support the rifleman's arm, and a shot from a high seat

can then be taken with a calm deliberation not always possible when on foot.

The blind, like the high seat, is designed to conceal the hunter's presence, although scent is not the prime consideration. Blinds (or 'hides') are placed at ground level, and are intended to conceal the hunter from the eyes of his quarry, rather than its nose. With the exception of pigeon-shooting hides or 'boxes' placed high in mature trees in roosting woods, hides and blinds are constructed at ground level. They are important wherever decoys are used, for example in pigeon shooting and in many forms of wildfowling, where the sportsman must

FIELD DRESSING

All sporting quarry, large or small, game birds or large mammals, must be dealt with correctly after they are shot, if their appearance and meat are not to be spoilt or wasted, and if attractive and often hard-won trophies are to be preserved and mounted afterwards.

Game birds require prompt but simple measures to ensure that they cool and stiffen readily after shooting, and it is best if they can be hung up on cords or hooks in a vehicle or game-cart, as is customary on large driven and covert shoots. Walking guns, dogging parties and individual rough-shooters must avoid cramming freshly-shot birds into the pockets of shooting jackets and waterproofs, even the large so-called 'game pockets'. Birds carried in this way will become soggy and crumpled, and their appearance at the end of the day will reflect no credit on the sportsman. Properly designed gamebags should be carried, and these are fitted with an outer pouch of netting, which enables game to cool and air to circulate freely.

Of the small mammals which are shot, it is normal to leave hares intact to be hung for several days before they are gutted and jointed for cooking or freezing. Rabbits, however, should be 'paunched' as soon as possible after shooting. This is a quick and easy procedure, involving nothing more than a quick incision through the thin, loose skin of the upper belly, which allows the entire stomach and lower gut to be removed in one smart pull, leaving the paunched rabbit clean and avoiding the taint caused by stomach contents and fluids leaking into the body cavity.

Deer and similar large game present proportionately greater problems for the hunter. All deer, wild sheep, goats and other big game should be eviscerated ('gralloched' is a widely used traditional term, from the Scots Gaelic *grealach*, meaning 'intestines') immediately after it has been shot. As with paunching a rabbit, this involves removing the stomach and all the lower digestive tract, the bladder and the genitalia, so as to keep the venison untainted and clean.

Once a deer or other large mammal has been shot it must be dressed promptly or the carcase may be spoilt. The old

practice of cutting the major arteries of the throat and bleeding the animal is now rarely necessary, owing to the massive haemorrhaging usually caused by modern, high-velocity rifles firing soft-nosed, expanding bullets. The first move must be to roll the fallen animal on to its back, shaking it slightly to and fro, which causes the paunch and intestines to lie down within the belly cavity and along the line of the back. It may be helpful to wedge the animal between two small rocks, or to pursuade a companion to hold it in position as the gralloch begins, to prevent the carcase rolling awkwardly, with legs and antlers getting in the way.

The belly skin should be pinched between finger and thumb just below the animal's breastbone, and a sideways cut should be made carefully to open up the body cavity. Two fingers should be slid through this incision and spread apart, to hold the belly skin clear of the stomach and gut, and the knife blade should be carefully introduced into the incision, cutting edge upwards and guided between the spread fingers. The cut should now be extended backwards from the base of the ribs to the anus.

In expert hands almost any sharp knife can be used, but the ideal stalker's knife will have two sharp blades, either of which can be locked firmly in the open position, with one

normal blade and a second, blunt-pointed gralloching blade. The latter is an extra safeguard to avoid puncturing the stomach or gut, with resultant leakage of stomach contents and juices into the beast's body cavity.

When gralloching male deer, the penis and scrotum are cut away carefully but not detached. The stalker should ease the genitalia back towards the anus, and careful cutting at this point enables the anus and lower gut to be worked forward through the pelvic girdle and into the body cavity without the leakage of urine or faeces.

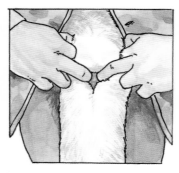
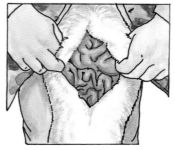

PAUNCHING A RABBIT *With the rabbit held between your knees, belly up and head towards you, cut a hole in the belly. Then use your fingers to open up the hole so that you can remove the guts.*

Game birds are hung up to cool and stiffen after shooting. Rabbits should be gutted, but hares are usually hung intact.

With the smaller deer, such as muntjac and roe, it is usually possible to cut forwards, severing the sternum and extending the cut up to the base of the neck. Some purpose-made stalking knives have a saw-type blade designed for this purpose, and these may be useful with an old or unusually tough animal, although a heavy, sharp blade will usually suffice. Such a cut exposes the chest contents, and it is possible to reach up inside

Dressing a deer keeps the venison untainted, and also reduces the total weight to be carried or dragged.

to cut the windpipe and the upper end of the food tract below the head, which frees the entire body contents so that windpipe, lungs, heart, stomach, gut and genitalia can be eased away as one unit. Many stalkers then select and save the liver and kidneys for their own consumption, and the heart and lungs for their dogs, placing these in separate, leakproof bags.

Adverse weather, lack of time, or an unmanageably large beast may make it impossible or undesirable to carry out the full-length cut from anus to neck, and a shorter, simpler gralloch

is done. This involves making only the first cuts from the sternum to the anus, allowing removal of the contents of the body cavity from the stomach backwards. The chest contents and the diaphragm are left intact. The remainder of the gralloch should be carried out without delay on return to camp or to the deer larder.

In wild country, and on the open hill in Scotland, it is customary to slit open the stomach bag and leave the gralloch exposed, and various species of scavenging, carrion-eating birds and mammals like the hill fox, the hooded crow and the raven

will come to it quickly. However, the woodland stalker on farmland or in areas where the public have frequent access should be at pains to conceal the gralloch, by burying it or covering it up, well away from tracks and footpaths where it might be offensive. Finally, once the gralloch is complete the beast should be turned over on its belly with limbs outspread to allow any remaining blood to drain freely from the body cavity.

Small species like muntjac and roe are easily carried, either slung over the stalker's shoulder or, less messily, in a capacious rucksack with a detachable, washable lining. Larger species like fallow, red deer and the massive wapiti present greater problems in carcase extraction and recovery.

In well-roaded woodlands and forest, a wheeled or tracked vehicle may be brought to within easy reach of the carcase, which can then be dragged out. Scandinavian stalkers have developed various forms of dragging mats and sledge-type bases on which to drag large deer carcases and minimize bruising and abrasion of the carcase. On the open hill in Scotland, ponies and Argocat-type vehicles cannot always get right to the spot where the beast has fallen and some dragging may be necessary. This is traditionally done

by fixing a hemp rope around the animal's head and muzzle, and the antlers of a stag make natural anchor points. Downhill dragging on steep slopes may call for a tail-rope to be fitted and restrained by a second helper, to stop the carcase tumbling downhill out of control, which may bruise and pulverize the venison.

In remote wilderness areas, the extraction of an entire carcase may be physically impossible, and priority must be given to saving and removing the prime venison cuts and the trophy antlers or horns. The lower legs should be removed, and the two haunches and two forelegs detached without skinning, which helps protect and preserve the joints when they are packed and carried away. The prime saddle cut should be detached from behind the bottom ribs, and if the antlers are to be retained for mounting with the frontal bone only, the head should be severed by cutting above the top vertebra.

However, if the hunter wishes to have his trophy mounted in the form of a full head-mount the animal must be 'caped', which means severing the neck at the first vertebra, but retaining the entire head skin and also a generous cape of skin which should be cut from behind the withers and down level with the animals forelegs. Once detached, the head should be carefully wrapped in the cape of skin, and taken back for professional attention by a taxidermist without delay.

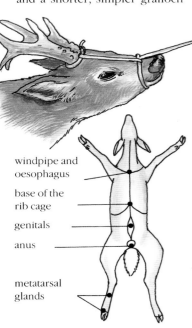

DRAGGING A DEER *A small deer can be carried to a road or track where it can be loaded onto a vehicle, but larger animals may have to be dragged by a rope fixed around the head or the antlers.*

DRESSING A DEER *Start by pinching the belly skin between your finger and thumb, just below the breastbone, and making a small sideways cut. Then put two fingers into the hole to lift the skin clear of the stomach and gut, and carefully extend the cut to the anus. Next, cut the windpipe and oesophagus (food tract) as close to the head as possible or, if you want the head intact, by making a cut at the base of the neck and reaching up inside to cut the pipes.*

windpipe and oesophagus

base of the rib cage

genitals

anus

metatarsal glands

To open the belly, cut from the rib cage to the anus

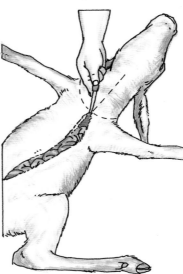

Sever the windpipe so that the entire body contents can be removed

WALKING-UP

Walking-up is a self-explanatory term, indicating a style of shooting in which game birds are flushed and mammals such as rabbits and hares are put on foot by the approach of the sportsman on foot, either working alone, or with his dog, or with a group of friends. It is a familiar and widely practised shooting technique, and its origins go back to the very beginning of sporting shooting.

Where areas of cover are believed to hold game, little could be more straightforward than to walk methodically through that cover, thereby creating sufficient disturbance to cause game to fly or run into view and offer the chance of a shot. When sporting shooting was in its infancy and sporting firearms were primitive and unreliable, it was considered perfectly

acceptable to shoot quarry like hares sitting, or to fire at a bird or into a covey squatting or running ahead on the ground. But as firearms developed and sportsmen became more proficient in what was known as the 'art of shooting flying', the unwritten code of sportsmanship called for ground game to be running and the birds to be flushed and on the wing.

Walking-up may be practised by the lone sportsman, perhaps accompanied by a flushing dog of the spaniel variety hunting through the cover within gunshot. However, this is best considered as one form of rough shooting rather than walking-up. 'Walking-up', as normally used, denotes a team or party of sportsmen, moving in unison to sweep across an area. The party need not be large, and may

consist of only three or four guns, or it may comprise as many as ten or twelve guns.

Walking-up grouse is a traditional and popular form of British grouse shooting, particularly in the early days of the season from August 12th onwards. It is usually an informal affair, with friends and families enjoying a day's shooting in the bracing environment and the stirring scenery of the uplands in late summer. It is also a practical and effective way of shooting grouse which have not previously been disturbed that season, which may tend to lie tight rather than to flush readily, and which may give off little or no scent for dogs in the warm, dry air.

Guns walking in a straight line and spaced approximately 30 yards apart, with spaniels and retrievers working through the

heather close to the guns, and perhaps accompanied by gamekeepers and other non-shooting companions in the line, will usually manage to flush all the grouse within the area they sweep across. Most will rise close to the guns, and shooting can be deliberate and selective. Second broods and late hatching may mean that coveys of half-grown cheepers will be encountered in the early days of a new shooting season, and the individual gun has time to assess the birds he flushes and to shoot or hold his fire as appropriate.

For walking-up to be an effective hunting method and also a

Part of a line of guns, with dogs, walking-up grouse on a heather-covered grouse moor in Scotland.

WALKING-UP IN LINE

30 yds

WHEELING

are important if sport is to be good and the day's shooting safe, and they should be instilled firmly from the outset. It is the duty of shoot organizers and experienced guns to ensure that everyone in the line knows what to do and how to behave. The quality of the sport and the enjoyment of the day will then be enhanced for everybody.

Walking-up in line can be carried out on other terrain and for other species. Guns may line out across a marsh in pursuit of snipe, across stubbles and ploughed land for hares and partridges, through low cover and scrubland for woodcock and blackgame, and through woodland for pheasants and woodcock. In every case a straight line is essential, and guns walking in cover should take particular care to keep in constant touch with their neighbouring guns on either side, whom they may not be able to see but whose movements they should be able to follow by sound. In thick cover, guns may find it helpful to whistle and call regularly, which serves both to help to create disturbance and flush tight-sitting game and to enable guns to maintain contact and thus know their safe arc of fire when game offers a shot.

There are occasions when a team of guns walking-up may need to abandon the normal straight-line formation. This may be necessary when beating out long, narrow coverts for pheasants or woodcock, especially late in the season when game is wary and tends to flush far ahead of the line or to break back over the guns. Sometimes it is profitable for guns to work forward in a three-sided or 'U' formation, with several guns and dogs beating through a narrow covert while two or three others move forwards ahead of them, along the covert side.

When birds break back, as often happens with woodcock and late season pheasants, it can be useful to have an additional gun hanging back behind the main formation, and such a 'rear-gunner' may get a good deal of the shooting. These variant formations can be highly effective, and need not be any less safe than keeping a straight line, always provided that each gun remains constantly vigilant, noting his position relative to his fellow guns and constantly assessing his safe arcs of fire.

WALKING-UP IN LINE *When walking-up in a line (above), the guns are spread about thirty yards apart and move forward at a measured pace, keeping in a straight line.*

WHEELING *Walking-up involves a series of sweeps across the moor, and after each the line wheels and makes a 180-degree turn, pivoting around one of the end guns.*

safe undertaking for the guns, certain fundamental principles must be observed. Most important of all, the guns must keep a straight line at all times, for only in this way can they avoid the chances of a shot being fired to the front or rear of the line and hitting a gun, beater or dog who has pushed too far forward or lagged behind.

To walk abreast in a straight line sounds absurdly simple, but the uneven, broken terrain typical of even the flattest and easiest moors makes it more difficult than it might appear. Walking guns must be constantly aware of their position relative to their right- and left-hand neighbours, and they must think three-dimensionally too. Grouse moors are rarely perfectly flat, and the line will frequently be moving along a slope where the end gun in a line of eight or ten others may be as much as two or three hundred feet above or below the gun on the other end of the line. Thus a shot at a high-flying bird, which would be perfectly safe on flat ground, might have tragic consequences if fired when other guns are walking on higher ground.

Another key principle in walking-up is for the line to

move at a steady, measured pace. Undue haste increases the risks of the line straggling, and guns walking quickly may fail to flush birds when they are sitting really tight. Too fast a pace over broken or boggy ground increases the risk of a fall, which is always to be avoided when carrying a loaded firearm, and an individual who is out of breath or overheated from fast walking is much less likely to shoot accurately and consistently than one who is relaxed, composed and comfortable.

When birds are flushed or a shot is heard, all guns, beaters and dogs should halt immediately. This response, which becomes instinctive with experience, confers a number of benefits. It maintains a straight, disciplined line; it ensures that all guns are standing in the best and safest position relative to one another to take advantage of whatever shots the birds flushed may afford; it enables shot game to be marked accurately and retrieved promptly; and it reduces the likelihood of the guns pressing forward over other birds from the same covey or party which might otherwise flush behind or in other unshootable directions.

A line of guns walking-up

grouse is best controlled by those who are placed at the ends of the line. These should be experienced individuals, and the intermediate guns should take their cue from them. Walking-up in line usually involves making a series of sweeps to and fro across moorland, and after each beat the line must wheel and make a 180-degree turn, pivoting on one of the end guns just as a line of soldiers on parade manoeuvre in relation to a right or left marker at the end of a rank.

To execute a neat wheeling movement in an extended line of guns, strung out across perhaps 300 yards of moorland, is a satisfying achievement, but it requires some thought and care. The 'pivot' gun must virtually stand still while the gun at the other end of the line may have to walk almost half a mile, and as the line swings round everyone must be on the alert in case game is flushed, and be ready to fire selectively, accurately and safely.

These simple but important principles for walking-up over moorland become second nature to experienced sportsmen, but these apparently obvious skills do not always come readily to novice sportsmen. But they

ROUGH SHOOTING

Rough shooting is an informal and enjoyable form of sport for an individual with his dog or for a group.

The term 'rough shooting' is both self-explanatory and misleading, for while this form of live quarry shooting is often more informal and relaxed than driven or covert shooting, it still calls for its own distinctive skills, disciplines and organization. Rough shooting can be a solitary or a group activity, but its essence lies in its simplicity, the variety of habitats and species which may be encountered, and the gun's need to be versatile and adaptable to make the most of the sport available.

Rough shooting may involve a single gun setting off with his dog for little more than an hour or two of 'pottering', or there may be several guns who join forces, with an assortment of dogs and perhaps also accompanied by friends, wives and children to help with a variety of tasks including informal beating-out of cover, carrying shot game and leading the dogs when they are on the leash. More democratic than covert shooting, the rough-shooting party will make various collective decisions about how the day's sport is organized, but it is still best if those who are most familiar with the area to be shot over guide the others.

A typical winter day's rough shooting in Britain and Ireland may begin early, perhaps even before first light, as the guns assemble and make their way to a marsh or pond where duck or geese are known to flight at dawn. The shoreline is an alternative venue if coastal wildfowl are the first quarry. Guns should move quickly and quietly into position, according to placings devised by those in the party who know the area and the birds' movements best. Thereafter, the sport will consist mainly of flighting and pass shooting.

After the morning flight is over, and a thorough picking-up operation has accounted for all birds shot, the rough-shooting party may pause for a short break, to stow the bagged birds in vehicles or gamebags and to discuss the next stage of the day over a warming cup of coffee (or something stronger). As the sun rises the heavy, warm clothing suitable for the pre-dawn chill may be exchanged for lighter wear, and the guns may exchange the heavy loads and large shot which are the duck-shooters' choice for lighter cartridges with smaller shot, more suited to tackling a variety of gamebird and wildfowl species.

Many flight ponds for duck are close to areas of marshland and wet bogland, which are likely habitats for snipe and various waders and wildfowl including golden plover and teal. The party may move off to such a spot, and if the marsh is extensive they will usually spread out in an extended line, applying the techniques of walking-up. Snipe are best tackled by guns walking downwind, and the team of guns, their friends and their dogs should work slowly and methodically, with minimum noise and with dogs close to heel. When birds are flushed and shots fired, the line must halt and wait until the pick-up is complete and guns have been reloaded before they move on.

The younger and nimbler members of the party should take the roughest ground and do most of the walking, and it may be possible to combine a walk-up with an informal drive, by placing the more elderly members of the party as standing guns along a road or track. Birds flushed forwards by the advancing line may present sporting shots, but each opportunity should be individually assessed. Perhaps a bird may fly too low to be a safe shot, and is best left for one of the standing guns.

The majority of bogs and marshes are crossed by drains and ditches, and thigh-length waders may be useful items in the rough-shooter's wardrobe to tackle such ground, quite apart from their value when duck shooting or coastal wildfowling. The narrow, water-filled drains often hold duck, especially teal, and hares are also fond of open marshes and will lie up there in dry, sheltered spots. Rushy clumps and the reedy fringes of marshland often attract pheasants, which were originally marsh birds and feed readily on the seed-heads of rushes, and a spaniel should be run through these areas to beat them out. In this way, an informal group of guns and their dogs, or even one solitary sportsman, can have a variety of different types of quarry and styles of shot within one area of land, and the bag on a rough shooting day can often be more diverse than on organized driven days.

The marshy land may occupy the party for an hour or more, and then the guns will reassemble and discuss the next stage of the day. Game shot should once again be stored properly, and the guns and their partners may be glad of a brief break to chat together and perhaps to change their footwear – especially if someone has received a bootful of cold marsh water.

Rough woodland and shrubby scrub-land can provide excellent mixed sport, and the next stage of the day might be to move off to such a spot. Rough-shooting parties often form a

The great beauty of rough shooting lies in its simplicity. Here, a rough shooter in America takes aim at a ring-necked pheasant which has risen from cover in a maize field.

convoy of cars and move about a good deal during the day, unless they have access to a large piece of land which can provide a full day's shooting. And a variety of habitats and species is one of the principal charms of a day's rough shooting.

In Britain and Ireland, woodlands which are not managed for covert shooting may often be rented for rough shooting, and farmers and landowners are often ready to allow rough shooting over such land. Private forestry companies and the Forestry Commission also often lease plantations for shooting, usually on a tendered-bids basis, and these areas can give good sport for the rough-shooter, with wild pheasants and woodcock as the principal game species. Pheasants can often be encouraged by a little feeding with wheat or maize, while woodcock come and go in unpredictable ways, according to the moon and the weather.

Rabbits have returned in good numbers to much of the British Isles, and can provide excellent sport when hunted from cover by eager spaniels, affording opportunities for some exciting snap-shooting as they bolt across rides and gaps in vegetation. But care is needed in this sort of shooting, to avoid the risk of endangering one's fellow guns or shooting an unsteady dog which may give chase and run just behind a bolting rabbit.

Woodpigeons are among the most testing of all European sporting birds, and their pest status means they can give fine sport throughout the year. Many a day's rough shooting will end with the guns going to a copse or plantation where pigeon are known to roost, and exciting shooting can be had if the guns are strategically placed. Even the solitary gun may have some excellent shooting for an hour or so before last light, and if the evening is windy the birds fly with a speed and verve which can test even the finest shooter's skill.

Such, in broad outline, is the variety and diversity which may go towards the making of a day's rough shooting. Variety of species and habitat, and informality and versatility on the guns' part, are the essential ingredients for this form of shooting, which still forms the mainstay of sport for a majority of shooters in northern and western Britain.

SHOOTING OVER DOGS

Shooting over dogs is one of the oldest and best-established forms of systematic gamebird shooting, which involves a precise and well-defined technique. Unfortunately, this expression is also often used rather loosely, which is misleading and inaccurate. 'Over dogs' always means shooting over pointers or setters, which range widely and find game by air scent, pointing or 'setting' it and flushing it when ordered to do so by their handler. It is quite incorrect to use this phrase to describe shooting over other breeds such as spaniels or retrievers working through cover close to walking guns, which is a form of walking-up, a quite separate shooting technique.

Bird dogs – a convenient generic term for the English pointer and the English, Irish and Gordon setter breeds – find game by ranging fast and widely, questing for scent carried on the breeze. A touch of scent will slow their gallop to a walk, and a sure 'find' will cause the dog to freeze into total immobility, nose pointing towards the game in cover. An English pointer typically stands to point, leaning forward with nose, back and tail forming a straight line and with no movement other than the merest tremble or a slight twitch of the tail tip, while setters often crouch low or drop belly-flat to the ground.

Bird dogs work with their heads held high to catch airborne scents, and those with natural working ability will tend to move in an instinctive quartering pattern, running to and fro across the wind and turning upwind with each new beat, thus effectively covering a wide sweep of terrain. With experience, bird dogs can learn to work in a crosswind or even downwind direction, which the lie of the ground may sometimes necessitate, but this is advanced dog-work which calls for steadiness in the dog and thoughtful management by its handler.

Bird dogs work at their best in open country where their powers of sustained galloping and wide ranging are put to optimum use. This form of hunting over dogs is seen at its best when the quarry is red grouse on open heather moorland, and this is the best scenario in which to describe how guns and bird dogs work together.

Pointers and setters are still widely used for grouse shooting on upland areas of northern and western Britain and Ireland where grouse densities tend to be too low for driving to be a viable technique. In many areas of western Scotland, Wales and Ireland, grouse are thinly scattered over large expanses of badly-drained moorland where the quality and management of the heather does not promote high grouse populations. In such habitat, a wide-ranging bird dog is quite the best means of locating grouse, and northern and western parts of the British Isles remain the strongholds of these gundog breeds.

Typically, a dogging party comprises not more than two guns, and it is unfair and ineffective to expect any bird dog to work for a long line of walking guns. If the dogs are not handled by one of the guns there may also be a dog handler present. A useful additional helper is a ghillie, to carry the bag of shot

game, hold fresh dogs in reserve until they are required later in the day, and lead a retriever for finding and collecting shot birds.

Grouse-dogging parties will usually spend a five-or six-hour day working their chosen ground in a roughly circular movement, returning to their starting point, and will not always be able to work directly upwind. Wherever possible, however, a start is made into the wind. The dog is 'cast off' on its first beat, and races out at an easy, loping gallop across the wind on a beat which may be as

much as 300 to 400 yards wide. Sometimes two dogs are run together, and in this 'brace-work' the two will work in unison, quartering to and fro in alternate, criss-crossing sweeps. Brace-work is the most attractive and effective form of bird-dogging, and a uniquely pleasing style of sport to watch.

The role of the guns at this stage is a rather passive one, following the dogs and watching their work, until there is a 'find'. The gun who knows what to look for may see the dog's pace falter or its gait and tail action change subtly as its nose picks up a 'touch', the bird-dogger's term for the first faint whiff of scent which is often the prelude to a find, slowing the dog as it gets wind of the full scent of grouse ahead and then freezes into sudden immobility.

POINTING AND 'ROADING IN'

POINTING AND 'ROADING IN'
The guns follow the dog (A) until it comes to point. Then they take up position on either side of it (B) and order it to road in. Game flushed, dog flattens (C).

their shots. Guns shooting over dogs should always be aware of the risk of damaging a dog's sensitive hearing or making it gunshy if shots are fired too close to its head.

On a grouse moor, the find may have been anything from a solitary snipe or a single old grouse to a large covey or pack of many birds. The guns should have comparatively straightforward going-away or slightly quartering shots, and each should take the birds on his own side. With a covey of grouse, two experienced guns should each achieve a right-and-left on most occasions – in theory, at least. Experienced guns can also shoot very selectively, holding their fire altogether if a covey of immature cheepers rises, and shooting the old birds first if the covey is well-grown.

Experienced bird-doggers know to reload immediately, while marking the position of fallen birds. Covey birds like grouse do not always rise together, and guns should be prepared for 'the lazy one' which rises some seconds or even minutes after the others have flushed. The leading pointer or setter should be ordered forward to 'work out the point', which involves a slow, systematic questing with nose held low and the dog's tail lashing to and fro in excitement. If any more birds rise the dog must again drop, and only when the handler is satisfied that the point has been thoroughly worked out should the picking-up begin.

European and North American sportsmen often expect their bird dogs to move forward, 'point dead' (point the shot or wounded game) and retrieve it to hand, and train their dogs accordingly. In Britain, however, this is not common practice and is generally discouraged on two main grounds. It is believed to lead to unsteadiness on point, and British-bred bird dogs are not bred for soft mouths or natural retrieving ability. At this point, therefore, a retriever or a spaniel used as a retriever is sent out to collect the shot birds one by one, the bird dogs remaining dropped or restrained on leads.

Where a brace of dogs are running together, both should stop instantly with the hind dog pointing his mate who has found – 'backing the point', as it is known – and neither should move again until commanded to do so. Most bird dogs back instinctively, but some can become jealous and rush up to 'steal the point' from the other dog, a serious fault which may cause birds to be flushed prematurely and out of shot. In competitive field trials this is a grave misdemeanour which leads to that dog's elimination from the trial. Any bird dog which tends to run in and steal another's point should only be worked singly.

When a bird dog finds, the guns should make their way quickly but carefully towards it, advancing steadily from the rear. In grouse-dogging, the dog may stop on point several hundred yards away, and the guns' approach may be over broken ground or up a steep slope. But the bird dog should be steady and staunch, holding its point for as long as is required for the guns to reach it, which may be many minutes. Many gamebirds lie well to a bird dog, but even grouse and grey partridge will become unsettled in windy, wet weather and may run ahead or flush wildly and unpredictably, while pheasants and red-legged partridges are always notorious for running ahead of a dog.

As they approach the dog on point, the guns should carry their shotguns ready in the 'high port' position, pointing upwards and forwards across their bodies, with thumbs ready to release safety catches and trigger fingers laid in readiness alongside the trigger guard (but *not on the trigger itself*). They should carefully take up their positions one on either side of the dog and about 8 to 10 yards away from it, and ideally slightly ahead of the dog's nose. Then all is ready for the handler to order the dog to break its point and 'road in', walking forwards quickly and decisively to flush the birds. This is usually signalled by a click of the handler's fingers.

A good dog should unfreeze and road-in immediately, dropping instantly to a belly-flat position when the birds take wing, or, if a hare has been pointed, when it runs. This reduces any likelihood of the dog giving chase and also gets it down well out of the guns' line of fire and away from the muzzle-blast of

DRIVING

Game shooters, especially in Britain, use the term 'driven shooting' as a useful blanket expression to signify all forms of sport in which gamebirds are flushed so as to push them forward and over a line of guns waiting at pegs and stands, or in butts. Thus 'driven game' may mean a formal day's shooting at grouse, partridge or pheasant, and also at snipe or woodcock in certain areas, principally in northern and western Britain. However, it is important to distinguish between the techniques of driving game from low cover on open ground such as heather, stubble fields, root crops and marshland, and the rather different procedures of covert shooting, which involve beating out copses and similar wooded areas to flush pheasants and woodcock.

Red grouse are birds of heather moorland, while partridges are found on arable farmland and grassland, and from the mid-19th century onward both species were increasingly shot as they flew forward over the guns, having been flushed by a team of what we would now loosely call 'beaters' but which were then termed 'drivers'. The latter word, now rarely used, gives a truer reflection of their role, which is to work in an extended line across a wide sweep of downland, fields or moorland, to flush the birds and move them forward over the line of standing guns, at pegs or in butts, which in grouse driving may lie as much as a mile or more away from the beaters' starting point.

On grouse moors where driving is the usual practice there

DRIVING SNIPE

DRIVING SNIPE *Snipe are driven upwind toward the guns (above) by beaters working about 60 to 80 yards apart.*

DRIVING PARTRIDGE *Partridge are driven downwind (right) toward a line of 8 or 10 guns (only 3 are shown here).*

On a driven grouse shoot in Scotland, the birds are driven toward guns stationed in 'butts' made of stone, wood, turf or bales of straw.

will be sufficient lines of butts to allow for five or six drives in a normal day's shooting. These will be carefully placed to take advantage of the flight lines of birds driven from particular areas of the moor, and there may be one or more additional, alternative lines of butts which will be used depending upon the direction of the wind, which can have a major influence on the direction in which driven grouse will fly. As the season progresses, grouse which have been driven several times become wary and 'butt-shy', and for this reason additional lines of butts are often positioned just over a ridge, or below the crest of a rise, to conceal them from oncoming grouse until the birds are almost on top of them.

Timing is especially important in grouse driving. Beaters and guns start the drive far apart and the drive is normally controlled by the head keeper, who will only order the beaters to start moving when he is sure that guns, flankers, flag-men and pickers-up are all in position. Portable two-way radios are frequently used on grouse drives to maintain close communication between the beating line and the butts. In partridge driving, the areas and distances involved are smaller, and guns and beaters may be within sight of each other almost throughout the drive.

On many grouse drives a large sweep of moor will be traversed by the beaters, birds flushed will often pitch down in front of the line and be flushed again later, and the guns may have to wait for some time before the first grouse appear. Each drive may take up to an hour to complete.

Driving grouse from August 12th onward is now common practice, although earlier generations preferred to walk-up the first grouse of a new season, reserving driving until late August, September and October. Early-season driving means that the birds may sit tight, especially in warm weather, and there may still be immature coveys of late-hatched birds, so the beaters should be more numerous and not too widely spaced at this time. The line should move steadily and aim to bring in a manageable piece of ground thoroughly. As the season progresses and grouse become more mature and wild, the beating line may be longer, with much wider gaps between the beaters, and the area swept may be much greater than in mid-August.

A line of eight or ten guns stationed in butts or at pegs some 30 to 40 yards apart represents a fairly narrow front across which to drive the birds, usually not more than 250 to 350 yards from end to end. To help funnel the flying coveys of grouse and partridge into the desired area, flankers and flag-men are de-

ployed to either side of the beating line and also as an extension of the line of guns. Theirs is a skilful role, and it is best if they remain unobtrusive, even to the extent of lying or crouching in long heather or behind knolls or hedgerows, and standing up and waving their flags only if birds show signs of swinging wide of the guns or breaking out sideways from the direction of the drive.

With a well-timed movement, a skilled flag-man or flanker can effectively turn a large number of birds back into the drive and over the guns, while an inept one moving at the wrong moment can make matters much worse. A flag-man near the butts or, in partridge driving, the guns' pegs, can usefully use a loud thunderer-type whistle, blowing it as birds approach to alert sportsmen who may have relaxed their vigilance.

Partridge driving embodies in miniature most of the principles of grouse driving. Much smaller acreages are involved, but shoot organizers must take careful account of the lie of the ground, the wind direction and the birds' preferred flight lines. These may vary from day to day with changes in wind and weather, and from season to season as the arable cropping pattern changes. It may be necessary to have a beating and flanking line which almost encircles the areas driven, especially if partridges are to be driven effectively upwind or across the wind. It is generally agreed that partridges are best driven downwind if possible, working inwards from the upwind end of the shoot.

Finally, where habitat is suitable, driving has an important part to play in snipe shooting. Where groups of more than three or four guns wish to tackle snipe on a succession of small-to-medium sized marshes or bogs, driving is usually the best procedure. Unlike grouse and partridge, snipe should be driven upwind whenever possible, with guns placed in a semicircle or U-formation in an upwind position. Three or four widely-spaced beaters with flags should suffice to drive snipe off even a very wide marsh, and it helps if they each have a whistle and blow blasts when snipe rise, as these small birds are often difficult for the guns to see until they have gained height.

DRIVING PARTRIDGE

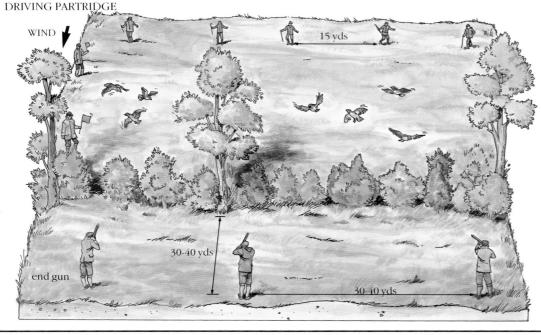

WIND

15 yds

30-40 yds

end gun

30-40 yds

COVERT SHOOTING

Covert shooting, while practised in various forms in many countries, is a distinctively British form of game shooting and is the principal type of formal game shooting in winter. As the term implies, shooting takes place in or close to woodlands, which may vary in size from small copses to larger woods and plantations, and all such areas managed for game are known collectively as coverts.

In a typical day's covert shooting, parties of beaters will work through a succession of five or six drives, and the object is to flush the birds steadily and progressively in such a way that they gain height and speed quickly, and so that the majority of birds pass over a strategically-positioned row of standing guns.

Typically, the management of the beaters is regulated by the head gamekeeper, and he may be accompanied by a team of eight to twelve beaters, each of whom will carry a stick. Many will use spaniels and terriers to help beat out and flush birds from thick cover. The flushing of the birds, the direction of their flight and the efficient management of the drive also depend upon the careful deployment of other helpers, including 'stops' who are placed individually to prevent running pheasants from moving too far forwards or sideways. Others may be called upon to lay out lines of 'sewelling', which are long strings or ropes bearing fluttering ribbons or bunting-like tags which encourage run-

ning birds to stop and take wing. On some drives, flagmen will be used, and as in the driving of grouse and partridges, their job is to turn flying birds in the desired direction and to further increase the height and speed of their flight.

The management and deployment of the guns is the task of the individual host or shoot captain. Customarily, the guns will draw for numbers at the beginning of the day, and the number drawn indicates the number of the stand or peg at which that gun will shoot during the first drive. Lines of guns usually number from right to left, and each gun normally moves up two places after each drive – for instance, a gun shooting on peg number 3 in the first drive will go on to peg number 5 for the second. While the conventions of numbering from right to left and moving up two places are customary, individual shoots may adopt slightly different procedures and the visiting gun should ensure that he knows what to do before the first drive begins.

Additional personnel also help in the running of an organized covert shooting day. These include a team of pickers-up, dog handlers usually accompanied by one or two steady and reliable retrievers, whose task is to mark and recover shot birds. Birds which fall dead in the open or close to the guns are easily recovered, and are often left for the guns to pick up with the help of their own dogs. The pickers-up concentrate on those

MOVING PEGS

The pegs are numbered from right to left, and the guns move up 2 positions at a time.

PEG POSITION

birds which fall in thick cover and in awkward corners, and are especially concerned to account for injured birds which may fly or run some distance into cover, often far behind the guns. Without an efficient picking-up team, many birds might be unaccounted for.

Shot game must also be carefully handled and sorted after each drive, and most shoots arrange for one or two people to man the 'game cart', frequently a Land Rover or other four-wheel-drive vehicle in which the shot game can be carefully

COVERT SHOOTING *The beaters flush the birds from woodland cover toward the line of guns positioned in the open at a suitable distance from the edge of the trees.*

hung up, and which can move easily from drive to drive during the shooting day. Other drivers and vehicles may also be required to transport the guns, their dogs and any non-shooting companions from one drive to another, and transport is often necessary for the beating team also, frequently a large trailer drawn by a tractor.

In the formal and disciplined context of a well-regulated covert shoot, shots may only be fired during the course of a drive, and guns must be unloaded at all other times and are usually carried in a leather or canvas sleeve or cover, only being taken out and loaded when each gun is in position at his peg or stand.

The drive will begin when the beater, stops, pickers-up and

line and are outlined against open sky. To fire at a low bird coming forward or crossing is a dangerous practice and puts unseen stops and beaters at risk. Likewise, low shots taken behind may endanger the pickers-up.

Ground game such as hares and rabbits are not normally shot on formal covert shoots, but it is important to have clear instructions about this from your host. Foxes on covert shoots can be a tricky question, and the shoot captain should give all guns clear guidance. Generally, however, foxes are not shot on covert shoots in areas which are hunted regularly by foxhounds, and to do so may cause offence and create bad relations with the hunt. In unhunted areas, however, it may be necessary to shoot foxes, although a formal covert shoot may not be an appropriate occasion for this.

During each drive, all guns should mark the fall of dead game and the direction taken by wounded birds, to facilitate a speedy and humane pickup by the dog handlers after the drive. 'Runners' – birds with broken wings but capable of running strongly – may go long distances, and guns should not hesitate to fire at any running bird to dispatch it promptly on the ground, always provided it is safe to fire such a shot. The alternative may be that a strong runner will escape to meet a painful and lingering end. Similarly, while guns should scrupulously avoid poaching birds which should be left for their neighbours, it is both legitimate and desirable to fire at any bird pricked or wounded by another gun, to stop it dead if possible.

To kill a bird which has been fired at and missed cleanly by another gun is known as 'wiping his eye', and can be the cause of good-natured humour or grave offence, depending upon the individual's temperament. Except when shooting with close friends, attempting to wipe the eye of other guns can appear like showing-off and should normally be avoided.

After three or four drives, most covert shooting parties will break for lunch, which may consist of a light snack in a shooting hut or barn or may involve adjourning to the estate house for a formal three-course meal with wines. A break of longer than an hour is not normally desirable, but the beaters particularly appreciate a break and a rest in the middle of the day. On some shoots, however, it is the practice to 'shoot through', especially in late December and early January when the hours of daylight are very short. This involves taking in all the drives in an unbroken succession, perhaps pausing briefly in the late morning for a light snack of soup and sandwiches, and ending the day's shooting around 2.30 pm.

At the end of a covert shoot, the head gamekeeper will normally 'brace-up' the pheasants in pairs comprising a cock and a hen bird, and the bag is normally laid out to be counted and inspected in the presence of all the guns and beaters. Where individual shoot cards have been provided, bearing the date, the names of the participating guns and a list of the drives shot, the day's bag should be recorded in the appropriate place. This information can later be entered in the individual game books which most shoots and dedicated individual sportsmen keep throughout their shooting careers.

It is customary for the head gamekeeper to present each gun with one brace of pheasants, and many shoots also adopt the thoughtful practice of giving any woodcock which have been shot to the lucky guns who bagged them. After the bag has been shared out in this way and before the group disperses to return home or re-enter the house for tea, every gun should personally thank the head gamekeeper and a tip is customary and will be expected. The amount to tip can vary, but a useful guideline is to tip £10-12 when the day's bag has been up to 100 head of game, and an additional £5 for each further 50 head in the bag.

Finally, a day as a guest on a formal covert shoot should be treated like any other social occasion, and you should thank your host both verbally as you leave and later in a short letter of thanks, for his hospitality and for all the fine sport which he has provided.

guns are all in position, and many shoots have devised their own systems of signalling by hand and whistle to indicate readiness, although hand-held portable radios are increasingly used for this. A traditional method of signalling the start of a drive is by the host or shoot captain blowing a blast on a hunting horn, which is the signal for guns to prepare to shoot and for the beating line to begin its advance. Similarly, the horn or some other clearly audible signal is normally used to indicate the end of the drive, at which point the guns must unload immediately, no further shooting taking place until the signal for the beginning of the next drive has been given.

Once in position at his numbered peg or stand, the individual gun should arrange his equipment carefully, placing his cartridge bag and his shooting stick or shooting seat in a convenient and comfortable position. He should also take careful note of the position of his fellow guns, of pickers-up and others behind the line, and of the layout and contours of the covert from which the birds will come.

Safety requires that every gun should be constantly aware of his safe arc of fire, and courtesy requires that each gun should appreciate the area in which he can legitimately fire at driven game without 'poaching' a bird which ought to be left for another gun to fire at. With few exceptions, birds driven from coverts should only be fired at when they have cleared the sky-

DECOYING

The art of decoying birds holds a special fascination, something akin to presenting an artificial fly of your own tying to a trout, and watching him fall for it. It is an historic art, used long ago by the Ancient Greeks and Egyptians to lure duck within range of a thrown net, and the art extends to the decoys themselves. At one extreme, they may be nothing more than crudely-shaped blocks of wood, but they can be works of art in themselves, carefully carved and painted with the breath of life in a time when market gunners could not order twenty plastic drakes or ten rubber ducks from the local store.

Decoys are set out to represent a number of birds feeding or resting, and the more decoys the rig contains, then the greater the illusion of safety and companionship. In the past, hunters would set out huge numbers of decoys. A Chesapeake Bay rig for duck, for instance, would be counted in hundreds, and this still holds true for goose rigs in certain parts of North America, but the general trend in decoying duck and geese is to substitute size for numbers.

Oversized decoys come in a number of forms. At one extreme, some hunters use silhouette goose decoys the height of a man. A more usual type are duck decoys of over twenty inches in length, rather than the standard eighteen inches. Another possibility is to include a couple of goose decoys in a duck rig. These are easily seen over long distances, and draw natural birds' attention to the duck decoys, advertising the product.

Big rigs of magnum-sized decoys are best suited to big waters and wide open spaces. On smaller, intimate ponds, they do not work as well as a few standard-sized decoys. Even then, you may need that little something extra to draw attention to the rig. A white, or black and white, decoy is highly visible, and European sportsmen might advertise a mallard rig with a piebald tufted decoy. In the old days they used a dummy

A wildfowler placing duck decoys on a flooded patch of field, to attract birds flighting in at dusk.

seagull, or even a swan; not to attact other swans, but because a big, white bird is visible over enormous distances. Duck are used to feeding and resting alongside swans, and so they would swing over for a look.

Another way to increase the visibility of a duck rig is to set out twice as many males as females, because the drake's plumage is so much more conspicuous than the rather dowdy,

Goose hunters setting out decoys in front of a hide built in the middle of a large stubble field.

camouflaged female. Geese and pigeon, of course, do not have such sexual variation in plumage.

Even with magnum-sized decoys, the more you set out, the more birds you will pull in. Of course, on small ponds you will pull in a few duck with six

decoys, but normally you will want a minimum of twice that number. You could double that number again for geese; forty would be better still, and some hunters will set out a couple of hundred.

To most ducks and geese, cover represents danger. Whether it is the bank of a lake or the hedge around a field, it may conceal a predator. Birds will draw best to a rig set in the middle of a field or lake, but then they could be out of range of your gun. The compromise is to place the nearest decoy a minimum of 20 yards from the cover where you are going to conceal yourself, and the furthest at a maximum of 40 yards, preferably a little less.

If you put decoys out at the extreme range of your gun, then as sure as anything you will have birds dropping in just beyond them and out of range. If you place the decoys too close to you, then besides the fact that some birds will shy away, you'll be hitting birds before the shot pattern has had a chance to open up.

In choosing the best layout for your decoys, your aim should be to create landing areas just in front of you. This means taking account of the ways in which various species choose to join a flock on water or on the ground. For example, diving ducks will pitch in at the head of the flock, but dabbling ducks will settle in behind the main group. Geese don't seem to mind where they land, and they will settle in front, behind and even among the decoys.

Another factor to consider is the direction in which your decoys are facing. To make your rig more realistic, you should set your decoys so that they're mostly facing into the wind, because real birds don't like being on the ground with the breeze dead astern to ruffle their feathers. However, as birds will quarter into a wind or even stand broadside-on to it, there's no need to set out your decoys like soldiers on parade.

The wind also affects the way that birds will approach the

decoys, as they generally prefer to land into the wind. In still conditions they will come in from all directions, but given anything of a breeze, their normal behaviour is to circle around and come up from behind the rig (the decoys facing into the wind).

For instance, suppose you have a hide on the bank of a lake, the wind is blowing from your right to your left, and you want to set out a rig for dabbling ducks, such as mallard. You know that dabblers won't pitch in ahead of the decoy flock, and that they will approach and land into the wind, so you set the bulk of your decoys upwind (to the right of your position) with

one or two stragglers further back, directly in front of your hide and looking for all the world as if they have just joined in at the back of the main flock. Decoyed birds will circle into the wind, aiming to land right in front of you. With the main rig set at between 20 and 30 yards out from the bank, the birds will be drawn into perfect gunning range.

When you're laying out decoys for geese, in a field, say, you should remember that these birds will settle behind, in front of or among the decoys. Birds making for the head of the decoy flock will be swinging across in front of you but, if the rig extends too far downwind,

you may find that birds settling in at the back are almost out of range. If this happens, the best plan is to move your rig slightly upwind, and arrange it in a figure-of-eight pattern which will encourage the birds to pitch into the middle of it.

Calling will both draw attention to your rig and create confidence in it. It can work well with ducks, but it is even more effective (and important) with geese, because they are far more vocal birds – a silent flock of geese on the ground is quite unnatural. You will certainly kill some geese over decoys without calling, but they are such gregarious birds that clever calls are a sure road to success.

RIG FOR DUCKS

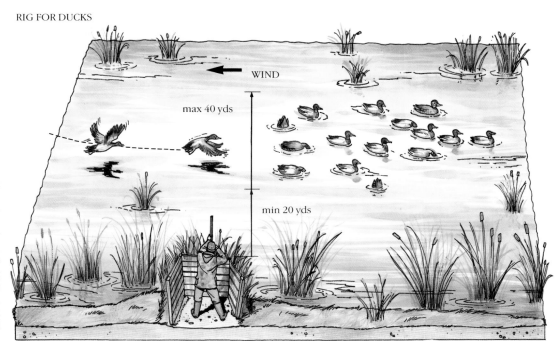

RIG FOR GEESE

RIG FOR DUCKS *This duck rig (above right) is set out to attract dabbling ducks, such as mallard, which will land behind the decoy flock.*
RIG FOR GEESE *Geese will land in front, behind or even among the decoys, but wherever they intend to pitch they will always land into the wind.*

JUMP SHOOTING

Duck tend to feed at night and rest during the day. Some of the places that they are to be found resting are on streams, rivers, ponds and lakes, but they will also be found on marshes, both freshwater and salt. On salt marshes, the chances of sport depend heavily on the weather, and high tide in rough weather can bring sea-roosting ducks in search of shelter in the flashes and the maze of creeks.

At its most simple, jump shooting is a leisurely walk along creek and river banks, or across marshes, shooting the duck as they jump ahead of you; but it is seldom that easy. What makes jump shooting so different from upland shooting, walking after grouse, partridge or pheasants, is that these upland gamebirds will head for cover a lot of the time, allowing you to get well within range before they blast out of their hiding places, whereas duck behave very differently. Let them see, hear or even smell you and they will be up and away.

The fact is that jump shooting has a whole lot more in common with deer hunting than bird shooting. If deer or duck know that you are coming, they don't wait about for a close encounter. So whenever possible, try to locate the duck from a distance, for instance by using binoculars or by watching for birds pitching onto a distant pond or creek.

Having located the birds, stop and think before you make your approach. Glass the ground between you and them, taking careful note of every hill and dale and any bush, patch of tall grass, reeds or any other area of natural cover that you can use to conceal your approach. You should also take notice of the direction of the wind. Even if the duck can't smell you, you might crack a twig or make some other noise that will alert them to your presence. If you make your approach from downwind of the birds, any small sound will be carried away from them.

For every time that you are able to pinpoint the position of ducks, there will be ten times when you can't see any at all, but feel sure that some teal or others are tucked away on the marshy ground or stream edges. Then there is nothing for it but to creep along as quietly as you can. Normally, it won't pay to walk straight along a river bank. Look ahead and try to spot any areas of tall reeds, or bays or curves in the river that might prove attractive to duck. Move away from the river bank and cut back in at an angle, using any cover to get in as close as possible to any potential hotspots. The secret is to behave as though every area you are approaching holds a flight of birds. Move in slowly and quietly and take those last forty yards at a snail's pace.

For most of the time in jump shooting, when you finally get the chance of a shot it will be at extreme range. A well-choked gun can be a great advantage, partnered with a heavyish load of quite large shot to carry a

good punch to knock down that fast-departing mallard drake.

When your prize has fallen on the opposite shore of the river, you'll see the need for another essential item of jump-shooting equipment: unless you're prepared to strip off and swim, you'll need a good dog, and not just any old dog. What you want is what the British call a 'no-slip' retriever. For water work it will probably be a labrador but, whatever breed you choose, it must walk quietly at your side, and be prepared to drop and stay for however long it takes for you to get a shot.

Jump shooting from a boat is

more correctly known as float shooting. It is really a job for two men, but there are many variations to the basic technique of gently floating with the stream and taking any shots as they are presented. On big rivers, where the duck are sitting out in the open, you might use a type of skulling or punting technique, with both men lying flat in the bottom of the boat and the stern man sculling ever so gently to keep the boat on course. To the duck it should look as if a big log is drifting toward them, and maybe they will let you get within range before they jump. On smaller streams, the technique depends more heavily on rounding a corner and taking the duck by surprise, or you might choose to carry a decoy rig and, when you

For successful jump shooting, you need a well-choked gun, a good pair of binoculars and a well-trained dog.

Patches of tall grass, reeds or other areas of natural cover will help you to get within range before the ducks jump.

birds in front.

Second, you should be aware of the risks involved in a capsize in cold winter weather when the rivers and streams are running high. Also, if you're not familiar with a river, check to see if there are any rapids or other hazards, and remember that a relatively unstable boat, such as a canoe, can be made to tip over just with the recoil if both men fire broadsides at the same time.

The legal position regarding float shooting in Britain is very different from that in America. In Britain, you won't be able to float shoot unless you have permission from the owner of the adjoining land, and so most British float shooting takes place on the coast, sneaking about in tidal estuaries and creeks. In America, so long as the stream is navigable, you don't need permission to float shoot although you may need permission to come ashore.

The weather is a great ally of the float shooter. An overnight frost may ice over ponds, but most streams stay open and that is where duck will congregate, and float hunters on big rivers such as the Mississippi know that when a storm lashes the main river, the duck will move to smaller and more sheltered streams. Naturally, such weather is also a great aid to the jump shooter, as it concentrates the duck on smaller waters.

find an area of abundant cover and lush river grasses, set the decoys out, camouflage the boat with long grasses against the bank, and wait for some duck to come to you.

There are two things to beware of in float shooting. First, it is probably far safer if only the bow man shoots, taking it turn about with his partner. In the heat of the moment, it is all too easy for an excitable stern man to lose all sense and take a shot over his partner's head. A sensible type will only take an occasional shot at crossing birds, broadside on to the boat, leaving the bow man to take the

When you're float shooting, take care not to capsize the boat – or to shoot at or near your partner or your dog.

PASS SHOOTING

In general, geese feed by day and will often fly considerable distances from their resting areas to their feeding grounds. In normal weather conditions these flights are carried out at high altitude, well out of shotgun range. However, when weather conditions cause the birds to fly lower, pass shooting can come into its own. At its most basic, pass shooting simply means positioning yourself at a spot where the birds are likely to pass overhead, and then waiting for one or more of them to come within range.

In North America, pass shooting is the predominant method used in the public shooting areas which are established around wildfowl refuges. The fields to which birds from these refuges will flight do, of course, offer the best shooting (over decoys), but you need a deep pocket full of money to buy your way in and, even then, it isn't easy to find an opening. Much the same applies in Britain, where inland shooting is

largely in private hands and the only public wildfowl shooting is along the shore, where geese flight in at dawn from estuarine sandbanks where they have roosted.

The normal practice around refuges in America is for the hunters to be given positions chosen by drawing lots, which makes it a matter of luck as to whether they are going to be under the birds when they pass. Along the shore, however, whether in North America or in Britain, hunters are more free to choose their own positions, paying regard to where the geese are thought to be feeding inland, where they have been roosting (and whether this has altered due to, say, a high tide with a strong wind to churn the surface and make roosting uncomfortable) and other factors such as wind direction. As the geese might come over at any point along a ten mile stretch of coastline, there is quite an art to coastal wildfowling and if you're not familiar with the area it's a

good idea to make use of the services of a local guide.

Even when your positioning is perfect, the geese may pass over you at three gunshots high; there again, they may not pass over you at all, because around the time of the full moon they will often avoid hunting pressure by feeding at night and resting during the day. On refuges, there may be no dawn flight at all at such times, the geese spending the day resting on their feeding grounds. The best hunting is usually to be had at or near the new moon, especially when the weather is bad and fog, rain, snow or high winds force the birds to fly lower than normal.

Geese don't like flying in fog any more than we like driving in it, because of the risk of hitting something. Fog at dawn will delay the flight time because the geese will sit it out, hoping for it to clear. When they do fly, they will go above thick ground fog and so be out of sight of the pass shooter – what you want is a

Pass shooting is a popular method of taking geese.

thin fog in which the birds will fly, staying close to the ground in order to keep sight of familiar landmarks that help them to navigate. If they have to fly within 150 feet of the ground, the pass shooter is in with a good chance.

Very heavy rain has much the same effect as thick fog on the behaviour of geese, because they don't like flying in it. When they do fly in rain, they fly lower than usual, although light or showery rain doesn't seem to have much effect on their flying.

In snow, geese realize that they will be hard put to find sufficient food in the short winter's day, so they tend to fly early, setting off with the first of the light. When a blizzard is coming, the geese can sense it

Along the shore, the pass shooter chooses a site where the geese will fly over on their way to feed or roost.

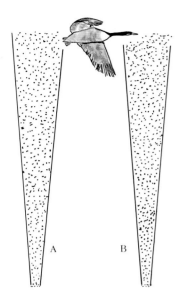 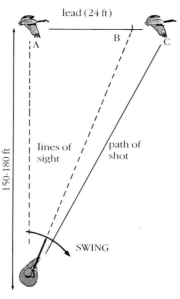

CONE OF SHOT *If you don't aim well ahead of the bird, the shot will pass behind it (A). The bird should fly into it (B).*

LEAD AND SWING *Swing ahead of the bird (A), firing at B and following through. The shot will hit the bird at C.*

and will feed greedily up until its arrival, when they will try to sit it out.

Times of high wind are the best of all for pass shooting, and the wind is one of the pass shooter's best allies, almost as important to him as his gun. Because of surface friction, the speed of the wind near the ground is less than it is higher up in the air. The effect of this friction is quite high at low levels, but it decreases rapidly with altitude and is virtually nonexistent by about 2000 feet above ground level. As a result, geese find it easier if they fly low when they are heading into or across a strong wind.

Pass shooting probably places more demands on gun and cartridge than any other form of shooting does. Even when they are forced to fly low by bad weather or strong winds, the geese will still be at the very extremes of range for anything other than a specialist water-fowling gun, loaded with a suitable cartridge and shot. In Britain, the fowler can use the popular magnum 12-gauge, or choose a 10, an 8 or even the mighty 4-gauge capable of throwing 4 ounces of large, heavy shot. In America, any gauge larger than a 10 is outlawed, which is somewhat ironic because the modern magnum 10-gauge cartridge contains 2¼ ounces of shot, which is more than the 8-gauge loads in use at the time these guns were banned. Maybe the conservation ideas behind the banning of heavy loads would have been better served by limiting the shot load, not the gauge.

Successful long-range shooting requires a dense pattern of pellets with enough striking energy to kill cleanly by shock and penetration, so the correct combination of load, shot size and choke is essential. Assuming a full choke barrel, a minimum of 1½ ounces of American no. 4 shot (English no. 3) will maintain good patterns out to the maximum killing range of the shot – just under 60 yards for most geese, but rather less for the big, heavy Canadas. Upping to no. 2 shot (English B) pushes the range out to beyond 70 yards while maintaining striking energy, providing you use full or extra-full choke barrels and at least 2¼ ounces of shot. Beyond that range, unless you are operating in Britain with a 4-gauge, 4-ounce rocket launcher, you have to accept that you are relying on fluke kills. You will certainly be able to pull down some really high birds, but for every one that you kill you will probably be wounding two more.

A bird 60 or 70 yards up is a long, long shot – it's at about the same height as the eighteenth floor of a highrise building. When you're taking your shot, swing through the bird and out in front of it before pulling the trigger, and keep swinging to follow through. Alternatively, estimate by how much you will need to lead the bird, say 24 feet or about 8 goose lengths, and aim that far ahead of it. Whichever way you choose to do it, don't expect to make big bags on pass shooting, which is possibly the sternest test of gun and marksmanship of them all.

FLIGHT SHOOTING

Geese and the majority of ducks, especially dabbling ducks, roost at some distance from their feeding grounds. On a reserve, this distance may be quite short, but in natural conditions it may be ten miles for geese and as much as twenty miles for ducks.

The typical flying pattern of wild waterfowl is to gain height as rapidly as possible and to stay flying high, out of gunshot, until the destination is reached. In that, duck and geese are the same, but there is one important difference: duck will normally rest by day and flight in to feed with the dusk, but geese usually feed by day and rest during the night. The main exception to this comes at the time of the full moon, when parties of geese will fly and feed by moonlight.

This is why the wildfowler is so concerned with the dusk and dawn flights; unless weather conditions are such as to keep the birds flying low between their takeoff and landing areas, offering the opportunity for pass shooting, the fowler will have to station himself at either the feeding or the resting area.

In Britain, the fowler who wants to shoot duck on the evening flight will often encourage them to visit a naturally-attractive, shallow flight pond by regularly feeding them with barley or frost-damaged potatoes. After a while, when the duck numbers have built up, they arrive one dusk to find the fowler waiting for them in a hide, and the shooting is brisk until the light has faded, which may not take long on a short winter's day.

In North America, the situation is very different. Putting out food (baiting) is firmly associated with now-illegal shooting practices which were common in the early part of this century, and if you bait you have every chance of ending up facing a judge. It is also illegal to leave too much grain on the stubbles after harvesting; the permitted amount is only that left by 'valid agricultural operations or procedures'.

People are often surprised to learn that ducks can be shot on an area without any water, because they associate them so strongly with ponds, creeks and marshes. However, what attracts ducks is food rather than water, and the stubbles, even if they have been harvested to a strict agricultural code, will still have sufficient waste grain to attract ducks, particularly mallard. If you have stubble fields on your shooting grounds, and they are within flying range of duck resting areas, you should be looking out for droppings and feathers on them. If you find them, you will know that the duck are flighting in with the last light of dusk, feeding through the night, and leaving with the dawn. Then you have to figure out how to get a shot at them.

There's little point in building a blind at the field side because duck will pitch into the middle of a field, well away from any cover that might conceal predators, human or otherwise. The only time you have any chance of getting a shot from the side of a field is when there's a wind blowing, the stronger the better. After circling, the ducks will make their final approach and landing into the wind. If the field is fairly small, you might be able to get a couple of shots from the upwind end – but not often. Even more pointless is standing in the middle of the field and waiting for the birds to fly in, because the ducks' keen eyesight will pick you out before they have even begun to circle, and they will fly on.

The best method is to make a blind in the middle of the field. Camouflaged nets draped over stakes will be effective, particularly if they are left out for a few days so that the ducks become accustomed to them. A net interwoven with stubble will do better still, as will a blind built from bales of straw, the less elaborate the better. One good way is to lay out two rows of three bales, with just enough space for you to lie between them, then sit up quickly to take a shot as the birds pass overhead. Decoys can help to funnel the ducks into your shooting area, bringing them over your position.

Where it is permissible to shoot throughout the 24 hours, as it is in Britain but not in the USA, the most convenient time to shoot is on a dark night because then the ducks will flight over a relatively short time at dusk. On moonlit nights the flight time will be extended, which may be less convenient, and if the sky is clear the ducks may be very difficult to see. However, when there is a light cloud over the moon, the birds will be clearly silhouetted against the milky white of the clouds, and this more than compensates for the longer flight time.

When you're after duck on salt marshes, conceal yourself in late afternoon and wait for the birds to flight in at dusk.

Duck can be shot in the morning, as they flight in to their resting areas, or in the evening, when they go to feed.

Much the same rules apply as the season progresses and the ducks change their attention to flight ponds and fresh and salt marshes. Find where the birds are feeding, then conceal yourself in the late afternoon and wait for them to come to you. Always remember that ducks circle before they land, and avoid the temptation to take a long shot. Freeze until they come down well within range, maybe on their second or third pass, and then take your shots.

Ducks will occasionally flight during daylight, especially during a gale that whips up large areas of water, driving the birds off to seek shelter on ponds and creeks. In coastal areas, as the tide creeps up over estuarine sandbanks and is chopped and churned by a gale, the hunter hidden away in some cover on a salt marsh can get good shooting at small parties of duck flighting for shelter.

GUN LAW

Great Britain, Northern Ireland and the Republic of Ireland are each subject to quite separate pieces of legislation on firearms. Sportsmen who intend to keep or use firearms in any part of the United Kingdom or the Irish Republic should ensure that they comply with the law in the area concerned. What follows is intended only as a general guide in layman's terms to field sports and the law in Great Britain. If you live in or are visiting Great Britain, your local police will provide more detailed information on British firearms law; for details of Northern Irish law, contact the Royal Ulster Constabulary, and for information on firearms legislation in the Republic of Ireland, the Garda Síochána.

Shotguns
You must obtain a Shotgun Certificate from your local police before you may possess, purchase or acquire a shotgun, which is defined as being a smooth-bore gun (other than an air gun) which has a barrel not less than 24 inches in length. Shotguns with shorter barrels, and pump-action and semiautomatic shotguns, require a Firearms Certificate. Before a Shotgun Certificate is issued, the police must be satisfied that the applicant can be permitted to possess a shotgun without danger to the public safety or the peace, and in addition they may refuse to issue a certificate if they are not satisfied that the applicant has a good reason for possessing a shotgun. The details of each shotgun you own must be entered on the certificate, and possessing a shotgun without having a valid certificate for it will render you liable on conviction to a fine, imprisonment or both.

You may sell, lend or give a shotgun only to someone who has a valid, current Shotgun Certificate, and both yourself and the person to whom you transfer the gun must notify the police within 48 hours of the transaction. Failure to comply with this is punishable on conviction by a fine, imprisonment or both. It is also an offence to sell shotgun ammunition to someone (other than an authorized dealer) unless that person produces his Shotgun Certificate, or the certificate of some other person together with a letter of authority from the holder to purchase ammunition on his behalf.

You may not make a gift of a shotgun to anyone under fifteen years of age; once over fifteen, and having a Shotgun Certificate, a person may be given a shotgun and ammunition, but no-one under seventeen is allowed to buy or hire a shotgun or to buy shotgun ammunition.

There are some circumstances in which you do not need a Shotgun Certificate. These include:
- when you borrow a shotgun from the occupier of private premises (including land) and use it thereon in his presence
- when you use someone else's shotgun on artificial targets at a place and time approved by the local chief of police
- when you are in possession of a weapon (for which someone else holds a certificate) in a theatrical or film production
- when you are under instructions from another person who holds a certificate and you are carrying a weapon for his or her use for sporting purposes only

Air guns
If you are aged seventeen or over you may buy or hire most types of air rifle or air pistol, and the appropriate ammunition, without restriction. It is an offence to sell an air gun to anyone under seventeen; you may give or lend an air gun to anyone over fourteen, but it is an offence to give one to anyone under that age. Certain very powerful air guns are declared specially dangerous by the Secretary of State and may not be obtained without a Firearms Certificate; if in doubt, ask the police.

Rifles and other weapons
Special regulations apply to weapons other than shotguns (as defined above) and low-powered air guns. These weapons include rifles, pistols, short-barrelled shotguns, pump-action shotguns, semiautomatic shotguns, and air guns with a muzzle velocity of 12 ft-lbs or more. In general, you may not possess, purchase or acquire any of these weapons or most types of ammunition for them unless you have already obtained a Firearms Certificate from the police; nor may you sell, lend or give such weapons or ammunition to anyone who has not got a Firearms Certificate. Failure to comply with the laws governing the possession, use and transfer of these weapons and ammunition may result in a fine, imprisonment or both.

The police will not issue a Firearms Certificate unless they are satisfied that you have good reason for having it, that public safety is not endangered, and that you are fit to be trusted with a firearm. They may impose special conditions, and may revoke a certificate. There are some limited exemptions to the need to hold a Firearms Certificate, for example for some members of rifle or pistol clubs. However, these exemptions still require approval from the police.

Game Licences
In addition to a Shotgun Certificate or Firearms Certificate, you will need a Game Licence if you want to shoot deer (see below), pheasants, partridges, red grouse, black grouse, ptarmigan, woodcock, common snipe, hares or rabbits. Game licences, issued for various periods of from two weeks to a year, are available from Post Offices.

Deer and the law
A Game Licence is required to kill or take deer anywhere in Great Britain, except where an owner or occupier or his agent takes or kills deer on enclosed land, or, in Scotland, where a person is authorized or required by the Red Deer Commission to kill deer.

The 1963 Deer Act requires the stalker in England and Wales to use a rifle of not less than .240 calibre and ammunition with a muzzle energy of at least 1700 ft-lbs. Air weapons are prohibited, as are longbows and crossbows; shotguns may only be used to kill deer to control damage under the appropriate provisions of the Deer Act 1963 and the Wildlife & Countryside Act 1981 Schedule 7. Shotguns must be 12-bore or larger and loaded with AAA buckshot or solid ball. Rifle bullets must be soft-nosed or hollow-nosed.

The law relating to the killing of deer in Scotland differs in some respects from that which applies in England and Wales. For the most comprehensive published statement on deer and the law in Great Britain, see the reference section (pp 163-177) of Richard Prior's *Trees and Deer* (Batsford, 1983).

ASSOCIATIONS & SOCIETIES

The Game Conservancy, Fordingbridge, Hampshire SP6 1EF (tel 0425 52381)
The only organization devoted solely to the study of game biology and the ecology of game management in Britain and Ireland.

The British Association for Shooting & Conservation, Marford Mill, Chester Road, Rossett, Wrexham, Clwyd LL12 0HL (tel 0244 570 881)
Founded in 1908 as the Wildfowler's Association of Great Britain and Ireland, the BASC now covers all forms of live game shooting, including game and deer.

The British Field Sports Society, 59 Kennington Road, London SE1 7PZ (tel 01 928 4742)
Actively involved in promoting and securing the political status of all field sports, including all forms of sporting shooting.

The British Deer Society, Church Farm, Lower Basildon, Reading, Berkshire RG8 9NH (tel 07357 4094)
A voluntary organization concerned with all aspects of the study and management of deer.

The Field and Country Sports Society of Ireland, Ferndale, Kilpedder, Greystones, Co. Wicklow, Ireland (tel Dublin 874 317)
A voluntary society for the promotion and support of shooting and other traditional field sports in the Republic of Ireland.

The Clay Pigeon Shooting Association, 107 Epping New Road, Buckhurst Hill, Essex IG9 5TQ (tel 01 505 6221)
The central body for the organization and regulation of clay pigeon shooting in the United Kingdom.

SHOOTING SEASONS

GAME BIRDS

Pheasant

Great Britain: 1 October–1 February; Northern Ireland (cock birds only): 1 October–31 January (a licence to shoot released pheasants is obtainable from the Department of the Environment (Conservation Branch), Stormont Castle); Irish Republic (cocks only): 1 November–31 January

Grey Partridge

Great Britain: 1 September–1 February; Northern Ireland: fully protected; Irish Republic: 1 November–15 November

Red-legged partridge

Great Britain: 1 September–1 February; Northern Ireland: a licence to shoot released birds is obtainable from the Department of the Environment; Irish Republic: 1 September–30 September

Red grouse

Great Britain: 12 August–10 December; Northern Ireland: 12 August–30 November; Irish Republic: 1 September–30 September

Ptarmigan

Scotland only: 12 August–10 December

Black grouse

Great Britain: 20 August–10 December

Capercaillie

Scotland: 1 October–31 January

Woodcock

Scotland: 1 September–31 January; England, Wales and Northern Ireland: 1 October–31 January; Irish Republic: 1 November–31 January

Common snipe

Great Britain: 12 August–31 January; Northern Ireland: 1 September–31 January; Irish Republic: 1 September–31 January

Jack snipe

Great Britain: fully protected; Northern Ireland: 1 September–31 January; Irish Republic: 1 September–31 January

Golden plover

Great Britain and Northern Ireland: 1 September–31 January; Irish Republic: 1 September–31 January

WATER FOWL

Moorhen

Great Britain: 1 September–31 January; Northern Ireland: fully protected; Irish Republic: fully protected

Coot

Great Britain: 1 September–31 January; Northern Ireland: fully protected; Irish Republic: fully protected

Duck

The following duck species may be shot in Great Britain, Northern Ireland and the Irish Republic from 1 September to 31 January. In Great Britain only, the season is extended to 20 February on the foreshore, that is, in or over any area below the high water mark of ordinary spring tides.

   Mallard, Teal, Wigeon, Gadwall, Shoveler, Tufted duck, Pochard, Goldeneye, Pintail

Canada goose

Great Britain: 1 September–31 January, extended to 20 February on the foreshore (see 'Duck' above); Northern Ireland: may be shot only under licence from the Department of the Environment if crop damage is occurring

Greylag goose

Great Britain and Northern Ireland: 1 September–31 January, extended to 20 February on the foreshore in Great Britain

Pink-footed goose

Great Britain and Northern Ireland: 1 September–31 January, extended to 20 February on the foreshore in Great Britain

White-fronted goose

England and Wales: 1 September –31 January, extended to 20 February on the foreshore; Northern Ireland: 1 September–31 January; Scotland: fully protected.

Please note: all species of geese are fully protected in the Republic of Ireland

DEER

Red deer stags

England and Wales: 1 August–30 April; Scotland: 1 July–20 October; Irish Republic: 1 September–28 February

Red deer hinds

England and Wales: 1 November–28 February; Scotland: 21 October–15 February; Irish Republic: 1 November–28 February

Fallow deer bucks

England and Wales: 1 August–30 April; Scotland: 1 August–30 April; Irish Republic: 1 September–28 February

Fallow deer does

England and Wales: 1 November–28 February; Scotland: 21 October–15 February; Irish Republic: 1 November–28 February

Roe deer bucks

England and Wales: 1 April–31 October; Scotland: 1 April–20 October

Roe deer does

England and Wales: 1 November–28 February; Scotland: 21 October–31 March

Sika stags

England and Wales: 1 August–30 April; Scotland: 1 July–20 October; Irish Republic: 1 September–28 February

Sika hinds

England and Wales: 1 November–28 February; Scotland: 21 October–25 February; Irish Republic: 1 November–28 February

Muntjac and Chinese water deer

No statutory close season exists for these species, but the British Deer Society recommends that they should not be shot between 1 March and 31 October

Deer in Northern Ireland

Those intending to shoot deer in Northern Ireland should contact the Department of the Environment (Conservation Branch), Stormont Castle, Belfast, for guidance on seasons and on the types of firearms and ammunition that may be used.

PESTS, VERMIN AND RABBITS

Authorized persons are permitted to shoot the following at any time except on Sunday in Scotland, and on Christmas Day and on Sunday in England and Wales in those areas where the Secretary of State has expressly forbidden Sunday shooting:

Birds: Collared dove, Woodpigeon, Feral domestic pigeon, Magpie, Rook, Jay, Jackdaw, Carrion crow, Hooded crow, Starling, House sparrow, Great black-backed gull, Lesser black-backed gull, Herring gull

Animals: Grey squirrel, Black rat, Brown rat, Fox, Rabbit, Coypu, Mink, Stoat, Weasel, Feral cat.

HARES

In Great Britain, there is no close season, but hares may not be killed on Sundays or on Christmas Day. On moorland and unenclosed non-arable land, hares may be shot only by the occupier and persons authorized by him between 11 December (1 July in Scotland) and 31 March. It is illegal to sell or try to sell hares from 1 March to 31 July inclusive. In the Irish Republic, hares may be shot from 25 September to 26 February.

BIBLIOGRAPHY

Akehurst, Richard *Game Guns and Rifles* (repr. 1985)
Marshall-Ball, Robin *The Sporting Rifle: A User's Guide* (1986)
Burrard Bt, Sir Gerald *The Modern Shotgun* (3 vols, repr. 1985)
Thomas, Gough *Shotguns and Cartridges for Game and Clays* (4th edn, 1987)
Jarrett, William S (ed) *Shooter's Bible* (pub. annually)

Moxon, P R A *Gundogs: Training and Field Trials* (15th edn, 1986)
Brander, Michael *Training the Pointer-Retriever Gundog* (1983)
Shaw, Vero *The Classic Encyclopedia of the Dog* (1881, repr. 1984)

Coles, C L (ed) *The Complete Book of Game Conservation* (1984)
Martin, Brian P *Sporting Birds of the British Isles* (1984)
Marchington, J *The Natural History of Game* (1984)

McKelvie, Colin Laurie *A Future for Game?* (1985)
Gooders, John *Field Guide to the Birds of Britain & Ireland* (1986)
Scott, Shirley L (ed) *Field Guide to the Birds of North America* (2nd edn, 1987)
Harrison, Colin *A Field Guide to the Nests, Eggs and Nestlings of North American Birds* (1984)
Burt, William H and Grossenheider, Richard P *A Field Guide to the Mammals, North America north of Mexico* (3rd edn, 1976)

Brander, Michael *A Concise Guide to Game Shooting* (1986)
Reynolds, Mike and Barnes, Mike *Shooting Made Easy* (1986)
Andersson, Stellan and Akerman, Jan *The Practical Gun* (1986)
Blatt, Art *The Gun Digest Book of Trap & Skeet Shooting* (1984)
Darling, John *Air Rifle Hunting* (1988)

Housby, Trevor, Oglesby, Arthur and Wilson, John *The Complete Book of Fishing* (1987)

INDEX

Page numbers in bold type (eg **131**) indicate main entries, and those in italic (eg. *74*) indicate photographs or diagrams.

CREDITS

AUTHORS:
Fid Backhouse
John Darling
Peter Eliot
Rob Knowles
Crawford Little
Colin McKelvie

EDITORIAL:
US Consultant Editor David E Petzal
UK Consultant Editor Colin McKelvie MA FLS MIBiol
Editor Ian Wood
Art Director Steve Leaning
Chief Picture Researcher Jane Lewis
Extra Research Marion Pullen

STUDIO PHOTOGRAPHY:
John Darling, assisted by Abigail Barker

ARTISTS:
Game Species Jim Channel, Tim Heywood, Colin Newman, Maurice Pledger
Guns John Batchelor
Techniques John Batchelor, George Fryer, Tim Heywood
With special thanks to Bernard Thornton Artists

MANUFACTURERS AND SUPPLIERS:

Air Logic
Scalemead Arms Co,
3 Medway Buildings,
Lower Road, Forest Row,
East Sussex.

Airmasters,
2 Hibbert Street, Luton,
Bedfordshire.

ASI,
Alliance House,
Snape, Saxmundham,
Suffolk IP17 1SW

W J Bowman (1984) Ltd,
East Markham, Newark,
Nottinghamshire.

Browning Sports Ltd,
37D Milton Park Industrial
Estate, Milton, Abingdon,
Oxfordshire OX14 4RT

BSA Guns (UK) Ltd,
Armoury Road,
Birmingham B11 2PX

Coleman UK (Crosman),
Parish Wharf Estate,
Harbour Road, Portishead,
Bristol.

Eley Ltd,
PO Box 705, Witton,
Birmingham.

Gunmark,
The Armoury,
Fort Wallington, Fareham,
Hampshire.

Leslie Hewett,
Upton Cross, Liskeard,
Cornwall.

Holland & Holland,
33 Bruton Street,
London W1X 8JS

Hull Cartridge Company,
Bontoft Avenue, National Avenue,
Hull HU5 4HZ

Intergun,
PO Box 1, Truro,
Cornwall TR2 4JJ

Parabellum Sports Ltd,
475 Upper Richmond Road West,
London SW14 7PU

Parker-Hale Ltd,
Golden Hillock Road,
Birmingham B11 2PZ

Sportsmarketing,
13 Grange Way, Colchester,
Essex CO2 8HF

Venom Arms Co,
Gun Barrel Industrial Centre,
Hayseech, Cradley Heath, Warley,
West Midlands B64 7JZ

Viking Arms Ltd,
Summerbridge, Harrogate,
North Yorkshire HG3 4BW

DETAILED CREDITS

Pages 6-7: *photo* Bruce Coleman (Nicholas Devere)
8: *illustration* Mansell Collection
10-11: *illustrations* John Batchelor
12-13: *illustrations* John Batchelor
Pages 14-57: *all photography* John Darling
14-15: *guns* Sportsmarketing, Bomber Prento, Leslie Hewett; *other items* Leslie Hewett
16-17: *guns* Winchester, Parker-Hale, ASI, Browning, Holland & Holland; *other items* Gunmark
18-19: *guns* Parker-Hale, Leslie Hewett; *other items* Parker-Hale, Leslie Hewett, Eley, Hull Cartridge
20-21: *guns* Sportsmarketing, Browning, Leslie Hewett; *other items* Holland & Holland
22-23: *guns* Winchester, Browning, ASI, Gunmark; *other items* Leslie Hewett, Gunmark, Hull Cartridge
24-25: *guns* Winchester, Hull Cartridge, Intergun, Browning; *other items* Gunmark, Parker-Hale, Leslie Hewett, Browning, Hull Cartridge
26-27: *guns* Browning, Winchester, Gunmark; *other items* Gunmark, Browning, Hull Cartridge
28-29: *guns* Winchester, Gunmark, Browning; *other items* WJ Bowman, Leslie Hewett, Hull Cartridge
30-31: *traps and clays* WJ Bowman
32-33: *shotgun ammunition* Eley, Hull Cartridge
34-35: *guns* Air Logic, Coleman UK, BSA, Hull Cartridge, Venom Arms; *other items* Venom Arms, Airmasters
36-37: *guns* Winchester, Parker-Hale, Browning, Hull Cartridge
38-39: *guns* Leslie Hewett

40-41: *guns* Winchester, Hull Cartridge, Viking Arms, Parker-Hale
42-43: *scope sights* Browning (Kassnar, Vistascope), Venom Arms, Parker-Hale (Pecar, Nikko), Leslie Hewett
44-45: *ammunition* Leslie Hewett
46-47: *gun* Browning
48-49: *guns* Parabellum Sports
50-51: *guns* Parabellum Sports
52-53: *ammunition* Leslie Hewett
54-55: *reloading equipment* Leslie Hewett
56-57: *accessories* Browning, Holland & Holland, Parker-Hale, Leslie Hewett

58: *illustration* Mary Evans Library
60: *photo* J Marchington
62: *photo* J Darling
63: *photo* J Marchington
64: *illustrations* Robert Morton
65: *photo* J Darling
66: *photos* J Darling (top), Spectrum Colour Library (bottom)
67: *photo* (Sally Anne Thompson/ Animal Photography
68: *photo* GL Carlisle
69: *photo* Ardea
70: *photo* Ardea
71: *photos* Sally Anne Thompson/ Animal Photography (top left), GL Carlisle (below left), NHPA (right)
72: *photo* NHPA
73: *photo* Robert Estall
74: *photos* B & C Alexander (top), Ardea (bottom)
75: *photo* B & C Alexander

76: *illustration* Mary Evans Library
78: *photos* Frank Lane Picture Agency (Lee Rue Jnr) (top), Ardea

(John Daniels) (bottom)
79: *photos* NHPA (top), Nature Photographers Ltd (Don Smith) (middle), Aquila Photographics (Robert Maier) (bottom), J Darling (right)
Pages 80-99: *all illustrations* Maurice Pledger
Pages 100-103: *all illustrations* Tim Heywood
Pages 104-115: *all illustrations* Colin Newman
Pages 116-117: *all illustrations* Jim Channel
Pages 118-119: *all illustrations* Tim Heywood
Pages 120-127: *all illustrations* Jim Channel
Pages 128-139: *all illustrations* Tim Heywood

140: *illustration* Mansell collection
142: *photos* B & C Alexander (top), Frank Lane Picture Agency (bottom)
143: *photos* Sporting Pictures (top), J Darling (bottom left), NHPA (bottom right)
144-145: *photos* Mike Millman, *illustrations* John Batchelor
146-147: *photo* J Darling, *illustrations* George Fryer
148-149: *photo* Colorsport, *illustrations* George Fryer
150: *photos* Sporting Pictures (top), Gunmark (bottom)
151: *illustrations* George Fryer
152-153: *photo* J Darling, *illustrations* George Fryer
154-155: *photo* J Darling, *illustrations* George Fryer
156-157: *photo* J Darling, *illustrations* George Fryer

158-159: *photos* J Darling
160-161: *photo* B & C Alexander, *illustrations* Tim Heywood
162: *photo* Animal Photography (VLOO)
163: *photos* APB Photographic (top), Frank Lane Picture Agency (bottom)
164: *photo* J Darling
165: *photo* Frank Lane Picture Agency, *illustrations* Tim Heywood
166: *photo* Mike Swan
167: *photo* B & C Alexander
168: *photo* B & C Alexander
169: *photo* J Marchington, *illustration* George Fryer
170: *photo* GL Carlisle
171: *illustrations* George Fryer
172: *photo* J Marchington
173: *photo* Bruce Coleman (Leonard Lee Rue)
174-175: *photo* Impact Photos (Mark Cator), *illustration* George Fryer
176-177: *photo* GL Carlisle, *illustrations* George Fryer
178-179: *photo* GL Carlisle, *illustrations* George Fryer
180-181: *photos* NHPA, *illustrations* George Fryer
182: *photos* Bruce Coleman (Nicholas Devere) (top), Animal Photography (VLOO)
183: *photo* Animal Photography (VLOO)
184: *photo* J Marchington
185: *photo* NHPA (David Woodfield), *illustration* S Leaning
186-187: *photos* NHPA (top), J Marchington (bottom)